BELIZE
A Natural Destination
SECOND EDITION

Richard Mahler
Steele Wotkyns
Color Photography by Kevin Schafer

John Muir Publications
Santa Fe, New Mexico

John Muir Publications, P.O. Box 613, Santa Fe, NM 87504

©1991,1993 by Richard Mahler, Steele Wotkyns, Kevin Schafer
Cover © 1991, 1993 by John Muir Publications
All rights reserved. Published 1991
Printed in the United States of America

Second edition. First printing September 1993

Library of Congress Cataloging-in-Publication Data
Mahler, Richard
    Belize: a natural destination / Richard Mahler, Steele Wotkyns;
color photography by Kevin Schafer. — 2nd ed.
       p.   cm.
    Includes index.
    ISBN 1-56261-141-0 : $16.95
    1. Belize—Guidebooks. 2. Natural history—Belize—Guidebooks.
I. Wotkyns, Steele. II. Schafer, Kevin. III. Title.
F1443.5.M33   1993
917.28204'5—dc20   93-22122
                                                CIP

Cover photo: Ocelot, photo by Kevin Schafer
Cover art: Susan Surprise
Designer: Susan Surprise
Maps: Jim Wood
Typeface: Plantin
Typography: Ken Wilson
Printer: Malloy Lithographing

Distributed to the book trade by
W. W. Norton & Company, Inc.
New York, New York

Contents

Acknowledgments

The authors wish to especially thank Rita Cadena for the inspiration to write this guidebook and the warm and wonderful people of Belize for making it possible. We also thank everyone at John Muir Publications for their patience and assistance; and the staff, volunteer pilots, and supporters of Lighthawk, the international environmental air force.

Richard Mahler wishes to especially thank Sue Dirksen; Robert Mahler; Lisa Enfield; Peter Bylen; Al Dugan; Victor Gonzalez; Ricardo Castillo; Rita and Rachel Emmer; Colin and Ellen Howells; J. Christian Headley II; Nasario Coo; Fallet Young; Bob Jones; Neil Rogers; Mick and Lucy Fleming; Jim and Marguerite Bevis; Bruce and Carolyn Miller; Bart and Suzi Mickler; Lin Sutherland; Klaus Eiberle; Ray Lightburn; Paul and Mary Shave; Charles Colby III; Alvin and Reyna Dawson; Doug and Lou Moore; Therese Rath Bowman; Logan McNatt; Elizabeth Corcoran; Marguerite Wood; Bill MacGowan; Rosita Arvigo; the staff of the Belize Tourist Board; Continental Airlines; and last, but not least, Don and Mary Mahler.

Steele Wotkyns wishes to particularly thank his parents; Michael Stewartt; Victor Gonzalez; the Belize Audubon Society; the Belize Center for Environmental Studies; Programme for Belize; Jan Meerman; Meb Cutlack; Matthew Gibson; Robert Hardy; William Schmidt at Nature's Way Guest House; Jerry Hoogerwerf; Bob Martin; Dick Guffey; Bruce J. Morgan; Tom Grasse; Karen Johnson at Preferred Adventures; Ernesto Saqui; Bardy Riverol, Jal's Travl and Tours; Henry Menzies Travel and Tours; Gus Gonzalez; Michael Konecny; Nick Brokaw; the Belize government, particularly the Ministry of Natural Resources, the Ministry of Tourism and the Environment; and others we have neglected to mention.

Kevin Schafer would like to thank Sharon Matola and other staff members of the Belize Zoo. Thanks also to Meb Cutlack and Katie Stevens, and Rachel and Rita Emmer, all good friends. An especially warm thanks to Ged Caddick, for his help and enormous patience in the field. Finally, an endless debt to my father, who introduced me to Belize and spent his last days there, happily.

Foreword

Media coverage, opinion polls, statements by political leaders, and the sheer number of international projects focusing on conservation activities all indicate that environmental concerns have reached a new peak of public attention globally. This increased attention stems from the concern that wild plants and animals face an increasingly uncertain future—an uncertainty that is a consequence of shrinking habitats brought about by human development.

Added to the pressure of encroachment by humans on wildlife habitat is the potential threat of climate change caused by global warming. It is thought that the increase of a few degrees in temperature and changes in rainfall can affect various species, causing some to migrate and thus disrupting the set pattern of species within a biological community. Considering that tropical moist forests contain more than half the number of species of life forms that inhabit the planet, it is important that efforts be made to conserve the tropical forests and their communities of wild plants and animals.

The tiny country of Belize, Central America, with its peaceful and stable political climate, has embarked on a course to preserve and conserve its natural patrimony. This effort is exemplified by the recent action of the Government of Belize to expand the Cockscomb Basin Wildlife Sanctuary from an area of 3,600 acres to 102,000 acres and by the establishment of the 92,000-acre Bladen Nature Reserve.

Belize, like many Third World countries, is undergoing profound changes as economic development proceeds. This evolution is partly characterized by increased demand for forested areas to be converted into areas of agricultural productivity. While such productivity will bring economic benefits to the people of Belize, it is our *hope* that the conservation efforts of both the private and the public sectors of Belize can also produce economic returns to the people, particularly those who have relied on the forest resources for their livelihood.

One mechanism whereby such economic benefits can be obtained is through "natural history tourism," which is commonly referred to as ecotourism. This type of tourism aims at the marketing of our natural heritage as a tourist attraction. Within the geographic boundaries of Belize, hundreds of species of tropical wild animals and plants can be found. In many instances, the population of some species threatened or overexploited in other parts of Central America can be found in a healthy state here in Belize. As we in Belize ponder our involvement in the fate of tropical forests, we turn our minds to the state of the natural resources that we will bequeath to future Belizeans. Through natural history tourism we may have found a means to be proud of what we bequeath. The great value and significance of *Belize: A Natural Destination* is that it shows the importance of a conservation ethic and promotes a long-term sustainable tourism industry through the marketing of the flora and fauna of Belize while at the same time preserving them for posterity.

Dr. Victor Gonzalez
Permanent Secretary, Ministry of Tourism
and the Environment, Government of
Belize

1
History and Culture

The highest building in Belize is a magnificent Mayan ceremonial temple. The serene Sky Palace of Caracol sits in a jungle clearing near the Guatemalan border, where it remained completely hidden from outsiders until the 1930s. Its status as the country's most important architectural structure—long after the highly advanced civilization that built it mysteriously disappeared—is testimony to the unique and colorful history of Belize. An understanding and appreciation of historical highlights is invaluable in answering the frequently posed question, "Why go to Belize?"

Perhaps the most obvious reason is the natural beauty and quiet atmosphere that greet any visitor to an uncrowded and undeveloped subtropical place, especially one that gets as much as 180 inches of rain per year. This sliver of Caribbean coastline and verdant mountains remains the most sparsely populated nation in Central America, less than thirty inhabitants per square mile. It is not the smallest, however. With its 8,866 square miles, Belize is slightly larger than El Salvador. But whereas the latter is bursting with some eight million people, Belize had an estimated 1993 population of 240,000, at least one-third of whom were crowded into Belize City.

Remarkably, Belize's modest population probably represents only a fraction of what the territory sustained a thousand years ago. At the peak of the vast Mayan empire, archaeologists estimate that a million Indians may have lived within the borders of what is now Belize, with

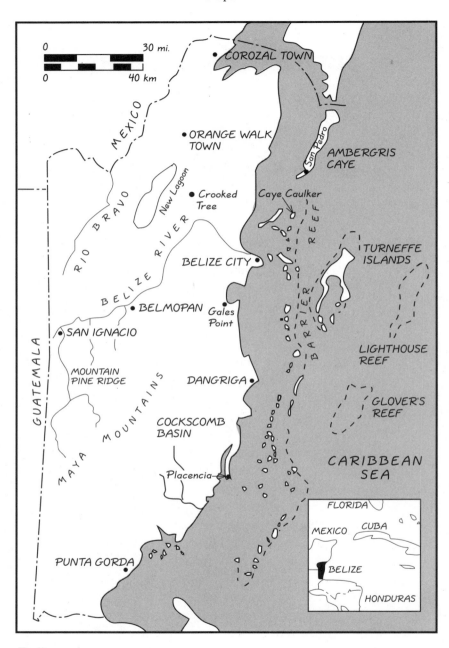

Belize

an equal number dwelling nearby in what is today eastern Guatemala and Mexico's Yucatán peninsula. A few thousand more Maya were scattered across Honduras and El Salvador.

The earliest Maya are believed to have spread into the Belize area from Guatemala and Mexico between 2000 B.C. and A.D. 300, after their ancestors had crossed the land bridge from Asia many centuries earlier. While the Maya of Belize are still very much shrouded in mystery, even less is known about their predecessors. There is evidence that archaic tribes roamed the area as early as 7500 B.C., at a time when Central America's climate and habitat was somewhat less tropical and given over to grassy savannas and broadleaf woodlands.

The early, or pre-Classic, Maya period extends from 1000 B.C. to A.D. 300. The Mayan civilization reached its height during the Classic era, from about A.D. 300 to 900. From around A.D. 1000 until the arrival of the Spanish five hundred years later, the Maya were plunged into a precipitous decline (the post-Classic phase), and the underlying structure of their society fell apart.

No one knows for certain why the civilization disintegrated or why many of its members migrated north into the northern Yucatán peninsula and left many of their city-states empty. Perhaps it was a prolonged war or a loss of faith in the godlike royalty who ruled with absolute authority. It is also possible that a series of earthquakes and other natural disasters contributed to the breakdown. Archaeologists are now collecting data that may some day help us settle such questions once and for all.

What is generally agreed on is that the area now known as Belize was for many years the heart of the Mayan empire. From A.D. 300 to 900, this land was the center of their complex collection of city-states, linked by trails, rivers, and Caribbean trade routes. Recent excavations have shown that Caracol, the country's largest site, is even bigger than Tikal, long considered the most significant Mayan restoration. Archaeologists now believe that Caracol defeated Tikal militarily as they competed for dominance during the Classic period (see chap. 6 for a more detailed discussion of Mayan history). The Mayan civilization is gone now (about 8% of Belize's current population are its descendants), but the major archaeological sites at Xunantunich,

Caracol, Altun Ha, Lamanai, and Lubaantun still reflect its impressive achievements.

What distinguishes the hundreds of Mayan sites of Belize from those of its neighbors is their relatively pristine character. For various reasons, notably a lack of funds and personnel, Belize has left its ruins pretty much as they were found. Indeed, newly discovered Mayan structures and artifacts are reported to the authorities almost every year by trekkers, scientists, and Indians who stumble upon them in the wetlands and jungle.

Belize's low population density has protected the sites to some degree from looters and land developers. Even today, the relatively low profile of the nation's tourist industry assures that travelers can visit these sites without the crowded conditions too often encountered at Mexico's Chichén Itzá, for instance. One of the biggest Mayan temples in the country, Altun Ha, is located just 34 miles north of Belize City and can be reached by car within 45 minutes. Yet it is virtually deserted much of the time.

In many ways, the ancient Maya were more advanced than their European contemporaries in Greece, Italy, France, and England. They were skilled astronomers and mathematicians and accomplished farmers and engineers. They developed a very elaborate religious system that incorporated many rituals and commemorated natural phenomena. Their calendar system, for instance, is precise within a matter of hours in tracking phases of the moon, planets, and stars. Over the years, the Maya became expert artists and craftsmen. Archaeological records indicate that they were also great traders. Excavations in Belize have yielded seashells from the Pacific Coast, obsidian and gold from northern Mexico, pottery from the Andes mountains, and jade from the Central American highlands.

Yet many dimensions of the Mayan way of life remain shrouded in uncertainty, and experts can only speculate on what their daily routine was like. By the time the first Europeans came to the region in the early 1500s, some Maya remained. Their intricate culture had mostly dissolved, although even today some remnants can be discerned. In the southern Toledo District of Belize, for example, Kekchí-speaking

Carved stone face at Mayan ruin of Lamanai (Photo by Kevin Schafer)

Indians still tell folktales that originated during the days of the Mayan empire and perform ritual dances held sacred by their ancestors.

European knowledge of Belize began in 1502, when Christopher Columbus sailed along its coast and named the Bay of Honduras. There is no evidence that the famous explorer actually anchored there. Other Spanish navigators followed throughout the sixteenth century, but few were willing to make the tricky crossing of Belize's barrier reef, and none saw fit to establish a permanent outpost. Other than a successful, plunderous raid on the Mayan trading city of Santa Rita (now Corozal), their initial presence was limited to a few minor explorations and some missionary work. Catholic churches were established at Lamanai in the early 1500s, but the Spanish clerics were ejected before a colony could be firmly established.

Perhaps the first permanent settlement of foreigners in Belize began in the early 1600s when Puritan traders, then based on the swampy Mosquito Coast of eastern Nicaragua, established several outposts on strategic barrier reef islands, including Tobacco Caye. The colonists apparently ignored the fact that Vicente Yanez Pinzon and Juan Díaz de Solis, among other Spanish explorers, had already claimed the area for Spain. Despite their own lack of interest in starting a Belizean colony, Spanish forces routed the Puritans from their trading posts in 1641.

Seemingly unknown to the Spaniards, a separate group of shipwrecked British sailors had started building their own tiny community on the Belize coast some three years earlier. They were a motley crew. Many were pirates and buccaneers who had learned of Belize through contact with the Puritan merchants. Gradually, over the next 150 years, more and more English settlers would move into the same area. They were later joined by a contingent of disbanded English sailors and soldiers who fought for the successful British liberation of Jamaica in 1655. Some of these early settlers were engaged in indiscriminate hardwood logging, others in piracy, and a precious few in farming. All would be forced to defend their primitive villages from sporadic attacks by Indians and Spaniards.

With few inhabitants, treacherous backwaters, and a dangerous offshore reef, Belize was an ideal hideout for these raiders of the

Caribbean. By the late 1600s, the most infamous Scottish and English pirates had established permanent bases in Belize, from which they mercilessly attacked the Spanish galleons carrying gold, silver, dyes, hardwoods, and other raw materials back to Europe.

The camp set up by one Scottish captain, Peter Wallace, eventually became Belize City. One theory holds that the word "Belize" is a corruption of the Spanish pronunciation of "Wallace." (Others insist that it is derived from the Mayan word *belix*, meaning "muddy water," or *belikin*, translated as "land that faces the coast." Yet another theory speculates the name derives from the French *balise*, a reference to the "beacon" used to guide plunderers back home at night.)

Just as they ruthlessly preyed on trading ships, the pirates of Belize began to plunder the virgin forests that surrounded them. The first documented lumbering was undertaken by buccaneer Bart Sharp about 1660. He and his comrades were especially eager to remove logwood (a source of textile dyes) and mahogany (an excellent hardwood prized for outdoor construction and fine furniture). Sharp and his cohorts called themselves "Baymen," after the Bay of Honduras to their south.

Unable to eject the Baymen by force, Spain finally signed treaties with Britain in 1763 and 1786 which secured cooperation in the suppression of piracy and protection of lumber interests. The British would be allowed to remain as long as they kept to certain areas and left the treasure-laden galleons alone. Unfortunately, this would not be the end of their territorial disputes in the region.

As they gradually turned more of their attention toward timber cutting, the white settlers began importing hundreds of African slaves from Jamaica and other British-controlled islands of the Caribbean. They relied on the brute strength of their charges to accomplish the difficult task of cutting the huge logs and hauling them to ships for export. By the 1700s, lumber was a booming industry and the English were going far into the Belizean interior to selectively cut the largest trees they could find.

Still, the British government could not seem to decide what to do with its de facto colony. The crown vacillated between lending aid to what had become known as the Bay Settlement and callously using the territory as a pawn in its ongoing diplomatic games with Spain. For almost two hundred years, the legal status of the region remained uncertain. At one point, English authorities even ceded authority over Belize to Spain, with the understanding that existing woodcutting concessions could remain. Other agreements barred the Baymen from erecting fortifications, governing themselves, and establishing plantations. The stout-hearted settlers, true to the lawless spirit of their forebears, generally ignored such treaties and set up their own laws. Eventually, with great reluctance, London sent official representatives to the Bay Settlement during the late 1780s.

This action infuriated the Spanish, who felt Britain was overstepping the bounds of its treaties regarding Belize. The showdown came in a conclusive 1798 skirmish off St. George's Caye, near Belize City, where a few hundred angry settlers and a British schooner drove off a powerful, battle-hardened wing of the Spanish Armada. Amazingly, even after the battle, England failed to officially seek title to the territory. Predictably, this made little difference to the Baymen, who proclaimed the date of their final victory over Spain as their independence day. Even now, September 10 is celebrated as Belize's "National Day," with a separate holiday on September 21 to mark independence from England in 1981.

Slowly but surely, British influence in Belize grew during the early 1800s. When Spain dismantled its New World empire and granted independence to Mexico and Guatemala in 1821, Britain's Foreign Office loudly rejected immediate claims to Belize by those two countries, which for separate reasons considered this "province" to be part of their rightful inheritance from Spain.

By 1826, the Baymen woodcutters had extended their timber harvesting to the Sarstoon River, the present southern boundary of Belize, and had become so prosperous that England could not help but take notice. At the same time, Guatemala remained adamant in its determination to annex the region and periodically waged war against the "trespassing" settlers. In 1859, fearing continued political instability would be bad for its now sizable business in the region, Britain finally signed a treaty with Guatemala in which the latter confirmed the present-day boundaries of Belize in return for British financing of a road from Guatemala's capital to Belize City. For various reasons, this promise was never carried out, thus explaining why Guatemala, which never formally ratified the 1859 agreement, remained hostile. (In 1991, Guatemala's newly elected president, Jorge Serrano, recognized Belize's independence and settled the long-running dispute, although the British continue to maintain a well-equipped 2,000-man garrison in the country as a deterrent to Guatemala and other would-be invaders.)

Similarly, Mexico's claim to Belize was not easily settled. Throughout the nineteenth century, the Mexican government insisted that the northern half—and perhaps all—of Belize was an extension of its Yucatán holdings. Tensions escalated during the Caste War of 1847-1858, when thousands of Indian and mestizo (mixed-race) slaves revolted against their masters in the Yucatán and fled across the border in search of British protection (slavery had been banned in Belize since 1838). Mexican authorities decided not to pursue the renegades across the border, and thus several thousand refugees became the nucleus for settlement in the northern districts of Belize, which remain largely Spanish-speaking. Mexico finally renounced any designs on Belize in an 1897 treaty with England.

Throughout much of the 1800s, authorities in London seemed to be sending the colonists a double message. On the one hand, British officials eagerly routed the attempts by Mexico and Guatemala to take over Belize. On the other hand, they barely inched their way toward granting the Baymen legal status as a colony.

Some historians have suggested there is a racial basis for this reluctance. During this period, only about 10 percent of the population was white, while 75 percent consisted of black slaves. Most of the balance were freed slaves, Creoles, or Mayan Indians. The European slave owners typically lived in the relative comfort of their Belize City homes while work crews of blacks labored in the hot, overgrown interior. In 1812, these slaves were put to work building St. John's Cathedral, an imposing brick structure still in use along Belize City's Southern Foreshore. Meanwhile, back in London, fierce debates were raging about the morality of slavery, which probably shoved this Central American backwater further into obscurity. By 1838, slavery was outlawed in the British Empire, including Belize (although former slaves were expressly forbidden from receiving land grants from the Crown).

In 1840, after establishing through various abolition-of-slavery acts that the Central American settlers were indeed its subjects, Great Britain declared Belize to be "the colony of British Honduras." But the declaration was in name only, and administration of the colony did not begin until 1862. It would be another nine years before British Honduras became recognized as a formal Crown colony, and it was not until the 1880s that the territory was administered separately from Jamaica.

With its formal establishment as a colony finally accomplished, development of Belize became much more organized. Oversight was badly overdue, since a lack of diversification in industry and over-dependence on imported goods had sent Belize into decline during the Victorian era. The concentration of landownership made it difficult for entrepreneurs to start projects that might wean the colony from its motherland. By the late nineteenth century, a single London-based company (Belize Estate & Produce) owned more than a million acres of land, or one-fifth of the entire territory.

During this period, Belize went through a series of profound cultural changes, yielding a multiethnic society that has remained remarkably cohesive. Many of the original English and Scottish settlers intermarried with freed slaves to form the Creole majority that still dominates the population. In the north, Mexican citizens fleeing the Yucatán's long-running Caste War crossed the border and began cultivating small farms. Many of their descendants now grow sugarcane, the country's most lucrative crop. To the south, Kekchí and Mopan Indians sought refuge from forced labor plantations in Guatemala, and a small contingent of weary Confederate war veterans arrived from the United States to found a plantation colony they called Toledo. From the Bay Islands off Honduras, a large contingent of Garifuna people had arrived. These were blacks of mixed African and Carib Indian ancestry forcibly expelled from the West Indies island of St. Vincent in 1797 (see chap. 5 for a detailed description of Garifuna history and culture).

Belizean man and national flag (Photo by Kevin Schafer)

Others immigrating to Belize in smaller numbers during the 1800s included Chinese sugarcane workers and Lebanese shopkeepers. A few ethnic Sepoys were also conscripted to the colony from India after an 1857 rebellion, and many West Indian plantation workers were recruited to do field work by the end of the century. A handful of expatriate Europeans and North Americans decided to make this their home, too.

Despite this steady influx of able-bodied foreigners, the economy of British Honduras remained stagnant during Queen Victoria's long reign. Thanks to reckless logging practices, most of the easily accessible mahogany and other prized hardwood was gone by the 1860s, and the availability of cheap steel (coupled with inexpensive foreign labor) lowered the demand for such trees in shipbuilding and other types of construction. The export of timber gradually declined as the virgin forests closest to the rivers and coastline were systematically thinned.

Early attempts to diversify the economy met with mixed success. The lack of roads, high transportation costs, and a limited pool of skilled labor stymied developers, and many new crops fell victim to exotic diseases and poor soil conditions. Periodic hurricanes devastated the country, uprooting trees and flattening houses. Then, as today, Belizeans were unable to produce enough food to feed themselves and had to rely heavily on expensive imports. Because their own food was cheap and labor plentiful, neighboring countries such as Honduras and Guatemala easily outproduced Belize in such valuable commodities as bananas, sugar, rubber, and chicle (a natural chewing gum base). Another problem facing Belize was its large population of freed slaves, who were effectively barred from obtaining vacant land that could be used for farming.

By 1900, British Honduras had grown to a population of 37,000. But the economy was moribund, wages were low, and discontent was endemic. The situation exploded after World War I, when thousands of returning Creole soldiers rioted in a violent expression of their demand for better social conditions. Joining in the chorus were hundreds of men who had helped build the Panama Canal, only to join unemployment lines back home. There was little improvement, however, as mechanization of the timber industry only increased unemployment and the depression years brought many businesses to a virtual standstill. A very destructive 1931 hurricane only compounded the colony's problems. By the late 1930s, Belize's deteriorating economic conditions prompted some residents to begin calling for independence. (Sensing this unrest, Guatemala renewed its claims to sovereignty and payment from Britain for the promised road to Guatemala City that was never built. Over the next 20 years, Guatemala became more adamant in its demands, and several forays across the frontier had to be repelled by the British.)

During World War II, many Belizeans again volunteered to fight but came back to a land where living conditions were miserable, work opportunities were limited, and political power was concentrated in the hands of a wealthy, mostly white elite. Fearful colonial administrators responded to the growing unrest by passing restrictive laws and banning public marches. But in 1950, after a sharp devaluation of the local currency, Belizeans decided they had had enough. The independence movement, led by George Price, an American-educated, cautiously liberal Creole divinity student, rapidly increased in size and influence. (Now over 70 years old, in 1990, Price began serving his second term as Belize's prime minister and his fifth decade as head of the People's United Party.) In 1954, voting rights were extended to all adults, and in 1955, a form of ministerial government was introduced. By 1961, London had finally agreed to begin the process of setting Belize free.

Full internal, elected self-government was instituted in 1964, modeled on the Westminster parliamentary system. Britain remained in charge of foreign relations, defense, and internal security. A bicameral assembly (House and Senate) was established, and its members were popularly elected. (After Price's P.U.P., the largest political party is the more conservative United Democratic Party, in office from 1985 to 1989.)

In 1973, the colony's name was officially changed from British Honduras to Belize. The reins of power were gradually turned over to local authorities, and on September 21, 1981, Belizean independence was formally declared. With British troops on full alert and the border sealed, the Guatemalan invasion that some had seriously feared never took place. (Curiously, Belizeans seem quite content to play host to foreign forces, and their country essentially remains a British protectorate.)

But while Belize has successfully thwarted foreign claimants since 1798, it is quietly experiencing a subtle transformation into a Spanish-speaking country. Large numbers of Guatemalans, Salvadorans, and Hondurans have crossed its borders since independence, many of them illegally. Belize does little to discourage the influx and has even established a U.N.-funded refugee camp, Valley of Peace, on the Western Highway near Belmopan. The vast majority of these newcomers are unskilled peasants, attracted by an abundance of available land as well as a tradition of peace and political stability.

The latter is a truly significant factor for people who have known only military dictatorships, political warfare, and genocidal terrorism. The party of Prime Minister Price, for example, has dominated Belizean national politics since 1954. A governor-general represents Britain's political interests in Belize.

Hand-cranked ferry at San José Succotz (Photo by Richard Mahler)

Compared to other Central American countries, Belize enjoys relative prosperity, adequate health services, improving sanitation, a good (compulsory) public school system, and little of the income disparity that divides its neighbors into feuding factions of rich and poor, Indian and Ladino. Literacy, estimated to be over 80 percent, is higher in Belize than in the vast majority of developing countries. As the economy has slowly diversified and the infrastructure has developed, the standard of living for most Belizeans has noticeably improved.

Still, Belize is heavily dependent on foreign aid—both governmental and private—for its survival. Most oil, food, manufactured goods, and consumer products are of necessity imported and often paid for through loans and grants provided by aid programs of the United States, Britain, and other EEC members. While the country's economic base is broadening, progress has been painfully slow. In candid moments, government officials admit that illicit trafficking in marijuana and other outlawed drugs has been a major contributor to the bottom line, perhaps more than 25 percent as much as the estimated $393 million 1992 gross domestic product (GDP). During the late 1980s, officials estimated that Belize was the fourth-largest supplier of marijuana to the United States. In 1990, one expert said twenty to thirty drug-laden planes departed each month from the country, bearing as much as $30 million worth of cocaine each. Other drug shipments are transferred in Belize to trucks, boats, and even television sets for transport to the United States and Europe. There was evidence that these shipments decreased during 1991 and 1992, but they seem to have increased again since that time.

The U.S. State Department notes that much of Belize's foreign exchange is derived from citizens who have immigrated to more developed countries and regularly send money to their families back home. Today, there are a third as many Belize citizens living outside the country as inside. The largest concentrations are in Los Angeles, New York, and Chicago (with 25,000 Belizeans alone).

Although timber is still an important Belizean export (most of it pine and cedar now, not hardwood), the major agricultural crops are sugarcane and citrus fruit, cultivated in the north and south, respectively. Bananas and fish products (mainly shrimp and lobster) are also important exports, along with honey, maize, plantains, beans, mangoes, papayas, cocoa, and rice. A small number of poultry and cattle are raised domestically, and light manufacturing (mostly clothing and furniture) now accounts for about 15 percent of the GDP. Agriculture is responsible for 85 percent of export earnings. Tourism, however, is closing in on farming as the biggest contributor to Belize's bottom line.

In 1992, estimated Belizean gross imports totaled $260.9 million, while exports totaled $161.5 million, for a deficit of nearly $100 million. The United States is by far Belize's most important trading partner, buying 52 percent of all exports and supplying 59 percent of all imports. Western Europe, in contrast, supplies only 17 percent of all imports. (The United States also maintains an important Voice of America transmitter in Belize and a large contingent of Peace Corps workers.)

In early 1993, annual economic growth was running at about 6 percent, slightly ahead of the country's 5 percent rate of inflation. Unemployment was around 15 percent, and the annual federal budget was about $85 million. Observers consider the Belizean economy "fragile," since it remains very vulnerable to fluctuations in the price of farm and plantation products, in addition to trade preferences imposed by other countries. In an attempt to improve the situation, Belize during the early 1990s added powerful new incentives for investors, including duty-free export zones near the Guatemalan and Mexican borders.

Many Belizeans are hopeful that their country can at least soon become self-sufficient in food, a top priority of each successive government. In 1993, simple foodstuffs still accounted for more than 25 percent of all imports. Foreign visitors are gradually changing the Belizean way of life. Indeed, tourism is now Belize's fastest-growing industry, and the government is actively supporting that development through a cabinet-level department of tourism established in 1989. By the end of 1992, Belize had enough hotel rooms to accommodate easily its more than 225,000 visitors annually (about half from the United States and Canada).

"Nature tourism," as one official labels it, has the potential for becoming the dominant theme of those Belizeans catering to foreign visitors. Today, both the government and the private sector of Belize are promoting a more diverse and challenging kind of tourism, which takes full advantage of the country's unique resources.

"Our commitment to ecotourism is strong and steadfast," declares Glenn Godfrey, Belize's attorney general and minister of tourism and the environment, in an open letter to foreign visitors. "We are unwavering in the protection of our environmental treasures. Come and see our unspoiled rain forests, with their abundance of natural beauty and great diversity of flora and fauna. As a person concerned about the world's environmental health, you will derive considerable satisfaction from knowing that you are making a positive contribution to the preservation of these natural wonders simply by visiting them."

2
Conservation and Responsible Tourism in Belize

At one time or another, most of us dream about getting away from it all on an idyllic vacation in the sunny tropics. We may picture ourselves sprawled on a sandy beach under the shady fronds of a swaying coconut palm, sipping a rum punch, and staring hypnotically at a shimmering sea. Or perhaps we envision ourselves gliding in ecstasy through warm, perfectly clear water, sharing a dazzling marine environment with multicolored coral, jaunty sea horses, and four-eyed butterfly fish.

Maybe you have even been lucky enough to take such a trip—only to return with the unsettled feeling that something vital was missing. Like eating a fluffy dessert full of empty calories, the experience was pleasing but not quite satisfying. Next time, we recommend an adventure in what we call "natural history tourism," which is exactly the sort of unique vacation Belize has to offer. In the pages that follow, we will take you to our favorite destinations in the unspoiled "high bush" of this plucky little country.

In many ways, Belize is light-years ahead of other underdeveloped nations in redefining tourism as an economic strategy that can preserve, rather than destroy, its priceless resources. Belize has won praise from international conservationists for the so-called sustainable development strategies it has implemented to protect its impressive treasures of nature and artifacts of Mayan history while at the same time making certain that its people benefit from the public

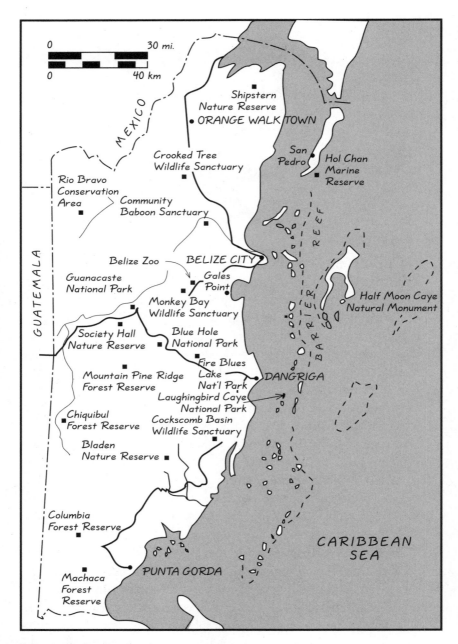

0   30 mi.

0   40 km

MEXICO

Shipstern
Nature Reserve

● ORANGE WALK TOWN

Crooked Tree
Wildlife Sanctuary

San
Pedro

Hol Chan
Marine
Reserve

Rio Bravo
Conservation
Area

Community
Baboon Sanctuary

REEF

GUATEMALA

Belize Zoo

BELIZE CITY

Guanacaste
National Park

Gales
Point

Monkey Bay
Wildlife Sanctuary

Half Moon Caye
Natural Monument

BARRIER

Society Hall
Nature Reserve

Blue Hole
National Park

Mountain Pine Ridge
Forest Reserve

Fire Blues
Lake
Nat'l Park

DANGRIGA

Laughingbird Caye
National Park

Chiquibul
Forest Reserve

Cockscomb Basin
Wildlife Sanctuary

Bladen
Nature Reserve

Columbia
Forest Reserve

CARIBBEAN
SEA

Machaca
Forest
Reserve

PUNTA GORDA

Belize's Parks, Reserves, and Monuments

lands set aside for environmental purposes. It has managed to succeed in this campaign despite constant monetary problems and growing pressure from agricultural and industrial interests. All that Belize's government officials have to do is look around them to see the danger of following another path.

Large portions of neighboring Guatemala, Mexico, and Honduras are now completely deforested, with plantations, timber interests, and slash-and-burn farmers quickly closing in on much of the remaining woodlands. In contrast, about 70 percent of Belize's land area is still covered with forest, only some of which has been thinly and selectively logged in the past. An even larger proportion—some 80 percent—of the country's pristine forest has been preserved (compared, for example, to the barely 2 percent of intact forest remaining in nearby El Salvador, slightly smaller than Belize but with about thirty times its population).

In 1990 alone, nearly 200,000 acres of verdant tropical jungle were placed under permanent protection by the Belizean government. The first of these remarkable achievements was establishment of the 92,000-acre Bladen Nature Reserve, encompassing an entire upper watershed in the country's southern Maya Mountains. In fall 1990, the Cockscomb Basin Wildlife Sanctuary was expanded with the stroke of a pen from 3,600 to 102,000 acres. Both areas contain some of the wildest and least disturbed subtropical habitat in all the Americas. Since then, officials have added more parks and reserves in the interior and offshore areas, and new proposals are up for serious consideration each year. When it comes to management of its resources, the credo of Belize seems to be, "Protect first and study later!" As a result, Belize needs to shift from establishment of parks and protected areas to long-term, on-the-ground natural area management. People from around the world should make every effort to help make this goal a reality.

Nature-based tourism is strongly and officially encouraged in Belize, partly as a justification for this determined conservation approach, which has come under some criticism from domestic advocates of more traditional growth-oriented projects. "We need the fuel, in terms of firewood, and we need the income from logging,"

Conservation class for Belize schoolchildren (Photo by Kevin Schafer)

concedes Victor Gonzalez, Belize's Permanent Secretary for the Ministry of Tourism and Environment. "Even though the industrial nations are crying out about the alarming rate of forest destruction, we in the Third World often lack the finances to stop it. It is very difficult for us to conserve." As Glenn Godfrey, Minister of Tourism and Environment, once explained, the ideal goal is to ensure that development in Belize does not adversely affect the ecology, social fabric, or future of the country. Godfrey and other politicians are hopeful that Belize can learn from the mistakes of others, weighing the advantages of badly needed foreign income against the irreversible damage that unbounded tourism and agriculture might inflict.

Environmentalists are well aware of what can (and too often does) happen when tropical travel is promoted with little regard for natural resources: protective mangrove trees are stripped by builders from sandy shorelines, fragile coral reefs are damaged by inquisitive but uninformed divers and snorkelers, commercial marine species such as conch and lobster are depleted to meet restaurant demands, and indiscriminate poaching may decimate wildlife populations so that exotic species such as gibnut, brocket deer, and sea turtle might needlessly grace a restaurant menu. Despite its own best efforts, Belize has not escaped this long list of injuries unscathed. Perhaps the parts of the country enduring the most intense development pressure are the coral reef formations immediately surrounding the most-visited cayes, Ambergris and Caulker. Coral reefs are the marine equivalents of tropical rain forests. "In most coral species, each individual polyp lays down a skeletal container of calcium carbonate that surrounds and protects its soft body," writes Edward O. Wilson. "Coral colonies grow by the budding of individual polyps, with the skeletal cups being added one on another in a set geometric pattern particular to each species. The result is a lovely, bewildering array of skeletal forms that mass together to make the whole reef—a tangled field of horn corals, brain corals, staghorn corals, organ pipes, sea fans, and sea whips." Some of these massive formations are thousands of years old.

However, Belize's barrier reef suffers injury every time a boat anchor is randomly cast and hauled in. Whenever these centuries-old marine architects are touched, they begin to turn black and die. Unfortunately, many collectors cannot seem to resist the urge to (illegally) collect sea fans, black coral, and other fragile underwater treasures. Commercial fishing throws the food chain out of balance when desired species are removed en masse. Important breeding and feeding grounds for lobster, conch, turtles, small fish, and waterfowl are destroyed when mangrove and sea grass beds are removed by developers. Over the long run, no one knows for sure what the cumulative effect of all these changes will be.

San Pedro, the main town on Ambergris Caye, already displays symptoms of tourism run amok. With its intense concentration of hotels, restaurants, bars, and souvenir shops, land prices jumped in the early 1990s to more than $100,000 for an unimproved 50-by-50-foot lot. The sewage system is overtaxed, and fresh water is scarce. Residents worry aloud about growing tension between the haves and the have-nots.

Meanwhile, in Belize's interior, habitat destruction in the form of deforestation and selective wood-cutting continues to cause serious damage to pristine ecosystems. "Today the refugees and their milpa [slash-and-burn farming of staple crops] are causing great problems for Belize," the former chief forest officer, Oscar Rosado, told a local magazine in 1990. "We must be aware of what could happen if immigration went unchecked and the situation got out of hand."

According to the government, as many as 10,000 refugees a year are entering Belize from other Central American countries, mostly Guatemala, El Salvador, and Honduras. They are drawn by Belize's relaxed attitude toward homesteading, and they bring with them a strong tradition of slash-and-burn agriculture. Unfortunately, these methods quickly drain nutrients from the shallow jungle soil, and new trees must be cleared every few years to secure fresh farmland. Many refugees also hunt wild game in the forests near their homes, supplementing their meager diets, even though hunting is forbidden in Belize without a license.

Just as significant, owners of large citrus, banana, and sugarcane plantations are lobbying government ministries to change the status of several forest reserves to allow more large-scale agriculture. The citrus industry has charged ahead in recent years, clearing vast tracts of pristine tropical forests; yet market prices for oranges are declining, and Belizeans pay the price for this deforestation in the fouling of their potable water by acidic, pesticide-laden runoff from citrus fields. In other areas, Mennonite farmers are rapidly clearing forests to plant corn, beans, and other basic food crops.

In a nation that still cannot feed itself, it is very tempting to give in to such pressures. In most instances, however, the Belize government is willing to gamble that there are more long-term gains to be realized in nature-based tourism than quick-profit farming.

Yet with the opportunities of tourism come fresh challenges. Such growth forces decisions about establishment of a better infrastructure of hotels, roads, police protection, and food distribution. Deterioration of cultural institutions and ancient Mayan ruins must also be checked. And last but by no means least, promotion of tourism must be carried out in a way that is not detrimental to the very wonders that foreigners are being enticed to visit.

Immigrant homesteading along the Hummingbird Highway (Photo by Richard Mahler)

As one of the world's most environmentally aware countries, Belize has already set a standard of behavior that speaks for itself. Later on in this book, you will read about the Community Baboon Sanctuary, the Cockscomb Basin Wildlife Sanctuary, and the Río Bravo Conservation Area, three among many innovative examples of how the demands of conservation can be successfully balanced with fundamental economic needs of the local population.

Another "appropriate scale" project in the southern part of the country demonstrates such sensitivity in action. In the largely undeveloped Toledo District, local organizers are working with a group of Kekchí and Mopan Maya who have opened simple thatch-roof guest houses for travelers who want to get a firsthand look at a subsistence farming culture that has persisted for centuries. Several villages have formed a collective and now speak with one voice in a scheme whereby some of the income derived from low-impact tourism can be used to develop something called "homesite farming." Homesite farmers rely on natural plants, growth cycles, and soil conditioning to make local land usable year after year. This has been shown to be a viable alternative to slash-and-burn techniques, with their renewed demand for forest acreage every two or three years (for a detailed description of the project, see chap. 5).

This innovative approach is proving to be a key to protecting Belize's only true rain forests, exclusive to the Toledo District, from further destruction. A 100-acre nature reserve, Río Blanco Falls, is the first protected area established following the express wish of Toledo villagers. Mayan residents of Santa Cruz and Santa Elena urged the government to declare the area a nature reserve, with assistance from the Toledo Ecotourism Association, to protect natural resources between the two villages. This is great news for visitors who want to experience Belize's rain forest and some of the lesser-explored Mayan ruins in Toledo.

Other money derived from the Mayan village tourism plan is being used to help set up a regional network of biosphere reserves, part of an ongoing campaign to protect the most biologically significant rain forests of Central and South America. The government, through its Conservation Unit, also expects to hire local Mayan farmers as guides and rangers, who will help protect these new reserves. This will provide them with a much-needed source of outside income.

While Belize's record of conservation achievements under Prime Minister George Price is admirable, especially for such a young and impoverished nation, there is a clear need for financial support from around the world to perpetuate its success and implement new strategies, such as the just-described Mayan village project. We are convinced that low-interest loans from the World Bank and grants from other international donors could provide critical support to the Conservation Unit and also be used to hire Belizeans to help restore long-neglected Mayan ruins, for example. It should be noted that the U.S. Agency for International Development (AID) has already acted on some of these suggestions. The AID program has, for instance, provided substantial funding for the study and restoration of Caracol, the spectacular Mayan ruin in extreme western Belize.

Many additional grants and loans are needed to take the pressure off the thinly stretched infrastructure of Belize. Road building and on-the-ground management of protected areas that employ locals are high priorities. There is also a clear demand for more tourism facilities, such as small guest houses and restaurants, that would be owned and operated by citizens of Belize rather than the foreigners who are now threatening to dominate the service industry. Again, decisions need to be made in view of their potential impact not only on the natural environment but also on the livelihood of the Belizean people.

Funding is needed to support management of protected areas and the hiring of local tour guides at destinations that already are being promoted. This list includes the Community Baboon (Howler Monkey) Sanctuary, Cockscomb Basin Wildlife Sanctuary, Crooked Tree Wildlife Sanctuary, Laughing Bird Caye National Park, Five Blues Lake National Park, Chiquibul National Park and Caracol Archaeology Reserve, Guanacaste National Park, Glover's Reef Marine Reserve, and Half Moon Caye National Monument, all described later in this book.

Support to ensure the success of such ventures could readily be generated through contributions from many international tour companies and conservation organizations that are hosting "adventure" trips to Belize and realizing enormous financial benefits through their subtle exploitation of the country's rich natural resources. It is important to note that some companies, such as International Expeditions, are leading the way in putting income back into the communities around these protected areas. (In chap. 5, we describe this company's collaboration with locals in Crooked Tree to promote the harvest of cashews, in tandem with natural history tourism, as sustainable natural resource development.) All companies for whom natural and cultural wonders represent the bottom line must contribute, however. A permanent fund or endowment might be established to which these groups are "strongly encouraged" to contribute. The money would then be directed in the form of grants or loans to Belizean enterprises involved in protected area management and conservation tourism. These funds, along with similar donations or loans from outside agencies, might be administered through a Belizean organization already sympathetic to these goals.

Tapping chicle from a sapodilla tree (Photo by Kevin Schafer)

Foreign-owned tour companies and conservation groups now reap enormous benefits from guiding travelers through Belize. Yet such organizations are often providing few direct economic benefits to the Belizean people. They may bring along their own tour guides and "facilitators," for instance, and often deal primarily with foreign-owned airlines, rental companies, hotels, and restaurants. We suggest that it is time these groups, taking the lead from tour companies such as International Expeditions, began putting at least as much into Belize as they are taking out. Taken as a whole, relatively small individual contributions from each could have a very powerful and positive impact.

Let us look briefly at a single practical accomplishment that could be achieved through this new source of income. One of Belize's most important freshwater ecosystems is the Mussel Creek/Cox Lagoon wetland complex in central Belize, only about 45 minutes west of Belize City by car. The Belize Audubon Society and Belize Center for Environmental Studies have both had an active interest in protecting this rich habitat for years. The value of this area is immediately apparent.

Mussel Creek/Cox Lagoon literally teems with life: water lilies cover the rippling surface of its slow-moving stream, roseate spoonbills create pink mosaics along the water's edge as they methodically dredge up microorganisms from the rich lagoon bottoms, white cattle egrets and wood storks soar in tight formation up the winding channel at dusk every evening, endangered hickatee river turtles and American crocodiles bob to the surface in search of their swimming prey, belted kingfishers plunge from tall kapok trees to snag tiny minnows from the waterway. As much as any natural wonder in Belize, the Mussel Creek/Cox Lagoon wetlands call out for protection.

If our proposed endowment were to come about, land along Mussel Creek and nearby Cox Lagoon could be protected before further encroachment by area farmers, fisherman, refugees, and developers. Local people are eager to act as guides for visitors while patrolling the area as reserve managers. Nesting sites of the imperiled Central American river turtle might be found, then guarded against the theft of their precious eggs by humans and other predators. In the surrounding villages, an influx of nature-minded tourists could lead to the establishment of an informal bed-and-breakfast network among Creole homeowners, not unlike the similar services already offered at the Community Baboon and Crooked Tree Wildlife Sanctuaries not far away (described in chap. 5). Local artisans would find a ready market for their wares. Within a single year, it is possible that the fragile Mussel Creek ecosystem could be protected. "The goal is to come up with a sustained yield use that does not exclude the needs of the local people," explains Arnold Brown, director of Programme for Belize, an organization managing a huge tract of pristine forest in the northwest part of the country known as the Río Bravo Conservation Area (see chap. 6). "That way, we can continue using the land for centuries to come."

If you are interested in helping to put these kinds of strategies into action, there are many very practical things you can do to help the environmental movement in Belize. One simple thing is to stop by their offices while you are in Belize City and contribute to the work they are doing. At the Programme for Belize headquarters in Belize City, at 1 King Street (tel. 2-75616), you will find descriptive information and maps concerning the Río Bravo Conservation Area. This is the place to inquire about accommodations at the Chan Chich Lodge, an unusual jungle resort built in the plaza of an old Mayan ruin .

Not far away is the Belize City office of the Belize Audubon Society, at 29 Regent Street (tel. 2-77369). (As of mid-1993, Audubon was planning to move their headquarters to the old customs building, so check before you set out to find them.) Travelers can pick up literature about the major parks, monuments, and sanctuaries Belize Audubon manages. As part of its educational outreach mission, the society also sells beautiful posters, wildlife guides, and such helpful materials as bird species checklists.

The Belize Center for Environmental Studies, at 55 Eve Street (tel. 2-45545), is a well-stocked information clearinghouse for anyone interested in details about the country's flora, fauna, and ecosystems. The center has played a critical role in assessing Belizean wildlife habitats and natural resources. Its leaders have used much of that information to convince the government that it must establish laws and policies to protect these environmental treasures, while at the same time assessing potential environmental impacts of development projects. Books, maps, and pamphlets are available on the premises.

Even if you make no direct contact with any of these groups, it is comforting to know that simply going to many of the destinations described in this book makes you a part of ongoing efforts to save a precious part of the planet. By joining the groups of your choice, you empower them to carry out their vital missions.

If you use the services of a so-called ecotourism travel operator, we urge you to take a careful look at their practices. Do they hire local guides and book guests into locally owned hotels? Are they actively involved in training, conservation, or other kinds of development work in the country they send travelers to? The Ecotourism Society is a nonprofit association that has established a rating system based on consumer evaluation of such operators. You can contact them at their Washington, D.C., headquarters by calling (703) 549-8979.

In the meantime, while you are in Belize, we hope you will keep in mind a list of "dos and don'ts" put together by one of the first truly "green" travel agents in the United States, our friend Karen Johnson at Preferred Adventures in St. Paul, Minnesota.

1. Respect the earth and understand how fragile and complex is the web of life that we are all a part of. Conservation is not just a matter of aesthetics. It is a matter of survival.

2. Leave only footprints—no graffiti and no litter! Never take "souvenirs" from historic or natural sites.

3. To make your travels more meaningful, do your homework. Learn in advance about the geography, natural history, and culture of countries you plan to visit.

4. Respect the privacy and dignity of others; try to understand how you would feel if you were in their place.

5. Do not buy products made from endangered plants or animals, such as ivory, tortoise shell, animal skins, and feathers. Read "Know Before You Go," the U.S. Customs Service list of wildlife products that cannot be imported.

6. Always follow designated trails. Do not disturb plants, animals, or their habitats.

7. Learn about and support conservation programs and organizations working in the countries you will visit.

8. Never harass animals or disturb plant life for the sake of a photograph; ask permission before taking pictures of local people.

9. Patronize travel agents, tour operators, airlines, hotels and resorts, and cruise lines that respect the environment and support conservation programs.

Here is one more item we would like to add to the Preferred Adventures roster:

10. Become a positive contributor to Belize's experiment in developing a new, responsible tourism ethic. You help such a country's conservation projects succeed by joining, by visiting, or by volunteering to participate in them. Your presence is itself a vote of confidence in the difficult decisions government leaders have made.

3

Practical Travel
Information

If you have spent time in Mexico or Central America, your first reaction to Belize may be one of great surprise. An English-speaking island in a sea of Spanish and Indian dialects, Belize looks and feels more like the relaxed, post-colonial British Caribbean than Latin America. And for travelers accustomed to the extremes of poverty, overcrowding, inefficiency, corruption, and militarism that are typical of some Latin destinations, the comparative tranquillity and prosperity of Belize will probably come as a welcome change. Its singular status as the only non-Spanish-speaking nation (and former colony) between Mexico's Rio Grande and South America's Guyana explains some of Belize's eccentricities, the most important of which are discussed below and in the section, Inside Belize.

As a subtropical country that is close enough to North America to be subject to its seasonal air currents, Belize has distinct periods of either warm and wet or cool and dry weather. Winters (January through April) are mild and relatively free of rain, while the balance of the year (especially June through October) is much hotter and damper, with a brief dry spell in August. The driest months are February and March, although rain can (and does) fall at any time of the year. Humidity is fairly high no matter what the season. Trade winds tend to keep things less sticky near the coast and on the cayes, although both areas are subject to sudden storms, and winds are frequently calm in midsummer. For detailed information, contact the Belize Weather Bureau at 25-2012.

Street scene at San Pedro, Ambergris Caye (Photo by Kevin Schafer)

Most visitors prefer to see Belize during the winter months of the Northern Hemisphere. Daytime coastal temperatures during this period are in the 70s and 80s. Even during the hottest summer months, shade temperatures seldom rise above 90 degrees F (38°C) near the coast. During the "cold" spells of December and January, the thermometer sometimes falls below 55 degrees F (13°C). Temperature extremes are greater inland, where mountain nights are generally cool, even plunging into the low 40s. The average temperature throughout the year is 79 degrees F.

Hurricanes are rare but can threaten Belize at any time between June and November. After Belize City was twice destroyed by severe storms earlier this century, an efficient warning system was set up, and hurricane shelters were established throughout the country. You will be warned well in advance if a potentially destructive storm is expected in Belize, which seems to be the case once every fifteen years or so. The last big hurricane struck in 1979.

Rainfall in Belize increases as one travels from north to south. About 50 inches a year falls in Corozal Town near the Mexican border, 65 inches in Belize City and the Cayo District, 95 inches in

Dangriga, and 170 inches around Punta Gorda, across a strait of water from Guatemala and Honduras.

English is the official language of Belize and is the mode of instruction in all its schools. Outside Belize City and environs, Spanish is widely spoken (many of the nation's newest immigrants, in fact, speak no English whatsoever). About two-thirds of the people speak a kind of "Creole" English not unlike the heavily accented patois of Jamaica and other former British island colonies of the Caribbean.

Spanish is most common in the far south, north, and west. An estimated 60 percent of the population is bilingual (mostly Spanish/English), and at least 30 percent regard Spanish as their mother tongue. The 9 percent of Belizeans identified as Garifuna or Black Carib speak their own language, as do the 8 percent who are Indian (mostly Mopan, Kekchí, or Yucatec). Most of the country's 6,000 Mennonites converse in an archaic Low German dialect.

Entry and Exit Requirements

To enter Belize, all nationalities must have valid passports plus "sufficient funds" ($50 a day minimum) and an onward ticket out of the country. In recent years, the last two requirements have not been strictly enforced, although there are occasional reports of border authorities turning away individuals whose appearance was deemed unsavory and/or who carried less than $30 per day for the duration of their intended visit. Do not be surprised if an immigration or customs official asks exactly where you will be staying and precisely how much cash you have, especially if you are a long-haired backpacker. For stays longer than 30 days, an extension must be obtained (for a $12.50 fee) from the Immigration office at 115 Barracks Road in Belize City.

Visas are not required from citizens of the United States, Canada, Mexico, Germany, France, the United Kingdom, and British Commonwealth countries and most members of the European Economic Community. Visa requirements vary; you are urged to check with a travel agent or Belize authorities if in doubt. Citizens of Latin American nations will note that since Belize was accepted as a full member of the Organization of American States in 1990, many visa requirements in the region have been dropped.

Visas may not be purchased at the border, although they can be obtained for $10 from the Belize consulate in Chetumal, Mexico, just north of the international crossing. These documents can also be arranged at Belizean embassies in Mexico City, Washington, D.C., and other capitals and, in some instances, through British consulates. Free transit visas are available at the border for periods of 24 or 48 hours, and visas are sometimes not demanded if the visitor has an onward ticket in hand. Those requiring visas for other countries after leaving Belize should obtain them before their arrival. Guatemala now has both an embassy and a consulate in Belize should visitors plan to cross into that country (see chap. 6 for further details).

Tourists are initially granted 14- or 30-day permits to visit Belize which can be renewed for up to six months. (After six months, travelers must exit the country for at least 24 hours.) As a tourist, visitors may not do any kind of work (paid or unpaid) without first obtaining a permit from the Department of Labor. With domestic unemployment hovering around 20 percent, permission is not easily granted.

Drivers should carry their own valid vehicle registration documents and licenses. International Driver's Licenses may be used in Belize, but domestic equivalents are also acceptable. You must obtain a temporary permit at Customs control waiving duty payment if the vehicle is not going to be sold in Belize. Third-party insurance is compulsory and can be purchased at border crossings or in major towns for about $60 a month. There is an exit fee of $2.50 per car, and any automobiles brought into the country permanently must pay a hefty import duty. Visitors are only permitted to use a Canadian or U.S. driver's license for 90 days, after which they must obtain a Belizean license ($20 plus photos and a medical examination report).

For those leaving Belize by land, there is no longer any departure tax. A $12 tax must be paid for all international air departures, unless the individual has spent less than 24 hours in the country, in which case there is no fee.

Immunization and Staying Healthy

No immunizations are required for entry, and public health standards in Belize are generally good. Public water supplies in most large communities are chlorinated, although there have been some reports about tap water contamination. Many travelers take the added precaution of drinking bottled water and other beverages or adding their own purification chemicals to local water. A drop of iodine or bleach can be used for each liter of water; however, stronger chemical solutions such as Bactrim and Metronidazole may be needed to kill some parasites and especially virulent bacteria. Be advised that giardia is a waterborne parasite that neither chlorine nor boiling is sure to kill.

Since Belizean pharmacies are rather limited, bring along whatever medications you ordinarily use and items such as contact lens solutions or prescription eyeglasses.

Mosquitoes and biting flies are quite common, especially during the rainy season, and it is advisable to carry repellent at all times. Cutter's, Jungle Juice, Repel, and Avon Skin-So-Soft Bath Oil are good deterrents, as is citronella oil and the consumption of garlic. Rubbing alcohol will soothe itching. Since most insects cannot fly well in a breeze, a fan is also useful.

Tropical diseases are reasonably under control in Belize, but mosquito-borne malaria and dengue fever are still reported. Yellow fever, cholera, and tuberculosis are rare but do occur. The cautious traveler who plans to spend extended time in the interior is advised to take antimalarial drugs and obtain gamma globulin (for hepatitis) as well as oral typhoid immunization and tetanus inoculation. It is a good idea to get a tetanus booster (usually combined with diptheria) every ten years. Outpatient medical attention is free of charge at government clinics and hospitals, and there are a number of private physicians' offices throughout Belize.

Snakes are found throughout Belize, even on the cayes, and care should be exercised when hiking or walking off the road. Only nine of the country's fifty-four snake species are poisonous, but they include the deadly tommygoff (also known as fer-de-lance) and several vari-

"No to Drugs" billboard on the outskirts of Orange Walk Town (Photo by Richard Mahler)

eties of coral snakes and rattlers. Scorpions, tarantulas, and ticks, plus carnivorous ants, are found in many parts of the interior.

On the cayes, the most common problems are overexposure to the sun, scratches from sharp coral or sea urchins, and the annoying bites of such otherwise harmless flying insects as no-see-ums and sand fleas. Stepping on stingrays can cause extremely painful wounds that are potentially deadly if not treated. The scorpionfish and jellyfish are also a hazard. Barracuda, eels, and sharks are common in these waters (especially the relatively harmless lemon and nurse sharks), but these animals will rarely attack humans unless provoked or drawn by the smell of bleeding wounds.

Remember to wear a shirt when snorkeling (to protect your back from sunburn). Bring along a hat, a long-sleeved shirt, cotton trousers, and sunglasses when outdoors during midday hours.

Food is generally safe in established hotels and restaurants. As in any underdeveloped country, there is some risk involved in eating from roadside stands and sidewalk vendors, particularly where unrefrigerated meat and unwashed fruits or vegetables are concerned. Cholera and hepatitis, easily transferred through such foods, are a continuing problem in Belize. Bottled drinks are safe. Remember that cooking seafood does not destroy ciguatera toxin, which tends to show up in big reef fish like grouper, sea bass, and red snapper. (Symptoms range from nausea and numbness to diarrhea and heart arrhythmia.) Avoid eating raw fish in Belize.

Safety

The U.S. State Department is a good source of up-to-date information about conditions in foreign countries. Contact the Citizens Emergency Center at (202) 647-5225. In mid-1993, officials were advising travelers to exercise caution against street crime in Belize City: walking alone at night was being discouraged. Several urban centers, notably Belize City and Orange Walk Town, have acquired reputations as being "unsafe" and even downright inhospitable to tourists. More recently, Caye Caulker has drawn a large number of complaints. There is a relatively high level of petty street crime in certain neighborhoods and some degree of drug trafficking. Production of marijuana and transshipment of cocaine remain lucrative businesses in Belize, despite aggressive attempts by the governments of the United States, Great Britain, and Belize to put a damper on such illicit activities. Visitors should inquire before setting out on foot into parts of these cities that might seem questionable. In Belize City, we recommend you take taxis. As you would at home, be aware of your surroundings and avoid carrying large amounts of cash or expensive jewelry. The most common form of harassment is strictly verbal, and the perpetrators will usually leave you alone if you ignore them or banter goodnaturedly. Anything beyond this should be reported to the authorities at once.

Another sort of hazard is posed by power boats. Several tourists have been badly injured and even killed in recent years while swimming in areas where fast-moving boats regularly travel. The most dangerous areas are off Ambergris Caye near San Pedro and in the "cut" at Caye Caulker.

As in other developing countries, it is a good idea to keep your expensive jewelry, flashy watches, and other signs of wealth at home. Carry your money and important documents in a money belt under your clothes. Keep only as much cash in your wallet or purse as you expect to spend that particular day. Make sure you have a duplicate of valuable papers (including passport) and a list of traveler's check identification numbers that are kept separate from the originals. If your hotel has a safe, leave valuables there. (Always obtain an accurate receipt for such items.) Immediately report any theft to local police and get a written report from them. To reach the police, fire department, or ambulance service in Belize, dial 90.

Airlines, Buses, Boats, Autos, and Railroads

Belize is currently served by two U.S. and four Central American airlines via the Phillip Goldson International Airport near Belize City.

From the United States, Belize can be reached most directly from Miami (American, Sahsa, Taca), New Orleans (Sahsa, Taca), Houston (Sahsa, Taca, Continental), and Los Angeles (Taca). Taca also makes connections from Washington, New York, and San Francisco.

Sahsa, a Honduran airline, also flies to Belize from San Pedro Sula and Tegucigalpa. Taca, based in El Salvador, schedules flights from San José, Guatemala City, and Panama City. The Guatemalan airlines, Aerovías and Aviateca, have biweekly schedules from Flores and Guatemala City, to Belize City. A domestic carrier, Tropic, flies twice a week between Flores and Belize City. Bonanza Airlines was scheduled to begin direct flights in mid-1993 between Belize City and Chetumal, Mexico, with connections from there to Mérida, Cancún, and Mexico City.

There is no direct service to Europe, although the situation could change at any time. Several carriers, notably Air France, KLM, and Lufthansa, have shown keen interest in establishing a Belize City connection. Now, most European visitors transfer at one of the American gateway cities, or in Cancún or Guatemala City.

Once in Belize City, frequent flights to smaller towns are offered by Tropic Air, Maya Airways, Sky Bird, and Island Air, all via the Municipal Airport. Tropic, Maya, and others will also arrange charters to Mexico, Guatemala, and Honduras as well as destinations within Belize (see Inside Belize).

There is minimal sea-passenger service directly to Belize, most of it through the southern village of Punta Gorda. A twice-weekly ferry shuttles between here and Puerto Barrios in Guatemala, with onward connections to Honduras. Private yachts, live-aboard dive boats, fishing vessels, and the odd cruise ship ply Belizean waters, but arrangements for passage must be made on a case-by-case basis. Cruise lines berthing at Belize City in 1993 included Classical (the *Aurora II* only), Royal Caribbean Princess, and Regency. See chapter 4 and Inside Belize for information about boats to the cayes and offshore islands or entering Belize by your own private craft.

Belize no longer has any railroads. The few railways established during colonial days have been dismantled, and today the nearest railheads are in Mérida, Mexico, and Puerto Barrios, Guatemala.

While the infrastructure of roads in Belize is improving, only one (the Western Highway) is currently smooth and well maintained. All others are of variable quality, ranging from rough dirt track to potholed pavement.

Overland entry to Belize by foreigners is only permitted from eastern Guatemala (at the Western Highway crossing between Melchor de Mencos and Benque Viejo) or Mexico's Yucatán peninsula (where the Northern Highway crosses the Río Hondo at Santa Elena and Chetumal). A second Mexican crossing was due to open in 1993 at La Unión, a village northwest of Orange Walk. The 1,300-mile drive from south Texas takes anywhere from three to seven days. Belizean buses—many of them purchased secondhand from American public schools—run regularly between Chetumal, Mexico, and Belize City. Seats can be reserved in advance, and ticket prices are reasonable. Batty Brothers and Venus are the two main companies, both charging about $8 for the four-hour trip.

Crossing into Belize from Guatemala is more problematic (see chap. 6 for specific details on crossing the frontier). Public buses do not cross the border; therefore, it is necessary to walk (or take a taxi)

Fort Street Guest House, Belize City (Photo by Kevin Schafer)

from one side to the other to buy an onward ticket and change vehicles. The crossing is open from 6:00 a.m. to midnight and sometimes closed for the midday siesta (noon to 2:00 p.m.). Guatemala charges a $5 fee for entering and leaving the country by land. Guatemalan and Belizean tourist cards are issued at the border, but visas usually are not.

While it is possible to rent a private car in Belize, many travelers are put off by the high cost ($100 or more per day) and limited availability of vehicles. Some tourists have also complained about unscrupulous operators who have allegedly overcharged them for insurance and unneeded repairs. It is possible to rent a car in Mexico and drive it into Belize, but agents will charge more if informed that this is your destination. If your Mexican car breaks down in Belize, you may have to pay for it to be towed back to Mexico for repairs and spare parts, both hard to find in Belize. Gas is also much more expensive in oil-poor Belize than in Mexico (about five times the price) and is sometimes difficult to find because of spot shortages. Rental agencies will not allow Belizean vehicles to travel into Guatemala.

Set your watch in Belize to central standard time, the equivalent of the American Midwest. Daylight savings time is not observed. Electrical current is the same as the United States and Canada: 110 volts a.c.

What to Bring

Visitors to Belize are allowed to bring with them virtually anything they might reasonably be expected to need during their stay, including fishing gear and diving equipment. Light, informal clothing is recommended. Firearms are prohibited without prior clearance, and pets are only allowed into the country with proof of rabies vaccination and a certificate of good health signed by a veterinarian. Radio transmitters (including CB sets) will be held until a license can be obtained from the government. Up to 200 cigarettes, 20 ounces of liquor, and one bottle of perfume may be brought in duty-free.

In contrast to Mexico and other Central American countries (except Panama), Belize is a relatively expensive country to visit. Almost everything, including food, is imported and subject to heavy duty taxes. Therefore, it is best to bring along all the clothing, equipment, film, books, maps, diapers, and toiletries you think you will need. If not, you can expect to pay much more than you would at home for such items, provided they are even available. If you wish to make friends among the locals, bring along fish hooks and small tackle items for men, cosmetics for women, books and small toys (e.g., balloons and magnifying glasses) for children.

Photography

Belize is a subtropical country posing special considerations for the photographer. Moisture, for example, can pose a serious problem. High humidity may cause condensation on (or in) lenses, promote the growth of fungus on equipment, and speed corrosion of camera parts. Rain can splatter on lenses and work its way inside a camera. Perspiration may make handling slippery. Precautions include a tight-fitting camera case, lens cleaning materials, and an absorbent cloth for your own sweaty hands and brow.

Light is another important factor in tropical photography. Midday sunlight is very intense and yields sharp contrasts; shoot in morning and late afternoon light for softer and richer effects. When taking pictures under the forest canopy, be aware of shadows and streaks.

A high-powered lens and/or sighting scope will help capture fast-moving and faraway fauna. Remember that most animals can see, hear, or smell you long before you see them. The jaguar, for instance, has eyesight six times as powerful as a human.

If you are going to be in Belize for some length of time, consider storing your film and other gear in airtight plastic bags, preferably with moisture absorbents.

Reservations

Reservations for airline tickets and hotel rooms are often needed and recommended during the "high season" in Belize, which begins just before Christmas and continues through April. A growing number of travel agents specialize in Belize (see Inside Belize), and most of the larger tourism businesses there can easily be reached by telephone or fax. Direct-dial calls to and from the country can be made without difficulty. Belize's international country code is 501, followed by a one- or two-digit region code that varies with each district. When calling direct from the United States or Canada, dial 011-501, drop the first zero from the local number, then dial the remaining numbers. Within the country, it is sometimes necessary to dial a zero before the local number.

At the Airport

The Phillip Goldson International Airport is located in Ladyville, about 20 minutes northwest of Belize City. Immigration and customs procedures are straightforward. Cars can be rented at the airport terminal building, and a bus leaves several times a day for major hotels in Belize City, at a cost of $3. Taxi rates are regulated by the government. The cost is $15 for the 10-mile ride into town. Some hotels and resorts will arrange private pick-up by van or cab. (Taxis can be identified by their green license plates.)

Tourist information is available at the airport, travel agencies, and in the lobbies of most hotels.

When leaving the country, bear in mind that Belize bans the export of marine curios, turtles, and turtle products as well as such national treasures as Mayan artifacts and endangered plants or animals. A maximum of 20 pounds of fish may be taken out of the country, but visitors are urged to either release their catches or consume them while in Belize. See the Appendix for a complete list of "dos and don'ts."

Anyone tempted to fly out of Belize with cocaine or other illegal drugs should be aware that baggage inspections are quite thorough, and even a small amount of marijuana can yield a stiff fine and/or jail term.

Camping

Camping throughout Belize is restricted by government regulation. Unless otherwise posted or granted, prior permission must be obtained from private owners before camping on deeded land or from the Ministry of Natural Resources if you are on government-owned land (tel. 8-22037 in Belmopan). Camping is still something of a novelty in Belize, although a growing number of tourism operators cater to campers, and camping is now permitted at many national parks and archaeological sites. Personal items on any camping trip in Belize should include a flashlight, insect repellent, rain gear, sun protection, first-aid kit, and waterproof shoes or boots.

Currency, Banks, and Credit Cards

Although the U.S. dollar is widely accepted, the preferred currency is the Belize dollar, stabilized at a fixed exchange rate of $2 Belizean to $1 American. Coinages from 1 to 25 cents are in use, with the latter referred to as either a "quarter" or a "shilling."

The best rates of exchange for foreign currencies are at the borders, with Mexican pesos sometimes obtaining an especially good rate. Belizean banks charge 3 percent for the exchange of foreign currency or traveler's checks, so it may be preferable to make such transactions with merchants, hotels, or individuals, who will almost always make a straight two-for-one swap for U.S. dollars.

The Belize Bank and Barclays, among others, will draft cash on Visa and MasterCard accounts, also for a fee. A maximum of $200 may be withdrawn in cash, with any higher amounts in traveler's checks (you may be asked for proof that you are leaving the country). Money can be telexed to the larger banks in Belize.

All banks are open Mondays through Thursdays from 8:00 a.m. to 1:00 p.m. and reopen from 3:00 p.m. to 6:00 p.m. on Fridays. After closing time, moneychangers can often be found in the vicinity of major banks. They will make exchanges at fair rates for most major currencies. Credit cards have long been welcome in the larger hotels and are becoming increasingly acceptable among tour operators and other businesses that cater to foreigners, although a 5 percent surtax is usually added automatically.

There is no black market to speak of in Belize. Financial rates are generally uniform from one institution to another.

Tourist Information

Employees of the government-sponsored Belize Tourist Board, located at 83 North Front Street in Belize City (or P.O. Box 325), are friendly and helpful. The local telephone number is 2-77213. The office is open from 8:00 a.m. to noon and 1:00 to 5:00 p.m. The board maintains an overseas office in New York at 415 Seventh Avenue (800-624-0686) which can answer questions and provide informational brochures. Belizean embassies and consulates can also provide basic travel materials. In Canada, contact the Belize High Commission at (613) 232-7389 or write 112 Kent Street, Suite 2005, Ottawa, Ontario K1P 5P2.

The Belize Tourism Industry Association, a private trade organization, is also a good source of information and advice. They are located at 99 Albert Street (upstairs) in Belize City.

Most travel agencies, hotels, and gifts shops have plenty of maps, brochures, and domestic airline information.

Communications

There are few public telephones in Belize, but most hotels will allow visitors to make calls at fixed rates. The larger of these will also make their telex and fax facilities available. Direct-access long distance service has been added at some hotels and the international airport. Some of the island and jungle lodges can only be reached by radio, which can be problematic. Mail service is inexpensive and reliable. Cards or letters sent from Belize usually reach overseas destinations within a week (U.S. and Canada) or two (Europe, Asia, Australia). Belize is known among collectors for its beautiful postage stamps, many of them depicting the country's flora and fauna. A special department for collectors is located at the main post office in Belize City.

Taxes and Tipping

In larger hotels and restaurants, a service charge is sometimes added to the bill. If not, tips are based on the quality of service, usually ranging from 5 to 15 percent, although many Belizeans do not tip at all in restaurants. Taxi drivers and boatmen are tipped at the discretion of the individual, but the practice is less common than in the United States. A 5 percent government room tax is automatically added to any bill for overnight accommodations.

Business Hours, Holidays, and Festivals

Normal business hours are 8:00 a.m. to noon and 1:00 p.m. to 5:00 p.m. Many stores are open during the morning only on Wednesday and Saturday, and a few are open evenings from 7:00 to 9:00. A handful of establishments do business on Sundays, although regular bus and airline schedules may be canceled or curtailed. Banks, shops, and government offices may be closed on the following holidays:

New Year's Day–*January 1*
Baron Bliss Day–*March 9*
Good Friday–*date varies*
Holy Saturday–*date varies*
Easter–*date varies*
Easter Monday–*date varies*
Labor Day–*May 1*
Commonwealth Day–*May 24*
National (St. George's Caye) Day–*September 10*
Independence Day–*September 21*
Pan American (Columbus) Day–*October 12*
Garifuna (Settlement) Day–*November 19*
Christmas Day–*December 25*
Boxing Day–*December 26*

4

The Offshore

The main—often the only—attraction of interest to most first-time visitors to Belize is the country's coral-studded barrier reef, a spectacular formation that runs almost the entire 185-mile length of the coast and swings from within 10 to 40 miles of the mainland. In sheer size, this magnificent natural wonder is surpassed only by Australia's Great Barrier Reef. One of the richest ecosystems on the planet, Belize's reef is punctuated by scores of beautiful islands (spelled "cayes" but pronounced "keys"), sand bores, patch reefs, and various underwater structures that are home to hundreds of animal and plant species, including 220 types of fish and untold hundreds of invertebrates. So rare and exquisite is this habitat that the United Nations has proposed preservation of the reef as a World Heritage Site, arguing that its deterioration or disappearance would result in "a harmful impoverishment of the heritage of all nations of the world."

While Belize is committed to protecting this precious resource, the difficulty is that authorities lack the funds needed to properly patrol Belizean waters. Several national parks and reserves have been established in the area, however, and regulations designed to protect coral, fish, and wildlife are now being enforced as well as circumstances will allow.

Belize now finds itself engaged in a delicate balancing act: it is vigorously promoting tourism, diving, snorkeling, and commercial

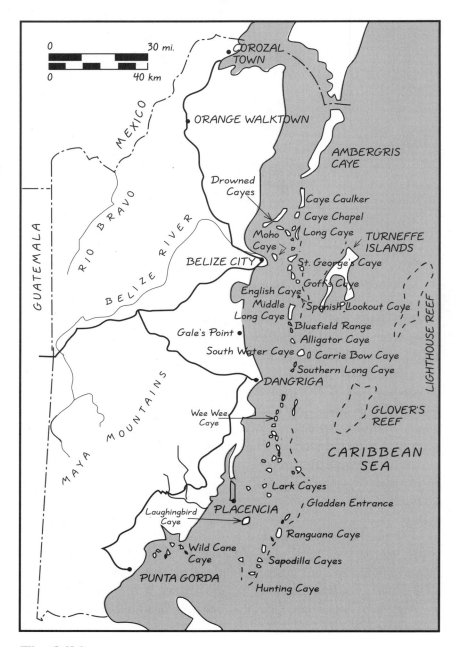

The Offshore

fishing on its barrier reef while at the same time trying to protect this exceedingly fragile environment from man's harmful influence. Certain species, such as lobster, conch and shrimp, are already being severely depleted, and some irreversible damage has been done to the reef by careless visitors.

One promising strategy for reducing the negative effects of tourism involves shifting at least some foreign visitors away from high-impact areas, namely, the Ambergris-Caulker-Chapel Caye corridor, toward lesser-known destinations that can more easily absorb the impact of newcomers. Rampant development on Ambergris Caye prompted the government to declare the northern two-thirds of the island off-limits to further exploitation—but not before one last major development broke ground. There is still talk of reactivating an abandoned airstrip on the north tip of Ambergris and founding a second town several miles away from fast-growing San Pedro.

Despite this trend, there are still dozens of islands along the southern half of the reef that are completely uninhabited and have much to offer visitors, including first-rate skin diving, snorkeling, and fishing. Also overlooked in most discussions of Belize's coastal waters are the several atolls, banks, and reefs that exist beyond the barrier strip. When taken as a whole, Belize has an estimated 350 miles of coral reef line and 280 square miles of island landmass. Much of this territory has seldom been explored by outsiders.

The atolls and southernmost cayes are not as accessible and offer more limited accommodations than the more northern barrier reef islands, but the extra effort and expense required yields some very unusual and rewarding experiences. For serious anglers and divers, these sites provide the chance to fish and dive in an almost undisturbed natural environment that teems with marine life.

Since many outer destinations are an easy day trip from the hotels on Ambergris, Caulker, and Chapel cayes, it may be more efficient to use those islands as a base for exploring the more remote offshore locations (see Inside Belize for accommodation and outfitter suggestions). Although there are places to stay and eat on the farthest cayes, cost and access may be a problem for travelers with tight budgets or time constraints. Those fortunate enough to have their own kayaks and boats will be pleased to know that the barrier reef provides innumerable safe anchorages and some of the finest sailing conditions anywhere. A couple of the islands also have private airstrips where casual visitors are allowed to land with prior permission.

The Barrier Reef and Cayes

Most of the 200-odd cayes of Belize lie in relatively shallow water along the barrier reef itself. The long, narrow stretch of water between the reef and the mainland, known as the Inner Channel, is also dotted with dozens of small islands, as are some of the country's larger inland lagoons. All these features are in actuality the summits of underwater ridges, plateaus, escarpments, or coral reefs.

The word "caye" is testimony to the varied history of the islands. It is a corruption of the Spanish *cayo*, translated in English as "islet." Early Spanish explorers were the first Europeans to set foot on the barrier chain, and they apparently stopped on them regularly to obtain fresh water and make repairs to their boats. The Spaniards no doubt encountered Mayan Indians, who established many fishing and trading outposts here over a period of centuries.

English, French, and Scottish pirates, along with Puritan traders, were next to arrive. They found the cayes ideal for their respective sea-based livelihoods, and to this day, old coins, bottles, and tools are sometimes found on the sandy beaches, along with ancient Mayan pottery and artifacts. Some of the European settlers remained as fishermen, whalers, and plantation owners, to be joined in the late 1800s by a wave of mestizo (mixed-race) immigrants from Mexico, eager to escape the brutal Yucatán Caste Wars.

Ambergris Caye

The largest and best known of the cayes, Ambergris is part of a wide limestone peninsula dangling south from the Yucatán coast of the Mexican state of Quintana Roo. In fact, most Ambergris residents are of Mexican ancestry and speak Spanish among themselves. Early

Belizean man and boy (Photo by Kevin Schafer)

in Belize's history, Mexico even laid claim to the island. Its land area is about the same as Barbados, although much of it is uninhabitable mangrove swamp.

To reach Ambergris (the name is a holdover from colonial sperm whaling days and refers to a valued substance taken from the animal once used in manufacturing perfume), most visitors take a boat or airplane across lower Chetumal Bay from Belize City, 35 miles to the southwest. Locals refer to passenger boats as "skiffs" and their smaller canoelike vessels as "dories." The crossing takes about an hour and 15 minutes by skiff.

Fishing was once the principal industry on the caye, but within the last twenty years tourism has taken over. Many fishermen now use their boats exclusively to cater to the needs of visitors. San Pedro, the island's only town, offers a wide choice of hotels, restaurants, gift shops, and travel agencies to suit every recreational interest and pocketbook, although budget travelers may find themselves pinched.

While San Pedro in some ways seems to be suffering under the strain of rapid growth, Ambergris Caye on the whole has much to recommend it. Away from the crowds, there is an abundance of birds and many other animals as well as idyllic scenery. Much of the island is covered with a high broadleaf forest interspersed with freshwater sinks that attract lots of wildlife. Visitors can spot flamingos, egrets, herons, pelicans, and frigatebirds. Bird Caye, located on the bay, or leeward, side of Ambergris, shelters rookeries for 30 species, including the reddish egret, greater egret, and cormorant. Spoonbills, avocets, and ducks also congregate here. Turtles like to nest on certain yet-undeveloped beaches, and even ocelots have been seen prowling through the mangrove forests. Thousands of shells litter the beaches. (The coral reef is less than a mile offshore.)

The island has the largest single concentration of visitor accommodations and services in Belize, yet it still manages to retain a laid-back atmosphere. The streets are sandy and belong to barefoot slow-paced strollers, since vehicles (mostly electric golf carts) are few and far between. The water is turquoise blue and immediately accessible. A cooling breeze sweeps in from the Caribbean much of the time, keeping insect pests at bay. People are friendly and tolerant, their life-style casual and simple. The tin-roofed wooden houses are cheerfully dilapidated, yet they are kept reasonably clean and colorfully painted. One gets the distinct impression that it is okay to simply relax all day if that is what one chooses. There is also a wide variety of food available, and some of the country's best cooks are happy to prepare meals (especially grilled seafood) just the way you like it.

For all these reasons, Ambergris Caye makes a fine base for excursions to nearby attractions and the more distant islands or atolls. Experienced guides are easy to find in this town of 1,500 smiling Belizeans, and some of the best outfitters for fishing and diving trips are also here, along with plenty of charter boats. Within a short distance of San Pedro, there are massive coral canyons full of caves and tunnels, and snorkelers report aquariumlike conditions. Within the confines of the reef itself, the Mexican Rocks area on the windward side is highly recommended. Conditions are also ideal here and among the island's thirteen lagoons for sailing, windsurfing, and sea kayaking.

Some words of caution are in order, however. Most of the 500 or so hotel rooms on Ambergris Caye are very basic by American or European standards. Furnishings and other physical amenities are usually minimal, so what you are paying for is location and service, not luxury. San Pedro has only five streets, and staying in town puts one close to the action—or noise, depending on one's point of view. Keep in mind that some rooms are less than 100 yards from the airport, and takeoffs go right over the town.

Be advised that the beach is very narrow in San Pedro, and there is virtually no chance of sunbathing within the town itself, what with boats, passengers, and cargo being constantly hauled on and off. You pay higher prices to stay in a hotel farther away from San Pedro because the beach is wider (and carries less traffic). Also, the ambience is decidedly less frenetic. If you stay outside the village, bicycles and motorbikes are often available for your use.

In general, the more sociable visitors will be happier in San Pedro, while those in search of a more tranquil setting would do well to investigate outlying accommodations on Caye Caulker and other more southerly islands. Quiet, upscale hotels on Ambergris include the recommended Ramon's Reef Resort, a family-oriented lodge with a complete dive shop; Rock's Inn, providing air-conditioned rooms with kitchens; Mata Rocks Resort, with studio apartments with kitchenettes; and the Holiday House, with single rooms, bungalows, and apartments as well as a dive shop. Moderate rates are charged at Lily's, Barrier Reef Hotel, and Victoria House, all engaging and friendly. Budget accommodations include Martha's Hotel, the Green Parrot (six miles north), Cruz Apartments, Lourdes Hotel, and Rubie's. Houses can be rented by the week or month.

There are many restaurants to choose from. Those with good reputations include Little Italy, the Jade Garden, Elvi's Kitchen, and Celi's. Recommended night spots include Big Daddy's Disco, the Purple Parrot, and Tarzan's, all located in the village. Other services include a bank, a pharmacy, a post office, and a library. An excellent source of general information is Josie Pollard at the San

Pedro Tourist Center (tel. 26-2378) and the weekly newspaper, the *San Pedro Sun*. See Inside Belize and the Appendix for further details.

Besides the usual water sports, volleyball, and bird-watching, activities on Ambergris include tours of the country's first-ever conch hatchery and a turtle-nesting beach on the northeast corner of the island. There are several ancient Mayan sites, but these are difficult to get to. San Juan, near the island's northern tip, is currently being excavated by Texas archaeologists. At least one local entrepreneur, Island Equestrian Trails, offers horseback riding, and sailing can be arranged through Islands & Reef Cruise at the Paradise Hotel pier. Annual events include the San Pedro Carnival (Feb. 10-12) and festival of St. Peter (June 29), which includes a blessing of the fishing fleet.

If You Go: Tropic, Maya, and Island airlines have as many as nine daily flights each to Ambergris from Belize City's municipal and international airports. Connecting flights are easily arranged to Corozal, Dangriga, and other Belizean cities. (If you are nervous about single-engine flying, the Tropic Air twin-engine aircraft are considered more stable.)

The island can also be reached by private or chartered aircraft, and San Pedro's airport is within walking distance of town. The flight from Belize City lasts only 15 minutes.

Boats regularly ply the channel between Ambergris and the mainland, departing from several locations in Belize City. The *Miss Belize* and *Andrea* are the best-known vessels and make two round-trips each day, one in the morning and one in the late afternoon, departing from the Bellevue Hotel pier on Baron Bliss Promenade. On weekends, there is just one round-trip, leaving Belize City around midday. The trip takes a little over an hour each way and costs about $10. Private boats can also be chartered, or you can hop a ride with a supply or fishing vessel (check the customs wharf near the Ft. George lighthouse). Ask around the various departure points such as the North Front Street Texaco Service Station, Bellevue Hotel pier, and Swing Bridge for information, and be prepared to bargain over the price.

Loggerhead turtle captured for an aquarium off the coast of Belize (Photo by Richard Mahler)

Once on Ambergris, there are regular boats to Caye Caulker and Caye Chapel (try the daily *Thunderbolt*), plus charters to virtually any scrap of reef or atoll you might care to visit, including the village of Xcalak, Mexico, located about 25 miles away. Caye Chapel also has an airport where pilots of domestic airlines are usually happy to touch down if requested. Private pilots are also welcome.

Hol Chan Marine Reserve
About 4 miles southeast of San Pedro, off the southern end of Ambergris, is a natural break (*quebrada*) in the barrier reef called Hol Chan, Mayan for "little channel." The channel is around 30 feet deep and has been protected since 1987 as a national marine reserve. As a result, it has become a major spawning ground that is strengthening underwater animal populations. More than 500 fish species have been identified here.

Hol Chan is rich in marine life, including many green moray eels and several varieties of sea urchin. (Be careful about getting too close to the near-sighted moray eels, which can chomp off a finger in the wink of an eye.) The sides of the channel are lined with coral, interrupted from time to time by small limestone caves and sink-holes, such as the spectacular Boca Ciega, a collapsed cave with a freshwater spring that teems with tropical fish. Humans share the clear waters here with everything from nervous squirrelfish to curious grey angels to parading parrotfish. Large schools of yellowtail snapper, horse-eye jacks, and blue-striped grunts cruise by, along with spotted eagle rays and purple cleaner shrimp.

Divers can take advantage of Hol Chan's shallow depth and stay down for an hour or more, drifting among the lovely spotted drum, hatfish, damsel, and butterfly fish. If the diver remains stationary, the shy hermit crab will make an appearance. Night diving can also be very rewarding, providing a rare chance to glimpse flaming scallops, octopus, spider crabs, lobsters, and other nocturnal species. Eerie bioluminescence will shimmer like tiny fireflies atop the water's surface, especially noticeable in the wake of passing boats.

The 5-square-mile reserve is divided into three distinct ecological zones, marked on the water's surface by anchored buoys. Zone A is the channel itself, one of the most northerly points in Belize's barrier reef system. Swimmers should be mindful of Hol Chan's strong tidal currents while diving or snorkeling in this area. Zone B encompasses broad sea grass beds and the Boca Ciega, which should only be explored by experienced divers. The sea and turtle grass serve as an important feeding and breeding ground. Zone C encompasses several mangrove cayes, a source of important nutrients and a critical habitat for the youngest sea creatures, who subsequently migrate into the sea grass beds and finally the outer waters. Above the surface, the mangrove islands provide a nesting area for several large bird species, such as herons, egrets, pelicans, rails, frigatebirds, and ospreys. The mangrove ecosystem is also home to sponges, anemones, sea urchins, crabs, jellyfish, mollusks, sea squirts, and sea horses.

As you wander through the reserve, remember that all flora and fauna are protected. Feeding the fish is discouraged, since it upsets the balance of nature and can lead to some potentially dangerous encounters with certain sharp-toothed animals.

Radio-equipped patrol boats regularly visit the area, on the lookout for anyone in trouble—or at odds with the law. The rangers also monitor anchoring activities, making sure private boats use mooring buoys whenever possible.

The Belize Audubon Society advises visitors to any coral habitat in the country that collecting these tiny organisms is prohibited and that overturning or disturbing any live coral will eventually cause them to die. One should always be very careful when stepping or dropping anchor on the ocean floor and try to avoid touching live coral at all costs as this can kill the polyps. Even a vigorous kick by a swimmer can stir up enough sand to clog their orifices. Contact with fire (also called red) coral can be especially painful. And here, as in other areas with lots of marine traffic, be careful of speeding power boats that may be unable to see you bobbing in the water: an encounter can be deadly.

Just outside the border of the reserve, at the swampy southern extremity of Ambergris Caye, is the Marco Gonzalez archaeological site. This small ruin, named after the young boy who found it, was once part of a large trade network linking inland Maya with settlements up and down the Mexican and Central American coast. Occupied between 200 B.C. and A.D. 1500, Marco Gonzalez has been excavated by Canadian archaeologists since 1986. They have confirmed that some of the structures are built entirely from conch shells. The location is not well marked and is best approached with the help of a knowledgeable guide. Be sure to bring mosquito repellent!

The Hol Chan Marine Reserve is jointly sponsored by the Belize government, the World Wildlife Fund, and the U.S. Agency for International Development. Assistance has also been provided by the U.S. Peace Corps, the Belize Audubon Society, and the New York Zoological Society. The reserve is the first park of its kind in Central America, and donations are welcome. Your contribution will encourage Belize and neighboring countries to expand such worthy experiments. A resident manager can be contacted for any necessary permits or further information at the Hol Chan visitors center across from Town Hall on Barrier Reef Drive (formerly Front Street) in San Pedro. This headquarters is well stocked with brochures and information about the underwater flora and fauna encountered in Belizean waters. It is a good idea to stop in before heading out to Hol Chan so you will have a better understanding of what you will be seeing later on.

If You Go: Because of its close proximity to San Pedro, Hol Chan can easily be visited for a half-day or even an hour by booking a boat through a hotel or simply showing up on the beach. Dive boats usually head out about 9:00 a.m. and 2:00 p.m. each day, returning in late afternoon. Expect to pay at least $15 for a round-trip. Several glass-bottom touring craft follow a similar schedule. Snorkelers and swimmers are welcome on board either type of vessel, and prices are reasonable. If you have small children who wish to snorkel, it is helpful to hire a guide who can help keep an eye on them in the water. They—and their parents—should wear water-repelling sunscreen and consider wearing a T-shirt to avoid burning. Watch out for sea urchins and fire coral!

Caye Caulker

Lying directly south of Ambergris, about 10 miles from San Pedro, Caye Caulker (also spelled Corker) is a popular destination among many visitors who want an experience more akin to San Pedro Town of the 1970s, before the latter was "discovered."

Caulker is "less" of many things San Pedro has become: less expensive, less crowded, and less noisy. However, it also has fewer hotels, restaurants, dive shops, and services than its northern neighbor. Therefore, some visitors try to visit both islands, content to absorb the "action" of Ambergris for a while and then slow the pace down on Caulker.

The island was dubbed Hicaco by the Spanish, their name for the coco plum palms found here. Over the years, the English pirates who settled here began pronouncing it "Corker," and, with their British accents, the word finally evolved into "Caulker."

The caye is fairly small, and the portion that is inhabited covers a few sandy blocks. There are only two streets. Like Ambergris, a good portion of Caulker is mangrove swamp. Visitors walk everywhere, since nothing is far away and vehicles are almost nonexistent. Only 750 people live here year-round, and within a few days time, it seems a traveler has waved or chatted with them all. This friendliness, coupled with comparatively modest prices and idyllic beaches, has enticed many first-timers to extend their stay on Caulker. A few foreigners, many of them budget-minded regulars on the so-called gringo trail, have stayed on for years and intermarried with the locals. An airport opened in 1991, and the island's tempo has speeded up somewhat, but by keeping the pace of progress on Caulker under control residents have been able to remain owners and operators of the rustic guest houses, home-style restaurants, and simple shops that cater to visitors. Property is still cheap enough that the citizens of Caulker can afford to buy it, although schools, marina, electricity, sewage, and water services are inadequate even for those who already live here.

The island offers many of the same attractions of Ambergris, including snorkeling, diving, and fishing. Anglers can catch one exotic game fish after another off the caye's main pier. Caulker natives have long been known as skilled fishermen (lobster, conch, snapper) and boat-builders, so you are sure to find skilled guides here for virtually any water-related activity. Particularly recommended is Jim Novelo's Sunrise Boat Tours and Charters (2-22195), which arranges trips as close as the Caulker reef or as far as the Glover's, Turneffe, and Half Moon atolls. Prices vary, but $6 to $10 per person should buy three or four hours of diving and cover at least two or three dive sites. A special attraction for divers is an underground cave system—said to be the largest of its kind anywhere—that is between Caulker and Ambergris. The Boca Ciega "blue hole" is worth the trip for any scuba enthusiast. Experts on the area's natural history and ecology include marine biologist Ellen MacRae at the Galería Hicaco, James Beveridge of Sea-ing Is Belizeing, and Bobby Heusner, who also runs camping trips by sailboat to smaller islands. Camping on Caulker itself is available from the proprietor of Vega's Far Inn. Other low-cost accommodations include Tom's Hotel, the Hide-A-Way, and Seebeez. At the top of the scale is the Tropical Paradise, offering hot water, fans, and a spa. Local

Walking path on Caye Caulker (Photo by Steve Wotkins)

restaurants of note include Celi's, Glenda's, Syd's, and Cabanas. Many of these eateries are simply open-air kitchens operated by local women outside their homes. Nightlife on the island consists of dancing and drinking at one of several bars or watching television. (Yes, even Caye Caulker has satellite dishes and cable.) See Inside Belize for a complete list of services and amenities.

The best swimming hole (the offshore water is otherwise very shallow) is in a channel that bisects the island just north of the village, known as the Cut. It was formed by powerful Hurricane Hattie in 1961, the same storm that virtually leveled Belize City. The water here is clear and fairly shallow, but beware of the currents (and an occasional saltwater crocodile). This expanding channel is a good illustration of what can happen when protective mangroves are removed from an island's outer boundaries.

Its idyllic surroundings, dominated by coconut trees, make Caulker a nice place to walk. A sandy path to the south end of the island brings visitors to the proposed Siwa-Ban Nature Preserve, named after the rare black catbird (*siwa-ban* in Yucatec Maya) found in this seaside forest habitat along with about 115 other species of birds. Sponsored by the San Francisco-based Siwa-Ban Foundation and founded by marine biologist and gallery owner Ellen MacCrae, the reserve would be modeled after the Hol Chan Preserve and would encompass 110 acres and protect mangroves, sea grass beds, and coral reef formations. MacRae was prompted to create the preserve project after bulldozers grading the Caye Caulker airstrip destroyed some of the best remaining habitat for the black catbird.

Among the few persistent annoyances on Caye Caulker are sand flies and mosquitoes, which can make hikes and beach excursions very uncomfortable in calm or rainy weather. Since most of the houses are built on tall stilts, these biting insects are less of a nuisance indoors. Another problem is a pack of seemingly unemployed young men, who panhandle, sell drugs, and engage in petty theft. The local authorities have been unable (or unwilling) to deal with these aggravating vagrants, who love to pester newly arrived tourists.

If You Go: Boats making the 20-mile (45-minute) trip to Caye Caulker leave Belize City about 11:00 each morning from the Haulover Creek moorings behind the Texaco Service Station on North Front Street, about 100 yards inland from the Swing Bridge. Other morning boats depart from the vicinity of the Swing Bridge itself. Later boats will charge more for the one-hour voyage. Keep in mind that the passage may be bouncy (but faster) on smaller, high-powered craft, which tend to zigzag through the mangrove cayes en route.

The legendary Chocolate is often touted as the best boatman for hire, but his reputation has spawned so many imitators that it is sometimes a challenge to find the original. Your best bet is to seek him out at Mom's Restaurant on Handyside Street, where he eats breakfast and picks up passengers for his fast-moving *Soledad*. He can also be reached at P.O. Box 332 in Belize City, telephone 2-22151. Another reliable operator among the dozen or so in business is Jerry, who ferries visitors to Caulker on *The Blue Wave*.

Skippers will generally drop you off at any pier you request. Boats head back from Caye Caulker to Belize City and San Pedro around 6:00 or 7:00 a.m., departing from the Reef Hotel (formerly Martínez) pier, also known as the "front bridge." The passenger boat *Andrea* stops at Caulker weekdays after departing San Pedro at 7:00 a.m. en route to Belize City. Expect to pay about $10 for the one-way trip. Although there are no regular passenger runs between Caulker and either Ambergris or Chapel Caye, boats can easily be arranged from these locations, usually very early in the morning.

Belize's domestic airlines make a total of 15 or more daily trips to Caye Caulker. Some travelers fly to airstrips on one of the two neighboring islands (Ambergris and Chapel) and later on make the remaining short hop to Caulker by water or air. You can call from either island if you wish to have a boat pick you up from Caulker.

Caye Chapel and Long Caye

Heading south from Caye Caulker, the next island in the barrier reef chain is Chapel, distinguished by the large groves of coconut palms planted by early colonials. It is easily visible across the horizon from Caulker and is about 15 miles northeast of Belize City.

Only one by three miles in size and privately owned, Caye Chapel is blessed with some of Belize's best beaches and the nation's second-longest airstrip. The latter is a paved runway serving the Pyramid Island Resort, which occupies almost all of Chapel and provides upscale services that include fishing, sailing, snorkeling, diving, tennis, volleyball, basketball, and even golf. There is also a gift shop, a restaurant, a bar, and a marina, all open to casual visitors.

Warships of the Spanish Armada spent a few days here nursing their wounds after the decisive 1798 battle that effectively ended Spain's claim on Belize. Some of the fleet's soldiers were buried here. Mayan artifacts have also been found, most recently at the site of a large vegetable garden planted by owners of the Pyramid Island Resort.

The Castaway's Hotel on nearby mangrove-studded Long Caye (also called Northern Long Caye) is run by an expatriate Englishman. It has eight comfortable rooms offered in the upmarket price range. As on Chapel, the small restaurant and recreational services are open to day visitors. Both islands provide good diving, snorkeling, and fishing in their offshore waters.

If You Go: Maya, Tropic, and Island airlines will land on Caye Chapel en route to or from Ambergris and Caulker at the request of passengers. A pier and full-service marina handle all boat traffic to and from the island, and the resort's helpful staff will arrange onward transportation to those who are dropped off here. Long Caye is only accessible by private boat.

St. George's Caye

During Belize's early years as a haven for British pirates and traders, its largest settlement was on St. George's Caye, located only 9 miles northeast of Belize City. It served as the Bay Settlement's informal capital for nearly two centuries, starting in the mid-1600s. Manatees and turtles were slaughtered here by the thousands, their smoked meat later sold to the crews of oceangoing ships.

The small island is best known as the focal point of a great sea battle between a ragged band of Baymen, a single British schooner, and seasoned Spanish naval forces. Despite the overwhelming odds against them, the Belizeans prevailed. Thus, the day Spain was defeated, September 10, 1798, has been a national holiday (St. George's Caye Day) ever since. On the island's southern tip there is a small cemetery where some of the early settlers were buried. A succession of tropical storms has washed most of the grave markers away (along with dozens of houses), but old coins and other historical artifacts are still found on the nearby grounds.

Today, there is not a great deal here to interest the casual or budget-minded traveler. Accommodations are only available at two locations. The expensive, highly regarded St. George's Lodge caters almost exclusively to experienced scuba divers (certification available). This resort is solidly built of tropical hardwood and has elegantly handcrafted furniture in its public areas. Power is supplied by windmills and solar collectors. Some cabanas are built on stilts right over the waters of the Caribbean; others are on the island's sandy soil.

The Bellevue Hotel also manages five cottages here, with transportation provided to and from Belize City. There are a number of piers (called "bridges") where day-trippers can tie up for an hour or so. A footpath encircles the island, and the snorkeling offshore is rated excellent. Visitors may run into Carl Bischoff, an Austrian immigrant and aquarium builder who uses the caye as the headquarters for a T-shirt and tropical fish exportation business.

St. George's Caye is home to a few fishermen and has several weekend cottages that belong to wealthy Belizeans. There is also a rest-and-recreation facility for members of the British armed forces who are based in Belize. Training is also carried out here for frogmen and other military specialists.

Like its island neighbors and Belize City, St. George's Caye suffered heavy damage during Hurricane Hattie in 1961 and would be very vulnerable should a similar storm sweep out of the Caribbean some day. Fortunately, all such islands are now part of a sophisticated radio-based warning system that will notify residents of any approaching storm well in advance of its arrival.

If You Go: There is no regular public transportation to St. George's Caye, but private boats can easily be hired to make the 20-minute crossing from Belize City. While en route, visitors will pass by a number of uninhabited mangrove cayes that have little or no dry land, including Mapp's, Swallow, and Riders cayes. Keep a pair of binoculars handy, since this dense foliage harbors lots of bird life. This is also a good place to observe the wooden sail-driven fishing ships known as "lighters" which ply the waters from Mexico to Honduras.

Moho and Drowned Cayes

Only a half-mile off the coast, opposite St. John's College on the north side of Belize City, Moho Caye is a very small island with a big past. It is the site of an ancient Mayan fishing settlement where thousands of pounds of old manatee bones have been found. The large mammals were apparently butchered in large numbers here and the meat then prepared for transportation to other Mayan communities. Fortunately, manatees can still be found in these waters. They can be seen in small, circular holes near the Belize Municipal Airport, where the Belize River enters the sea. The docile creatures have become very rare in much of their range, which extends as far as south Florida, but are holding their own in Belize thanks to government protection.

During colonial times, Moho was used as a quarantine area for sufferers of smallpox and other contagious diseases. A small graveyard marks the final resting place of many unlucky victims. The tiny caye, recently the site of a sportfishing and diving resort, is privately owned.

East of Moho, in the shallow Inner Channel waters, are a dense maze of mangrove islands known as the Drowned Cayes. While there is almost no dry land among them, these lush cayes provide excellent anchorage during storms and are an important habitat for the manatee. Several local tour companies provide trips to breathing holes where a glimpse of this marine mammal is almost guaranteed.

English, Goff's, Rendezvous, Sergeant's, and Spanish Lookout Cayes

Each of these tiny cayes retains the kind of charm visitors typically associate with exotic, deserted tropical islands. They are only a few acres in size, consisting of little more than a mound of sandy beach and a dozen or so coconut palms. Even native Belizeans like to visit them for an afternoon or weekend of snorkeling, fishing, and picnicking. No regularly scheduled transportation serves these cayes, but day trips can easily be arranged through the larger Belize City hotels and travel agencies.

Goff's Caye (Photo by Kevin Schafer)

As you approach these cayes from Belize City or points farther north, you will pass sugar barges taking their loads out to oceangoing cargo ships that cannot anchor any closer because of the shallowness of the water. Within the Inner Channel depths vary from about 100 to 150 feet. They quickly plunge to 1,000 feet or more beyond the barrier reef.

Sergeant's Caye has only three coconut trees surrounded by a long expanse of gorgeous beach. The island used to be much larger but almost disappeared as a result of Hurricane Hattie. Situated directly on the reef, it is ideally suited for snorkeling and diving both "in" and "out" of the reef ecosystem.

English Caye, located just to the south of the swampy Gallow's Point Reef, has been an important navigational aid for hundreds of years and marks the entrance of the deep English Caye Channel that large commercial ships follow into the Belize City harbor. The largest of these vessels anchor several miles offshore, where they are met by barges and other craft. The island is dominated by a brick lighthouse, where oceangoing ships stop to pick up one of the two pilots who must help navigate them through the Inner Channel. There is a small house where the lighthouse keeper lives. Visitors are welcome, and overnight stays can be arranged with special permission.

Goff's and Rendezvous cayes are mere specks of palm-shaded sand off the major shipping lanes which make excellent stopping points for snorkeling, fishing, swimming, and diving. Both are perched right on the edge of the reef, which allows visitors to swim in either deep or shallow water. Overnight camping and anchorage is allowed. Local fishermen frequently visit Goff's and Rendezvous cayes in their shallow-draft dories. Most are in search of lobster and conch that will be sold to the restaurants of Belize City and San Pedro.

Spanish Lookout Caye is 10 miles southeast of Belize City and 1 mile west of the main barrier reef. It was once used by British pirates to spy on Spanish galleons. There is now a small bungalow-style lodge, Spanish Bay Resort, with five units and an accompanying restaurant, dive shop, and complement of experienced fishing guides. The Belizean-owned facility caters to nature lovers, divers, and snorkers. It is well positioned for divers and anglers who wish to patrol the outer reef and Turneffe Islands.

Bluefield Range, Alligator Caye, and Middle Long Caye

Along Belize's barrier reef, the word "range" refers to the marshy clusters of mangroves that seem to be half land and half water. At least part (and in many cases, all) of every caye seems to fit this description; therefore, we have eliminated any mention of the scores of islands that are virtually impossible to set foot on. The Belize government has imposed a ban on purchase of these and other unoccupied islands in the hope that many (if not most) of them can some day be included in a national park system.

Bluefield Range is unusual in that it supports several habitats. A couple of the mangrove cayes are permanently soggy, while the largest has a thin strip of high ground that accommodates Ricardo Castillo's Beach Huts. Ricardo and his family have built guest cabanas and a restaurant on stilts right over the water. There are also several tent sites available on a pleasant stretch of beach at $3 per person per day. This beach is a favorite stopping point for sea kayakers headed south. Cabanas are $75 a night, including meals.

Staying with Castillo provides visitors with an unusual opportunity to observe traditional Belizean lobster fishing firsthand. Ricardo is a lifelong fishermen and free diver, originally from the boat-building village of Sarteneja, on the Shipstern Peninsula. He will take you along as he checks traps over a meandering route above nearby sea grass beds. Lobsters are still plentiful enough in these waters that they can be enticed into bait-free traps that rely entirely on the animal's natural inclination to seek refuge during the day in dark places such as wooden cages equipped with trapdoors and anchored with stones. Ricardo is a by-the-book member of Belize's large fishing cooperative and immediately throws back any undersized lobster, along with the occasional crab or fish that wanders into his traps. Later, you will dine on fresh lobster cooked to perfection. Boats hail Castillo via marine band radio from as far away as Guatemala to make dinner reservations in the tiny restaurant.

Bluefield Range is a good base for excursions to other nearby cayes and reefs, plus the many pristine diving and fishing sites hereabouts. Ricardo serves as an experienced guide to little-known underwater limestone caves, coral canyons, and cayes. Trips can easily be arranged for snorkelers and nature buffs to uninhabited islands where crocodiles and exotic birds make their homes.

Recommended nearby destinations include Columbus Caye, which has an underwater sinkhole more than 140 feet deep where large jewfish and sharks have been sighted. Caye Glory, a submerged coral formation off Southern Long Caye, is an important breeding ground for grouper and other fish. Snorkelers and divers in this area will see black coral and the occasional sea turtle.

Saltwater crocodiles and waterfowl are plentiful on Middle Long Caye (also called Alligator Caye), a few miles north of Bluefield Range. This large, swampy island is the site of Moonlight Shadow Lodge, a rustic cabana-style resort with a small restaurant and aquarium operated by a native Belizean, Rudolfo Avila. For years,

Rudolfo Avila outside his Moonlight Shadow Lodge on Middle Long Caye (Photo by Richard Mahler)

local fishermen have used Middle Long Caye's tiny beaches as campgrounds, and this is a good place to get to know native Belizeans firsthand. The manager of Moonlight Shadow will be happy to arrange tours throughout the area. There is no telephone or radio on the island, but Avila can be contacted via Ricardo Castillo's VHF-band marine radio. Daily rates at Moonlight Shadow are in the moderate price range, with meals included. As the name implies, there are plenty of large amphibious reptiles here, but they are crocodiles, not alligators (locals used this term, despite the fact that there are none in Belize).

Tobacco Range, Twin Cayes, South Water Caye, and Carrie Bow Caye

Farther south from Belize City, lying 10 to 20 miles off the town of Dangriga, several little-known cayes offer attractions and services to visitors eager to explore the reef in relative solitude.

Tobacco Range has been used over the centuries as a fishing camp and trading center. On Tobacco Caye itself, travelers have several choices of modest accommodations, including Jackson's Reef End Lodge and Rosie's Guest House & Store. These rustic resorts are operated by local fishermen and their spouses, who rely on them to supplement their income during months when sea creatures are breeding or the weather is too foul to venture out on boats. Excellent, well-informed guides are available here at modest prices, and camping can be arranged.

Much more luxurious services are available on South Water Caye, a picturesque island a few miles south of Tobacco Range. The Blue Marlin Lodge has 15 double rooms and 6 bungalows, plus a restaurant, a bar, a volleyball pit, a billiard table, and complete dive and fish shops. Fishing boats, guides, and a dive master are also available for the eager anglers and scuba enthusiasts drawn to this picturesque, flat island. Game fish found near South Water Caye include tarpon, snook, grouper, bonefish, permit, marlin, sailfish, tuna, and wahoo. Blue Marlin is a PADI dive training facility and has been widely praised for the quality of its instruction. The island is clean and quiet, home to various ospreys, royal terns, green herons, kingfishers, and crocodiles.

At the opposite end of South Water Caye, Dangriga's Pelican Beach Resort maintains a more modest hideaway on the grounds of an abandoned Catholic nunnery which caters to snorkelers and nature lovers. A cabin and dormitory are available for rental, and the hotel will send over a resident cook on request.

Like the Tobacco Range cluster, South Water Caye sits on the outer edge of the barrier reef, and marine life is abundant—so abundant that the Washington, D.C.-based Smithsonian Institution operates a major research station less than a mile away on tiny Carrie Bow Caye. On South Water itself, the England-based Coral Caye Conservation Association has conducted underwater studies since 1986, working with Belizean students interested in pursuing careers in environmental studies.

Nearby Carrie Bow Caye, only about an acre in size (it was twice as big before the mangroves were chopped down and several devastating storms struck), is leased from the Bowman family, which also owns half of South Water Caye and operates the Pelican Beach

Resort in Dangriga. Scientists from all over the world come to Carrie Bow Caye to study the hundreds of species of underwater plants and animals found in nearby waters, including mangrove and other important flora and fauna. As many as five scientists at a time are working on the island, whose waters provide some of the Caribbean's best snorkeling. Over the years, these experts have set up a baseline of valuable data that are being used to track the impact of agriculture, fishing, storm systems, pollution, and other influences on the fragile coral reef ecosystem.

Visitors are welcome at the research center by prior appointment, which can be arranged (along with transportation) through Tony Rath or Therese Bowman Rath at the Pelican Beach. Overnight accommodation in the house and dormitory is limited to Smithsonian personnel. The underwater marine area surrounding Carrie Bow Caye teems with many varieties of multicolored fish, sponges, and coral and is easily accessible from the island's concrete pier. Again, beware of strong currents through the reef cuts.

The Smithsonian, active in the area since 1977, is also conducting research on Twin Cayes, several miles northwest of Carrie Bow. Studies in this area, which is not permanently occupied, concentrate on the flora and fauna of the mangrove ecosystem. In one curious (and unsuccessful) experiment, scientists attempted to rebuild nearby Curlew Caye by planting mangrove at the site of the island, which became submerged some years ago by a series of hurricanes. Man-O-War Caye, not far away, is an important rookery for several species of large water birds, including the magnificent frigatebird. If you pass by during mating season, the male can be seen puffing out his immense red-colored throat balloon.

A small, privately operated marine research station is based on Wee Wee Caye, about 8 miles farther south. It is operated by Paul and Mary Shave of the nearby Possum Point Biological Research Station on the Sittee River.

The Southernmost Cayes

As visitors head farther south in Belizean waters, the barrier reef gradually swings away from the mainland. These cayes are remote and, for the most part, uninhabited. Aside from fishing shanties, rustic cabins, and sandy campgrounds, there are few overnight accommodations.

In large measure because they are so inaccessible, these islands and the marine life surrounding them are almost exactly as they were centuries ago when the Maya paddled among them in dugout canoes. Bird-watchers can expect to glimpse dozens of species here, including many varieties of tern, gull, pelican, booby, heron, and egret. Grackles, vireos, hummingbirds, cuckoos, and pigeons also breed on the cayes. During the winter, many migratory birds pass through these cayes on their way to and from North and Central America.

Some of the cayes are also home to a surprising number of land-based animals, such as lizards, iguanas, frogs, crabs, snakes, and even large mammals like opossums, raccoons, and armadillos. The larger islands of the barrier reef are home to the occasional paca (gibnut) and peccary.

Several of the southern cayes, including Laughingbird, Bugle, Colson, and Lark, are popular destinations for day trips out of Placencia, where the services of boats and guides are easily arranged. Other than excursions out of Placencia, Punta Gorda, and Dangriga, the best way to visit these pristine areas is by private boat. A small and expensive lodge—the Little Water Caye Resort—is located on Little Water Caye, and a similar facility was under construction in 1993 on nearby Hatchet Caye.

Be careful about stopping on inhabited islands, since Mosquito Caye and several others are privately owned. The government has placed a moratorium on the sale and development of unowned islands, although temporary fishing camps are allowed. After virtually all the trees were cut down on islands in the Triangles/Spanish Caye area, a permit system was adopted for removal of mangrove. Some small cayes have already disappeared as a result of island deforestation followed by big storms; experts fear others could be washed away in a major hurricane. Officials became more aggressive in their enforcement in 1992 after the owner of Hatchet Caye blew up part of a surrounding coral formation.

Island-hoppers heading south will find a campground on Rendezvous Caye, directly east of Placencia (not to be confused with the island of the same name near Bluefield Range), and Colson Caye nearby. Overnight visits are now discouraged at Laughingbird Caye, a national park, in order to encourage the return of nesting gulls. Another recommended campsite is on Raguana Caye, farther to the south. There is also a small, moderately priced lodge on the island, the Ranguana Reef Resort.

By the time one reaches the Toledo District, the barrier reef is out of sight across the northeastern horizon. Because the archipelago is a considerable distance from the mainland, travelers should expect to pay a hefty price for the trip and to stay overnight. A campground, a picnic area, and sparsely furnished cabins are available for general use on Hunting Caye; a second facility is said to be under development. There is also a small outpost of the Belize Defense Forces on Hunting Caye charged with interdicting smugglers and other lawbreakers.

The waters of the Sapodilla complex remain almost completely unexplored by anyone except local fishermen and vacationers from Guatemala. The coral walls that plunge steeply into the ocean's depths offer spectacular viewing opportunities for experienced divers. The islands have secluded, shaded beaches that make idyllic camping and picnicking spots. British scientists began a long-term ecological study of the Sapodilla Cayes in 1992.

From Punta Gorda, excursions can also be arranged to the Snake Cayes, small islands hugging the coastline a few miles north of town. Many of these are swampy mangrove ranges, but a few have enough high ground to support significant numbers of coconut palms, wild figs, buttonwoods, and other native trees. These cayes are not a part of the barrier reef system and instead lie on their own coral reefs emerging from a limestone ledge that extends several miles into the Caribbean Sea. One small island, Wild Cane Caye, is the site of an important ancient Mayan ceremonial center that is now being excavated. Sportfishing in the area is rated excellent (especially around river mouths), and several hotels and guest houses in Punta Gorda make a good base of operations. The town is also a jumping-off point for trips to Guatemala and, from there, Honduras and the Bay Islands. In recent years, several resorts specializing in sportfishing and diving have opened on secluded beaches north and south of Punta Gorda, around Punta Negra and Punta Ycacos. Contact Kingfisher Sports in Placencia or Nature's Way Guest House in Punta Gorda for details.

The Atolls

An atoll is a ring-shaped coral island and associated reef that fringes an enclosed, relatively shallow lagoon. While such formations are common in the South Pacific and other tropical oceans of the world, only four of any size exist in the Caribbean. All but one of the Western Hemisphere's large atolls are located off the barrier reef of Belize. Because of their isolation from the mainland, atolls are often home to many species of flora and fauna that can rarely be seen anywhere else. Their waters tend to be exceptionally clear and unpolluted, which makes them ideal for diving, fishing, and snorkeling. The islands themselves frequently are used as breeding grounds by birds and other animals that prefer an undisturbed habitat for raising their young. Belize has moved swiftly to preserve the pristine quality of its offshore atolls. A trip to one or more of these destinations takes some extra effort (and money), but the rewards are unmatched.

Turneffe Islands

Like its companion atolls, Glover's Reef and Lighthouse Reef, the name Turneffe has been given is deceptive. It really refers to a cluster of about thirty-five tiny coral islets and mangrove ranges (also known as "wet cayes") that encircles a shallow lagoon punctuated by seaward channels. The Turneffe Islands comprise the largest of the country's three atolls, measuring a maximum of 30 miles long and 10 miles wide and covering a surface area of 205 square miles. It is also the nearest, separated from the barrier reef by a 6- to 10-mile channel that plunges to a depth of 1,000 feet. During the Classic and Late Classic periods, Mayan fishermen and traders established

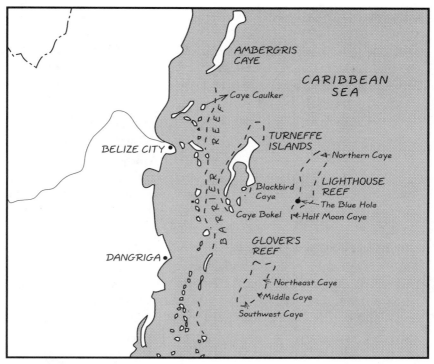

The Atolls

small outposts here as well as at Glover's Reef. Later, pirates set up camps here (complete with enslaved Indian women) and preyed on Spanish trade ships. In the early twentieth century, the Turneffe Islands were well known for their sponges and coconuts, largely wiped out by diseases and hurricanes in recent decades. Only a few fishermen, coconut collectors, and tourism operators now make this their home.

The water is more crystalline here than on reefs closer to the mainland, where some turbidity is caused by the muddy runoff from mountain-draining rivers. Visibility in the warm (74- to 84-degree) water is often in excess of 100 feet in any direction.

At Turneffe, most of the cayes are covered with thick forests of red and black mangrove that form a rich and vital breeding ground for conch, lobster, and fish as well as water birds. On close inspection, many of the islands on the west (or leeward) side are little more than a dense mass of mangrove trees clutching at the shallow sandbeds. On the eastern (or windward) side, a few acres of land in the archipelago rise high enough above the tide line to support human habitation, and several of these sites (easily identified by coconut palm clusters) are occupied by either sportfishing/diving lodges or commercial "fish camps" operated by individual Belizeans. Openings between the mangrove thickets are called "bogues," and they connect the shallow interior lagoons with outer waters.

The most unusual complex occupies a stretch of east-facing beach on 4,000-acre Blackbird Caye and is described by its American backer, Houston-based oil and real estate entrepreneur Al W. Dugan, as both a living marine and land resource management community and an environmentally sensitive resort. Blackbird Caye Resort (named for the great-tailed grackles found in abundance) provides a little-disturbed setting for visits to the nearby coral reef, turtle nesting areas, saltwater crocodile habitat, manatee breathing holes, and breeding areas for several bird species. Nearby Soldier's Caye is a sanctuary for nesting roseate terns and white crowned pigeons, both rare in Belize. Animals native to the Turneffe archipelago include boa constrictors, raccoons, lizards, and land crabs.

A Texas A&M University research station at Blackbird Caye studies the behavior of bottlenose dolphins, which frequent nearby lagoons. This is the first such research undertaken in a diverse environment in which mangrove islands, coral reefs, and sea grass beds form a delicately balanced ecosystem. Movie director Francis Ford Coppola, who maintains a home in Belize and has visited Blackbird Caye several times, is providing elaborate underwater communications equipment for this venture.

A cabana-style lodge is used by nature-oriented tour groups and scientific research teams that arrive by boat from the mainland. Besides marine ecology studies, activities include diving, snorkeling, fishing, hiking, and beachcombing. Blackbird Caye Resort accommodates as many as 16 visitors with a full-service kitchen, fishing guides, certified dive instructor, electricity, and hot water.

Blackbird Caye has become a mecca for marine science internationally and for Belizean students studying reef ecology. A large research vessel, the *Heraclitus*, is anchored nearby and will help coordinate scientific work and diver training through at least 1995. The ship is the home of Klaus Eiberle's Blue Planet Divers Diving School, catering to casual visitors as well as those in Blackbird tour groups. The section of the reef where the resort is located has remained essentially untouched for centuries. Although local fishermen, coconut growers, and visiting divers have had minor impact, this is one of only a few areas in the world where amateurs, professionals, and academics can get a firsthand look at such an unusual habitat. The government's long-term goal is to permanently preserve this and other sections of the Turneffe atoll as a national park, which developers are also advocating. Blackbird Caye Resort and other existing concessions would be required to operate with a minimal impact on the environment. This is accomplished through the use of solar energy, rain collection devices, state-of-the-art sewage treatment, reverse osmosis saltwater processing, and retention of native plants and wildlife.

The first accommodations for visitors on the atoll were built to house sportfishermen on Caye Bokel, at the southernmost tip of the atoll. Turneffe Island Lodge is owned by Dave and Jill Bennett and managed by Hugh and Theresa Parkey. There are 8 rooms at the lodge (6 doubles and 2 quads), plus a dining room and several boats outfitted for diving and fishing. Turneffe Island Lodge caters primarily to experienced divers, who are attracted to such popular nearby underwater destinations as the Elbow and the shipwreck *Sayonara*. Wall-diving off the reef is a favorite pastime among visitors.

Turneffe Flats, midway up the east side of the atoll on the northeast tip of Blackbird Caye, is built on the site of an old fishing camp that dates back to the Mayan era. The American-owned lodge can accommodate a total of 12 guests among several bungalows. Beach camping is allowed by advance reservation. The facility specializes in fly-fishing, although divers, bird-watchers, and snorkelers are also welcome. Guides, boats, equipment, transportation, and meals are provided.

The least expensive diving/fishing resort on the Turneffe Islands is the Golden Bonefish Lodge on Cockney Point Caye, at the southeast corner of the archipelago. Fishing packages, which include transfer by 22-foot skiff from Belize City, are from Saturday to Saturday. Sightseeing tours on the reef and mainland can also be arranged by the lodge's representative, Doug Moore of One Moore Tours. For nonfishing guests, 6-day rates begin at $550 (half the fishing package cost). Accommodations are bungalow style, with meals included.

The waters around the Turneffe atoll, especially the shallow coral-debris "flats," are alive with permit, barracuda, and bonefish. Tarpon are plentiful from March through June around Turneffe's channels and inlets, and larger species found in deeper water include mackerel, bonito, marlin, blackfin tuna, grouper, sailfish, and wahoo.

Divers are especially fond of the atoll's steep dropoffs and tall coral heads adorned with colorful tube sponges, fan coral, gorgonians, and occasional shipwrecks. Black coral and sponges are especially evident in the inland waters of Vincent's Lagoon. Mauger Caye, at the atoll's north end, is a popular location for divers. It is identified by its lighthouse, in place since 1821.

In the Turneffe Islands group, two areas have been recommended by the Belize Center for Environmental Studies for establishment as government reserves. Vincent's (also known as Northern) Lagoon is a breeding ground for the Morelet's crocodile and Caribbean manatee, both endangered. Soldier Caye, east of Blackbird Caye, is the nesting site of several species of birds. There is also a small rookery on Blackbird itself. An increase in human activity could have a negative effect on all these areas.

The archipelago's relative isolation and low level of human habitation currently provide even the casual traveler with the chance to see many unusual species in their natural environment. Visitors to the larger islands report a surprising amount of animal life, including boa constrictors (locally called wowlas) as long as 15 feet. Interesting side trips include Dog Flea Caye, where an old man and his son extract palm oil from local coconuts using wind-powered equipment, and Calabash Caye, site of long-abandoned coconut and sponge-gathering operations. Fungus wiped out most native sponges in the 1930s, and coconut trees were leveled by Hurricane Hattie in 1961.

If You Go: There is no regular transportation to the Turneffe Islands. The vast majority of visitors arrive as part of sportfishing or diving packages offered by the handful of resorts based on the islands (transportation from Belize City is prearranged by private vessel). Because it is close to the mainland in comparison to the other two atolls, Turneffe can be reached fairly easily through arrangements with local charter or live-aboard boat operators, either as a final destination or a stopping point en route to the Lighthouse Reef and/or Glover's Reef atolls. Expect to pay at least $70 per person for the 90-minute trip from Belize City. See Inside Belize for further details.

Lighthouse Reef
A largely uninhabited offshore atoll (50 miles east of Belize City), Lighthouse Reef is 28 miles long and between 2 and 6 miles wide. The center lagoon is almost completely surrounded by coral formations. Its six islands are widely separated and form a nearly perfect semicircle.

The atoll is best known to most visitors as the site of the 45-acre Half Moon Caye National Monument. Established in 1982 as Belize's first nature reserve, the monument protects a large nesting colony of red-footed boobies along with several other rare species of sea fowl, including the magnificent frigatebird (an archenemy of the booby). The 4,000-member booby colony is one of only two in the Caribbean (the other is on Tobago Island off Venezuela), and the nesting area can easily be observed from a special viewing platform. The boobies are so named because they showed no fear of early sailors, who killed them easily and indiscriminately for food. Red-footed boobies are usually dull brown, but most of the Half Moon Caye birds have white feathers accentuated by pale gold head and long blue-gray beak.

Red-footed booby at Half Moon Caye (Photo by Kevin Schafer)

The Belize Audubon Society, caretaker of the sanctuary, has counted 98 bird species on Half Moon, among them the osprey, white-crowned pigeon, and mangrove warbler, which all nest on the island. Several species of iguanas and lizards also live here, and both hawksbill and loggerhead turtles lay their eggs on the caye's beaches, where one may also see the largest species of land crab in Belize.

Camping and hiking is allowed on Half Moon Caye, with permission of the resident warden (who can provide maps, information on sanitation facilities, and camping assignments). An unmanned lighthouse, first built in 1820 and now completely solar powered, provides good views of the atoll and bird colonies. German U-boats refueled here during World War II, but there is no evidence of their visits.

The underwater area immediately surrounding Half Moon Caye is also protected and is full of marine life: over 220 species of reef fish have been identified. Conch, which has almost disappeared from local waters, is gradually being reintroduced. The marine park is easily accessible from a broad sandy beach or the leeward pier. Swimmers, divers, and snorkelers are all welcome, provided they stay in designated areas and observe marine conservation rules.

Some distance north of Half Moon is Sandbore Caye, which also has a lighthouse. Despite the presence of such stations, many ships have gone down in nearby waters. One Spanish trade ship, the *Juan Batista*, sank about a mile offshore in 1822 and is said to have carried a cargo of still-unrecovered gold and silver bullion.

A popular destination located 8 miles north of Half Moon Caye is the Blue Hole, an almost perfectly circular limestone sinkhole that is over 300 feet across and 412 feet deep. Created by the ancient collapse of an underwater cavern some 12,000 years ago, the Blue Hole was the subject of a 1984 film documentary by underwater explorer Jacques Cousteau, who concluded that a network of caves and crevices extends beneath the entire reef. Sport divers (limited to a depth of 130 feet) are able to admire its outstanding stalagmite and stalactite formations while swimming in crystal-clear water that appears to be a peculiar shade of deep blue when seen from the surface. The hole is also an important habitat for shrimp and jewfish, but you should not expect to see much besides an occasional shark or tuna if you dive here. Surrounding waters are only about 20 feet deep.

There are other popular dive sites in the area, where depths plunge dramatically from 30 to several thousand feet. The wide variety of marine life includes some deep-water species that seldom enter Belize's shallower reef areas. Look for enormous sponges, grouper, hogfish, and snapper.

Vegetation on the cayes themselves is rich and varied, thanks in part to the natural fertilizer provided by thousands of birds and reptiles. Ficus (fig) trees, ziricote, gumbo-limbo, sea grape, spider lily, and coconut palm are all found here.

There are no developed facilities on the atoll other than the exclusive and expensive Lighthouse Reef Resort, a 20-unit full-service diving facility on Northern Two Caye which has its own private paved airstrip for shuttling guests from Belize International. The lodge specializes in weeklong diving and fishing packages, with all meals, guides, and other services included in a single price. The resort grounds encompass 16 acres (not counting the airport runway). There are plans to open a second lodge on the same island. Contact a local travel agency for current information on its status. All other visitors to the atoll must bring their own food, drink, and fuel. Permission to land on the strip must be obtained in advance.

If You Go: Day trips to Half Moon Caye and the Blue Hole start at about $75 per person for groups of several individuals (the trip takes 6 hours from Belize City or San Pedro). Other vessels charge $150 and up for more extensive trips. It is possible to be dropped off for a few days of camping and then picked up at a time of your own choosing. Some of the live-aboard dive boats based in Belize City (and elsewhere) make trips to Lighthouse as well as the two other atolls. Because of its remote location, trips to the atoll by individuals or couples are fairly costly, so it is wise to arrange to make the trip with others to reduce the per-person expenses. Boats may dock only at the pier on the leeward side of Half Moon Caye, and deep-draught vessels must anchor only in designated areas. Charter flights can be made to the Northern Caye strip with permission of the airport's owners.

Glover's Reef Atoll

Glover's is a splendid offshore atoll, the most remote island group in the country, located about 20 miles east of the barrier reef and 70 miles southeast of Belize City. Rising from a depth of over a thousand feet, Glover's Atoll consists of a well-defined, oval-shaped coral formation (15 miles long and 5 miles wide) that surrounds a deep lagoon. More than 700 patch reefs are found inside the 75-square-mile crystalline lagoon. The many coral pinnacles arising from within are an important breeding ground for grouper and snapper. Surrounding walls begin at 30 feet and drop suddenly to more than

2,000 feet. The atoll is named after pirate John Glover, who used the remote island cluster as the base for his raids against Spanish galleons heading in and out of the Bay of Honduras. During the early 1970s, a visiting team of international scientists pronounced this the biologically richest atoll in the Caribbean Basin.

There are six small islands along Glover's Reef. In 1990, the most ecologically significant of these, Middle Caye, was purchased from its private owner by Wildlife Conservation International, a unit of the New York Zoological Society. This 15-acre island has been called the "keystone" to the salvation of Glover's Reef, in that representatives of conservation groups such as the Belize Audubon Society and the Belize government are now able to use Middle Caye as their base for monitoring activities around the atoll. Marine ecologists and enforcement officers can study the atoll's rich fauna and simultaneously protect the remote area from such human disturbances as overfishing and unregulated diving. The University of New England and Belize Fisheries Department have proposed a long-term, large-scale ecological study of the area in which commercial fishing will be strictly managed. Eventually, it is hoped that Middle Caye will be the headquarters for a marine park and include environmental education as well as field research facilities.

It is also hoped that all of Glover's Reef will become part of a comprehensive park or reserve system sponsored by the government. There is increasing concern that fishing and diving in this fragile ecosystem may quickly degrade what remains one of the world's most pristine marine environments.

There were two lodges operating on the atoll in mid-1993, and a third was planned. Privately owned Southwest Caye, on the archipelago's southernmost tip, is home to the exclusive Manta Reef Resort, a haven for anglers and divers from all over the world. Like its counterparts on Turneffe and Lighthouse, this complex caters to fishermen anxious to hook bonefish, permit, and tarpon, which are abundant in these waters. Conditions are also excellent for barracuda, snapper, grouper, marlin, wahoo, sailfish, and other billfish. Open since 1989, Manta provides lodging on the 12-acre island in thatched-roof cabanas and transportation for divers in small V-hull boats. It may now also be possible to fly to the island by chartered plane.

The more rustic and much less expensive Lomont's (Glover's) Reef Resort, located on palm-covered Long and Northeast cayes, also specializes in extended diving, snorkeling, and fishing trips for individuals and small groups. Members of the Lomont family, who manage the eight cabanas, campground, and tiny restaurant, live on Long Caye. They brag to visitors that they can guarantee access to underwater locations where no one has ever dived or fished before. Given their location, the boast is probably accurate. Canoes, power-boats, food, guides, and recreation gear are available, but bear in mind that there is no electricity, telephone, or indoor plumbing.

Northeast Caye is also used by sea kayakers, particularly on expeditions organized by Slickrock Adventures of Moab, Utah, which paddle here from Colson Caye off Placencia. Except for a few fishermen (in boats from as far away as Guatemala and Honduras) and a lighthouse keeper on Southwest Caye, the reef itself is usually deserted. Conditions for diving are excellent, and there are a number of underwater shipwrecks at the north and south ends of the atoll. The coral walls drop abruptly to a depth of over 2,600 feet a short distance from the shoreline. Marine life is very abundant here.

If You Go: The operators of Lomont's Reef Resort and Manta Reef Resort provide transportation to and from the atoll as part of their diving and sportfishing packages, which usually last from one to two weeks. Because of its distance from the mainland, one can expect to pay a minimum of $150 for a charter boat to Glover's Reef, probably departing from Punta Gorda or Big Creek. An alternative is to sign on with one of the several live-aboard dive boats that regularly anchor off the atoll. Transportation to Lomont's Reef Resort is arranged by the owners from Sittee River, where the family also rents a guest house and campground. For further information, see Inside Belize.

5
The Coast

For the purposes of this guidebook, the coastal destinations of Belize are generally defined as those located within 30 miles of the mainland coast. A noteworthy exception to our rule are all but one of the coastal Mayan ruins. We have included a detailed description of Altun Ha in this chapter (descriptions of all other Mayan sites are in chap. 6) because it is the only major ruin we consider to be an easy day trip from Belize City. For the same reason, the Belize Zoo, the Monkey Bay Wildlife Sanctuary, and the Community Baboon Sanctuary are discussed in this section, even though they are located about 30 miles inland from the coast.

Coastal Belize has a distinctive cultural personality, since it was the first part of the country settled by Europeans. The vast majority of the nation's people live along this narrow strip, including most of the Creole and European-descended population. The climate is warm and humid; the terrain is swampy and crisscrossed by waterways. Nature lovers can find plenty of wading birds here, and anglers can hook a wide variety of fish in the jungle rivers.

From the point of view of most travelers, however, the Belize coast has limited appeal. This area is the most cultivated in the country, particularly in the north, and lacks the dramatic scenery and abundant wildlife of the offshore islands and interior mountains. Yet some attractions we highly recommend, such as the Placencia Peninsula, have been overlooked by many visitors in the past, and others, such

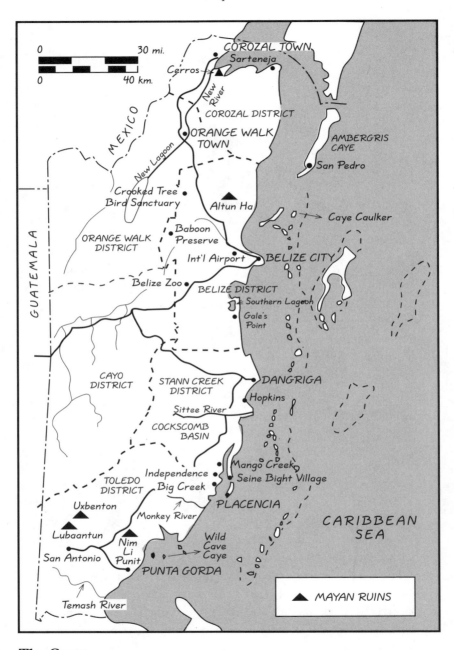

0   30 mi.

0   40 km.

MEXICO

GUATEMALA

COROZAL TOWN

Sarteneja

Cerros

New River

COROZAL DISTRICT

New Lagoon

ORANGE WALK TOWN

AMBERGRIS CAYE

San Pedro

Crooked Tree Bird Sanctuary

Altun Ha

ORANGE WALK DISTRICT

Baboon Preserve

Int'l Airport

Belize Zoo

BELIZE DISTRICT

Caye Caulker

BELIZE CITY

Southern Lagoon

Gale's Point

CAYO DISTRICT

STANN CREEK DISTRICT

DANGRIGA

Sittee River

Hopkins

COCKSCOMB BASIN

TOLEDO DISTRICT

Independence

Big Creek

Mango Creek

Seine Bight Village

Uxbenton

Monkey River

PLACENCIA

CARIBBEAN SEA

Lubaantun

Nim Li Punit

Wild Cave Caye

San Antonio

PUNTA GORDA

Temash River

▲ MAYAN RUINS

The Coast

86

as the Shipstern Nature Reserve, the Gales Point Manatee Community Sanctuary, and the Community Baboon Sanctuary, did not exist until recently. For these reasons, we hope you will spend at least part of your tour of Belize in its coastal zone.

Corozal District

The serene northern coast of Belize, particularly the seldom-visited Corozal District (which borders the Mexican state of Quintana Roo), masks a turbulent past. A series of bloody massacres of mestizos and whites by enslaved Indians throughout the Yucatán peninsula led to a long retaliation in the mid-nineteenth century known as the Caste Wars. Thousands of people, Indians and mestizos alike, fled to safety across the Río Hondo in what was then the colony of British Honduras. Their expertise in farming was welcomed by the colonial authorities, and today their descendants make up the majority of the population in this, Belize's northernmost district. As a direct result, Corozal is also one of the country's most extensively cultivated areas (primarily sugarcane) and almost exclusively Spanish-speaking. The main city, Corozal Town, and surrounding areas are good places to include in your itinerary as an escape from the sometimes hectic pace of travel in other parts of Belize. Except for the sticky summer season, there are almost constant trade winds off the water, and extremes of precipitation and temperature are unusual here.

The Corozal District was originally settled in 1849 by refugees from an Indian massacre in Bacalar, Mexico. For a good visual description of this history, see the fine mural by Manuel Villamor Reyes in Corozal Town's municipal building. (If the town hall is closed, the Reyes mural can be seen though windows on the ground floor.) In 1986, the painting was restored and updated to show the economic exploitation of immigrant workers in the district during the 1850s and 1860s.

The word "Corozal" is modified from the Spanish name for the cohune palm tree, which ancient Mayans considered to be a symbol of fertility. This area—and most of northern Belize—has always been relatively prosperous because of its fertile soil and benign climate. Corozal Town, located about 85 miles from Belize City and less than 10 miles from the Mexican border, consists of a mixture of clapboard houses and concrete block buildings. All are built on foundations of the Mayan ceremonial center of Santa Rita.

In 1955, Hurricane Janet destroyed much of the town, which until then featured adobe (mud-and-straw brick) buildings. Its population in mid-1993 was estimated to be about 10,000. Surrounding Corozal Town's Central Park you will find a modern Catholic church, a library, the city hall, an Adventist church, and government offices. There are also several old brick "pillboxes," used as defensive fortifications by the British during the last century. Although Corozal Town is built along the shoreline of Chetumal Bay, there is no beach here and the water immediately adjacent to the city is somewhat polluted.

Corozal Town is one of the most tranquil communities in all Belize—unless you plan a visit coinciding with one of several major fiestas: Christmas, Lenten Carnival, and Columbus Day. The sleepy community wakes up for these holidays, turning each of them into boisterous, Mexican-style parties.

The economy of the entire Corozal District centers on the sugar industry. The old Aventura Sugar Mill, about 5 miles south of Corozal Town, started operations in the 1800s. Although the processing plant no longer operates, its chimney stands as a symbol of an industry that generates an estimated 80 cents out of every dollar earned here. There is also the foundation of an old Spanish colonial church on the site. Raw sugarcane is now processed at two other area mills: La Libertad and Tower Hill. Tours of the sugar mills now operating are available by prior arrangement; they usually shut down from July until December.

About 7 miles to the north of Corozal Town, just off the right side of the main road to Chetumal, Mexico, is picturesque Four Mile Lagoon. Locals use this as a favorite picnicking, swimming, fishing, and weekend hangout. It is recommended for foreign visitors as well, especially those interested in sailing, windsurfing, and kayaking, all well suited to these calm waters. Campsites are available with permission from the owner.

Besides the ruin of Santa Rita, now nearly obliterated by the modern roads and buildings of Corozal Town, an interesting coastal Maya site known as Cerros (and sometimes Cerro Maya) is an easy boat ride across Corozal Bay. More fully described in chapter 6, Cerros is a late Pre-Classic trading center that boasts tombs, ball courts, and a magnificent temple with an excellent view back across the bay to Corozal Town.

About 8 miles northeast of Corozal Town, near the tip of the Corozal Peninsula, is the pleasant coastal village of Consejo Shores. A number of holiday homes have been built in the area and are sometimes available for rent (or purchase). This is considered a good departure point for day trips to Ambergris Caye and the Shipstern Peninsula. The Adventure Inn, a beautifully landscaped cabana-style resort, offers full services for sportfishermen, boating enthusiasts, and those interested in exploring Mayan ruins as far away as Lamanai. Windsurfers, sailboats, kayaks, bicycles, and fishing gear may all be rented here and are available at no extra cost for the hotel's guests. The facility has an excellent open-air bar and restaurant. You can take a taxi from Corozal Town or inquire about transportation at the Adventure Inn office there on Fourth Avenue near Third Street.

Accommodations in Corozal Town itself are rather limited, and the restaurants are generally undistinguished. One exception is the Caribbean Trailer Park and Motel, opposite Corozal Bay at the southern entrance to the city. This inexpensive facility, which includes a very good restaurant, has been operated for many years by Jo Wills, an American expatriate who goes out of her way to offer expert advice and answer questions. Tony's Inn, located a short distance away, is also recommended for its more upscale rooms, restaurant, and services. Nestor's Hotel, at 123 Fifth Avenue, and the moderately priced Maya Hotel (great view of the bay) on the Corozal-Orange Walk Road are popular among experienced budget travelers. There are several decent Chinese restaurants in Corozal Town, notably the King of Kings on Third Avenue. Crises and Dubie's serve above average Belizean cuisine. The former is especially recommended for its home-style atmosphere and excellent beans-and-rice dishes. Nightlife in Corozal is limited to a few bars, some of which occasionally have live music on weekends.

If You Go: For the best experience while in Corozal, we recommend Henry Menzies of Menzies Travel and Tours, Ltd., based in Ranchito Village at the south end of Corozal Town (office, 4-22725; fax, 4-23414). Since Menzies lives and works next to the airport, it is very convenient to have him meet your party there. A native of the area, he is particularly helpful if you want to tour local Mayan sites or quickly and efficiently get across the border to Chetumal and destinations in Mexico beyond. Menzies offers unique tours in Mexico such as a day trip to Bacalar Lagoon (lagoon of 7 colors) and to the Mayan ruins of Kohunlich, Xpuhil, Becan, and Chicanna. Commercial airfares from the United States to Cancún can be one-half the cost of airfares from the United States to Belize International. Henry Menzies can meet you or your group in Cancún. From there it is possible to see the famous Mayan ruins of Tulum, swim in the dazzling Xel-Ha lagoon, or visit the Mayan ruin at Cobá and the nearby Sian Ka'an Biosphere Reserve—if you are on a tight budget and wish to visit some of neighboring Mexico's attractions. Good service is also reported by travelers using Jal's Travl on Fourth Avenue in Corozal Town: tours and airplane tickets are available.

The Venus and Batty bus lines have frequent service to Corozal from Chetumal, Orange Walk Town, Belize City, and smaller communities. Local buses, which stop wherever the passenger desires, run about once each hour during the daytime and evening. Express buses operate about four times each day. The express trip from Corozal to Chetumal takes about 20 minutes and to Belize City around 3 hours. The time can double for all destinations on local runs. Tropic Air offers twice daily flights to San Pedro (on Ambergris Caye) from the Corozal Airport.

There are three banks in Corozal Town.

Orange Walk District

Slightly inland from Corozal but still influenced by the coastal climate, Orange Walk District is one of the least-visited areas in Belize. Like its neighbor to the east, the most accessible parts of Orange

San Pablo post office and store, typical of area's mestizo-owned businesses
(Photo by Richard Mahler)

Walk are highly cultivated in the form of sugarcane and citrus plantations as well as Mennonite farms of corn, sorghum, rice, and vegetables. There is no seacoast, and most of the pristine wildlife habitat is
either privately owned or inaccessible. An exception is the Río Bravo
Conservation Area, described in chapter 6. Orange Walk District is
home to the spectacular ruins of Lamanai (also described in chap. 6)
and Belize's largest lake, the New River Lagoon.

The best base of operations for visitors is Orange Walk Town, a
bustling mercantile center of about 13,000, located roughly 60 miles
north of Belize City on the banks of the New River. Major roads
from here lead in four directions and link the more than twenty villages of the Orange Walk District, consisting mostly of Spanish-
speaking mestizo, English-speaking Creole, and German-speaking
Mennonite farmers (see chap. 7 for a complete description of the
large Mennonite community in Belize).

Also settled by refugees from the Caste War, Orange Walk Town
has the badly eroded ruins of two forts, Mundy and Cairns, that

recall the scene of bloody battles between Belizean settlers and the district's earlier occupants, the Icaiche Maya. The latter bitterly fought the settlers in an unsuccessful attempt to rid the area of intruders. The final battle took place on September 1, 1872. One of the last remnants of this stand-off is the old flagpole in front of the Orange Walk City Hall.

Before settlement by the mestizos occurred in the late nineteenth century, the Orange Walk District was dominated for over one hundred years by loggers. During that time, all the timber taken from the region was floated down the New River into Corozal Bay. From there, it was transferred through the Inner Channel to Belize City and finally shipped to the outside world. Now agriculture is king. Sugar has been the most important crop for many decades (surpassing chicle and corn earlier this century), and Belizean rum (distilled at the Cuello processing plant under the Caribbean label) makes up one lucrative market for the cane that is grown and harvested here. Other cane is rendered into molasses and, of course, sugar. One growing environmental concern for the government is the waste effluent from this industry that is sometimes dumped untreated into area rivers. Belize's Ministry of Tourism and the Environment is ever-watchful of the effluent situation and is taking steps to regulate the industry. Steps are also now being taken to convert such organic by-products into electricity, which is very expensive in Belize, and methanol, which can be used as a gasoline additive. The region is also an important producer of citrus, papaya, and beef cattle.

For the natural history tourist, Orange Walk Town does not offer much as yet. However, if you are interested in seeing some of Belize's more than 110 native species of orchids, Godoy & Sons offer a tour that will bring you face to face with Belize's national flower: the delicately beautiful black orchid. Carlos Godoy at 4 Trial Farm Road (tel. 3-22969) guides this unique trek to see some of the many exotic species that thrive in Belize. Operating under a government permit, he gathers and propagates orchids and bromeliads that would otherwise be destroyed by logging and farming. For the serious orchid enthusiast, Godoy can also facilitate the customs and legal procedures that are required to export these precious flowers. Members of the Godoy family also run nature tours and boat trips up the New River to Lamanai and other destinations.

If You Go: Buses from Belize City to Orange Walk run daily at about one-hour intervals. Check the Venus or Batty Brothers bus service for fares and schedules. A private car or express bus can make the trip in an hour. Local buses take slightly longer. There is also frequent service from Chetumal and Corozal Town, and connections can be made in Orange Walk Town for Sarteneja and villages en route to the Shipstern Peninsula. All through-buses stop for about 20 minutes in Orange Walk Town, where passengers can buy food and change money.

Accommodations in Orange Walk Town include the Victoria Hotel (formerly Baron's), Chula Vista Hotel, Jane's Guest House, and Hotel Mi Amor, all located along the Northern Highway (which doubles as the city's main street). Some of these locations are very noisy, and be advised that there are at least a dozen brothels in Orange Walk, fronting as hotels and/or restaurants, which can become rowdy on weekend nights. Cocaine and marijuana are sometimes sold openly here, despite severe government penalties.

There are several good Chinese restaurants in Orange Walk, and the larger hotels also serve acceptable food. Lee's serves some of the better Chinese fare. HL's Burgers is a favorite among locals for American-style fast food. Eddy's Cabin, while off the main road at 46 San Antonio Road, is a fine, inexpensive stop for Belizean cuisine. Similar fare is also available at the Golden Gate Café and Orange Walk Restaurant.

Several hotels arrange tours to Mayan sites and boat trips along the district's various inland waterways, which are home to a wide variety of birds and other animals (see Inside Belize for further information). Some of the more reliable tour operators are the aforementioned Carlos Godoy and Mayaworld Safaris (2-32285 or 2-31063; daily 14-passenger canvas-topped boats to Lamanai). As of spring 1993, Mayaworld employed one of the best Belizean guides for archaeology, Wilfredo Novelo. Ask for him by name—you will not be disappointed. We also recommend Jungle River Tours (Antonio & Herminio Novelo, tel. 3-22293) for a superb day trip of birding on the New River and getting familiar with wonders such as the carved Lord Smoking Shell stela at Lamanai. Guided local boats can also be chartered from Atilano Narvallez at the village of Guinea Grass, west of Orange Walk Town on the New River. His well-marked house is near the river and pier.

Indian Church

A highly recommended destination near the Lamanai ruins (a 20-minute walk or 10-minute canoe ride) is the Lamanai Outpost Lodge, which overlooks the 28-mile-long New River Lagoon just outside the Spanish-speaking village of Indian Church. Opened in late 1992 by expatriates Colin and Ellen Howells, this impressively landscaped, cabana-style retreat offers canoeing, swimming, wind-surfing, fishing, nature treks, and even therapeutic massage. As you would expect in this remote location, prices are upmarket. Tours to the nearby Río Bravo Conservation Area, Mennonite farms, and Mexican border village of La Unión are available. The lodge is a bird-watchers' paradise, with a sweeping view of the nearby lake, for-est, and Mayan ruins. It was constructed using largely local materials and labor in a manner that minimizes any negative impact on the environment. Septic systems, for example, are set up to percolate "gray water" back into the soil, and mulch is used to retard erosion and discourage weed growth. Among the many amenities are a pon-toon boat to while away the days on New River Lagoon. The Out-post's excellent restaurant and bar are open to casual day visitors. Fresh food is grown on the premises or in the nearby village. Most employees are Guatemalan refugees who settled here in the early 1980s. The lodge may be reached in about two and one-half hours by either auto or auto/boat combination from Belize City. From Orange Walk Town, take the Yo Creek road to San Felipe and turn left for the final 12 miles to Indian Creek. For more on the Lamanai ruins, see chapter 6.

The Shipstern Peninsula

Sticking like a hitchhiker's thumb into the northern end of Chetumal Bay, the Shipstern Peninsula is one of the least developed areas in all Belize. Until recently, it could only be reached by private boat. Only a few thousand Spanish-speaking people live in this vast expanse of unspoiled and often waterlogged jungle, savanna, and mangrove swamp, most of them concentrated in the isolated fishing village of Sarteneja, which perches on a small patch of dry ground near the peninsula's northeast tip.

Before 1988, the few roads that had been cut through this moist Corozal District forest were impassable much of the year due to muddy conditions and high water. The main road has since been improved, and closures are uncommon. A four-wheel-drive vehicle is still advisable during the wet season, however.

Progresso, Chunox, Little Belize, and a few other small settlements punctuate the picturesque landscape en route to Sarteneja, but the peninsula's main attraction is the privately operated Shipstern Nature Reserve and Butterfly Breeding Centre. This 32-square-mile nature sanctuary is not far from the government's large Freshwater Creek Forest Reserve. The modest headquarters and visitors' center of the Shipstern Nature Reserve is located about 10 miles south of Sarteneja.

Managed by the Switzerland-based International Tropical Conservation Foundation, Shipstern Nature Reserve's 22,000 acres include northern hardwood forests and mangrove shorelines that are almost totally undisturbed by man. The tract is named after the abandoned village of Shipstern, located in the southern part of the reserve, and is considered an exceptional example of a heterogeneous forest in regeneration from devastating tropical storm damage. (Most of the mature trees were destroyed by Hurricane Janet in 1955.)

The flora and fauna have made a remarkable recovery during the past three decades, and hundreds of plant and animal species have been recorded here, including scores of migratory birds from North America that winter in Shipstern. The reserve is developing a public environmental education program, in cooperation with the Belize

Audubon Society. By educating Belizean families, especially children, it is hoped that new attitudes and methods can be substituted for age-old habits that are destructive to various ecosystems. Facilities for scientists and trails for casual visitors are slowly being developed within the reserve, as funds allow.

In 1990, the Shipstern Nature Reserve opened its Chiclero Botanical Trail, located in thick forest near the headquarters building. A booklet explains the traditional uses of dozens of trees identified along the path, including their medicinal and ceremonial applications. One of Shipstern's main goals is to show how countries like Belize can make conservation areas self-supporting through low-impact tourism and the controlled production of natural products within reserve boundaries, an approach known as agrobotany. A fascinating example of agrobotany in action is Shipstern's ongoing breeding of live butterfly pupae such as the colorful Dynamine for distribution around the world, primarily to England. Great Britain now has over 60 man-made butterfly habitats, and special public parks for these colorful insects have also been constructed in the United States, Japan, and Singapore.

Visitors can tour the Shipstern Butterfly Breeding Centre and view these delicate and magnificent creatures in the four stages of their life cycle: egg, caterpillar, pupa (also called chrysalis), and adult. Wild pupae from 25 of the region's nearly 200 species are collected for breeding at the facility, and as many as 10,000 dormant specimens a month are shipped off to simulated jungle environments, where they emerge a few weeks later as tiny winged ambassadors of Belize. After their release the butterflies usually live from 1 to 7 weeks. A single female will lay between 100 and 200 eggs during that short life span.

In early 1990, villagers in Sarteneja started a second butterfly farm, developed under the auspices of the Belize Biotropical Farming Company (contact director Linda Sealey for information about tours). Several dozen families now are involved in the breeding and rearing of butterflies for export. They grow plants in their gardens, where the insects like to feed and lay their eggs. Pupae are then gathered by hand and delivered to European buyers. A by-product of such operations, which include backyard cages used for gender-controlled breeding stock, is an increase in the wild butterfly population. While deforestation and the use of pesticides have destroyed many natural butterfly breeding grounds in many tropical nations, the moist forest of the Shipstern Peninsula remains largely untouched. It is the only protected area in the country that includes the more seasonal hardwood trees, as well as vast saltwater estuaries that are an especially important habitat for many wading and fish-eating birds. Bird-watchers can expect to see several species of flycatcher, toucan, warbler, aracari, and parrots. Among the colorful birds recorded here are the Yucatán jay, reddish egret, wood stork, and black catbird (previously assumed to be restricted to the offshore cayes).

All five species of Belize's native cats, along with tapir, paca, coatimundi, deer, peccary, and armadillo, roam the Shipstern forests and savanna. Five different jaguars were sighted within a 5-mile radius of the Shipstern Nature Reserve's headquarters during 1990. Plans are under way to reintroduce howler monkeys, which became locally extinct after a series of fierce storms in the 1950s knocked down most of the tall trees these primates favor. The howler population was further weakened by an epidemic of yellow fever, which is highly contagious.

The village of Sarteneja was almost completely washed away by Hurricane Janet. One resident was killed, and only three brick structures—the school, clinic, and old sugar mill—survived the flood. Yet the clapboard, tin-roof settlement has been rebuilt several times in its history, always around a well located in a massive piece of seemingly solid stone. Legend has it that this particular well, once used by seafaring Maya, has never gone dry. Sarteneja is a Spanish word meaning "water between the rocks." Bear in mind that rainfall totals here are much lower than in the south, and extended droughts are not unheard of.

The Maya apparently abandoned the original village about A.D. 1700. During the mid-1800s, Yucatán settlers fleeing the Caste Wars reestablished Sarteneja, which became widely known for its skilled boat builders. To this day, Sarteneja's fishermen sail as far south as Guatemala and Honduras in their beautiful handcrafted sailing vessels. They sell their catch in Belize City, San Pedro, or Chetumal on the way home, then turn around and start another fishing expedition a few days later. Every Easter, a huge sailing regatta is held in the small Sarteneja harbor and prizes are awarded for the fastest and most elegant boats.

Although more than 400 Mayan sites have been pinpointed on the peninsula, only one ancient structure has been excavated. While the world's archaeologists organize themselves, local residents continue to dismantle many of the old buildings block by block to make modern houses of their own. Jade, gold, copper, and shell artifacts periodically turn up here but are usually sold to traders or kept in private collections. Farmers sometimes drag the Mayan limestone bricks out of their fields and grind them up as ingredients for plaster and cement.

Small-scale pineapple, papaya, mango, grapefruit, and orange plantations are gradually invading the forests of Shipstern Peninsula, although most villagers are still closely tied to the sea. Most of Sarteneja's supplies, for example, come by boat across the Inner Channel from Chetumal, the capital of Mexico's state of Quintana Roo. While these waterways are generally too shallow for large craft, a growing number of foreign sportfishermen are now exploring the waters off Shipstern in search of barracuda, grouper, snook, yellowtail, and tarpon, which are all plentiful. The native shrimp, lobster, and conch, once very common, have been severely depleted by commercial fishermen.

A couple of cayes and reefs offer snorkeling possibilities here, but they are difficult to reach without a chartered boat. The area's murky lagoons are important feeding grounds for such rare birds as the flamingo and spoonbill, as well as manatees and crocodiles. Arrangements can be made with local travel agents and guides based in Orange Walk Town and Corozal Town (see Inside Belize for suggestions).

You might also want to make a side trip to Chacan Chac Mol, a small lake southwest of Sarteneja. Also, the Shipstern ruins are an infrequently explored ceremonial center with access through the Shipstern Nature Reserve. You must arrange this in advance and obtain permits from the reserve management.

If You Go: All-weather gravel roads to Sarteneja branch off the Northern Highway from several points in and around Orange Walk Town. The trip by car takes one hour from Orange Walk Town and two hours from Belize City, in good weather. The daily bus from Belize City leaves from the Texaco Gas Station on North Front Street at about noon, returning around 3:00 a.m.

From Orange Walk Town, take the northeast road toward Progresso and turn right just before that village toward the Mennonite settlement of Little Belize. From there, go to Chunox and on to Sarteneja. The Shipstern Nature Reserve headquarters is 3 miles before the village of Sarteneja.

Venus Bus Lines has a daily service to Sarteneja from Belize City with a stop in Orange Walk Town en route. Domestic airlines ferry passengers to Sarteneja via Corozal, and boat transportation can be easily arranged from Corozal Town, Ambergris Caye, or Consejo Shores.

Lodgings have come and gone in the village over the years. At last report, the only accommodation was at Diani's Hotel and Restaurant, described as simple and budget priced. There are no overnight facilities at the Shipstern Nature Reserve and Butterfly Breeding Centre, which is a short taxi ride (or 45-minute walk) from the village.

The best time to visit the breeding center is on a bright sunny day, as the butterflies tend to hide amid the foliage in overcast and rainy weather. The Butterfly Breeding Centre and Visitors' Centre is open daily (except New Year's, Easter, and Christmas) from 9:00 a.m. to noon and 1:00 p.m. to 4:00 p.m. Guided tours are $12.50 for groups up to four, $2.50 each for groups of five or more. Booklets are available for self-guided tours of the nature trail.

Tours to other areas, including night trips into the jungle to observe some of the forest's unusual nocturnal wildlife, can be arranged in Sarteneja by simply asking around town for a knowledgeable guide. If the tour will include parts of the Shipstern Nature Reserve, permits from the reserve management need to obtained in advance.

Information about the Shipstern Nature Reserve and Butterfly Breeding Centre can be obtained through Jan Meerman, Manager, P.O. Box 1694, Belize City.

Belize City

Belize City is the country's hub, located at the mouth of the Belize River on the Caribbean Sea and midway between the Mexican and Guatemalan borders. A seaport town with a population of about 65,000, it is the nation's largest urban center. Simply called "Belize" by locals, the city supports and manages a growing tourism industry as well as many other services and businesses. It also provides a base for Belizean conservation groups.

We trust that if you bother to take more than the usual passing glance at Belize City, you will find that it is more than just a "point of departure," as most travelers assume. Yes, foul-smelling trenches remain from the once open-air sewers, and dingy, shoddy clapboard structures are the norm. But the city's underlying charms include many elegant colonial-style buildings and a friendly, small-town atmosphere in which outsiders are readily accepted. Touring Belize City one often has the sensation of being caught in a time warp. It is as if such standard twentieth-century amenities as automobiles and electricity have only arrived here during the past several years. And this is not far from the truth.

Belize City's smiling residents and relaxed pace are among its greatest attractions. From hotel employees to restaurant workers, taxi drivers to conservation leaders, travel agents to bank tellers—almost everyone is eager to share helpful information with visitors. Please note, however, that walking alone in certain areas is not recommended because a small but aggressive contingent is quite persistent in demanding money or selling drugs. At night, a single person on foot may encounter even more significant trouble: the dangers of being attacked and robbed exist here, as they do in many large urban centers. Taxis within Belize City's limits are inexpensive and readily available. We advise you to use them, and do not walk alone at night or with valuables on your person. Although there is a municipal bus system, its routes are confusing and not well posted.

The first full-time residents of what is now Belize City are believed to have been Mayan Indians, who maintained a busy fishing camp on nearby Moho Caye for several centuries. Bones and other artifacts excavated at this site suggest there was abundant marine life, including a large number of turtles and manatees. In the late 1600s, after the area had been mostly abandoned by the Maya, Scottish and British pirates began to settle during the rainy season at the mouth of the Belize River. These buccaneers and their African slaves harvested tropical hardwoods in the interior and used the broad, slow-moving waterway to float the precious timber to oceangoing vessels anchored offshore. By the eighteenth century, the settlement of Belize Town, as it was called then, had been solidly established by members of what the British referred to as their Bay Settlement (named after the nearby Bay of Honduras). Historians say the city is built on a foundation of loose coral, logwood chips, and rum bottles. This pile of debris seems to be sinking, as much of the urban area is now barely above sea level.

To make matters worse, several violent hurricanes and accompanying tidal waves have battered Belize City over the years. They occur primarily in autumn, as evidenced by Hurricane Hattie's destructive visit on October 31, 1961, which took hundreds of lives and nearly leveled the town. This was the prime motivation for Belizeans to move their capital 35 miles inland to Belmopan, even though most residents chose to take their chances by staying in Belize City. (Only about 6,000 people reside permanently in Belmopan, and a large percentage of government workers commute every day.) In 1978, Hurricane Greta wreaked havoc on a relatively unprotected Belize City. In spite of Mother Nature's unpredictable and destructive forces, the city remains home to a third of the country's population.

A number of impressive landmarks have withstood the various storms and can be taken in during even a brief tour of Belize City. At the gateway to Belize Harbor is Fort George Lighthouse, dominating a finger of land that was originally the easternmost point on Fort George Island. The channel separating the island and mainland was filled in during the 1920s, long after it had fulfilled its function as an army base. Views of nearby cayes covered in mangroves now await visitors to the site, and brown pelicans often fish in small groups near the shore.

Clapboard house, Belize City (Photo by Sue Dirkson)

Next to the lighthouse is a small park and the Baron Bliss Memorial, a tribute to the "Fourth Baron Bliss of the former Kingdom of Portugal," Henry Edward Ernest Victor Bliss. An Englishman by birth, this eccentric adventurer first sailed to Belize in 1926 and instantly fell in love with its soothing climate, unspoiled waters, and palm-studded islands. The baron arrived in Belize too ill to come ashore as a result of food poisoning he suffered in Trinidad. He spent several months aboard his yacht, the *Sea King*, trying to recover and fishing in the harbor. Bliss was impressed by the way fellow sportfishermen and colonial officials alike treated him kindly and with great respect. He learned as much as he could about Belize without even having the physical ability to come ashore. Before Baron Bliss died aboard his boat, he specified in his will that a trust fund of almost $2 million be established for the sole benefit of Belizeans. So far the interest generated from the trust fund has been used to help construct a public building in Belmopan, a Corozal health clinic, the Belize City water supply, the Bliss Institute public library and museum, and other projects. Baron Bliss also stipulated that a portion of the funds be used to stage an annual yacht regatta in Belizean waters.

This is the focal event of the national holiday on March 9 honoring his contributions.

In the heart of Belize City is a large old colonial-style building that provides space for the main post office as well as the Belize City headquarters of such ministries as the Department of Natural Resources. Here you may purchase the colorful stamps of Belize, among the most beautiful in the world. They depict brocket deer, storks, marine life, tapir, jaguar, macaws, and many other native animals. A special counter for stamp collectors is on the Queen Street side of the post office. Parcel post is now handled next door on North Front Street. Upstairs on the right side of the Paslow Building, the best maps of Belize (divided into north and south sections) are available from a government office for about $10 each.

Facing the main post office is Belize City's Swing Bridge, reportedly the only such manually operated bridge remaining in the world. It was constructed in Liverpool, England, and has been cranked open for Haulover Creek boat traffic since 1923. Daily, at about 6:00 a.m. and 5:30 p.m., policemen stop pedestrians and vehicles on either side of the bridge while men insert long poles into a capstan and gradually open a passageway allowing high-masted vessels to pass upriver or out to sea. Unfortunately, this area is where a visitor is most likely to encounter aggressive and sometimes hostile panhandlers. The experience of seeing the Swing Bridge operate is worthwhile, however, and early in the morning the hassle is usually less intense.

Across from Belize City's motley Central Park is the Supreme Court Building. Built in a classic British colonial style and with a dome-topped clock tower, it stands on the site of the original settlement courthouse built in 1818. The courthouse has been rebuilt here twice: it was demolished in 1878, and a famous fire that took the life of then-governor William Hart Bennett destroyed the courthouse again in 1918. For an interesting slice-of-life experience, step into one of the courtrooms and watch the Belizean justice system in action.

Near the courthouse on Bliss Promenade (also called the Southern Foreshore) is the Bliss Institute, which, with its modern-looking circular second floor, looks out of place amid the Victorian gingerbread of Belize City's oldest neighborhood. The institute displays (poorly) some ancient Mayan artifacts from Caracol and other archaeological sites. It also houses a public library, auditorium, and art gallery as well as the National Arts Council. Slide shows and seminars on science, history, and culture are held here. Plans have been announced to build a bigger and better museum in Belmopan, but finished results are unlikely before 1995.

Headquartered on the south side of the Swing Bridge is Belize City's public market, relocated in 1993 to a modern three-level structure at the foot of Regent Street. A rival "temporary" market has operated since 1991 from a warehouse on North Front Street, about three blocks west of the Fort George Lighthouse. This is a place that mixes healing with agony. Besides the usual fruits and vegetables, you can purchase medicinal herbs from vendors whose wares include the bark from the negrito tree, used in the treatment of dysentery. You will also see sea turtles such as the loggerhead and hawksbill, placed upside down and slowly dying. Even though international trading of these and other endangered species is prohibited by the CITES convention on endangered species, local sales are apparently still legal. The sight of these giant marine creatures dying is certainly not for the faint of heart.

The oldest Protestant church in Central America is located at the far south end of Regent Street across from Government House, itself a historical landmark. St. John's Anglican Cathedral is one of the oldest buildings in Belize. Built by slaves in 1812 from bricks brought over as ballast in the hulls of ships sailing from Europe, the church was the site of several coronation ceremonies for the Indian kings of the Mosquito Coast. These were members of an indigenous ruling class that once presided over the indigenous tribes of what is now the Caribbean coast of Honduras, Nicaragua, and Costa Rica. Inside the church are dozens of plaques commemorating the lives of prominent Anglican colonists.

Across Regent Street from St. John's Cathedral, the graceful palms of its well-groomed grounds swaying in the breeze, Government House serves as an elegant place to stay for visiting dignitaries. Belize's prime minister also keeps an office here. The handsome wooden buildings were designed by acclaimed British architect Christopher Wren and constructed between 1812 and 1814.

Several hotels, restaurants, and stores deserve mention here as some of our favorites in the city. The 4 Fort Street Restaurant and Guest House (the name is the same as the address) gives travelers a very hospitable base of operations. The food and service are among the best in Belize. Located in a grand colonial-style building (once the home and office of a physician), 4 Fort Street is frequently used by locals as a meeting place. American proprietor Rachel Emmer has considerable experience in Belize and can be helpful in fine-tuning your trip. Book in advance, as this guest house is quite popular. Directly across the street, in a warehouse adjacent to the boat landing for British military forces, is the National Handicraft Sales Center. Operated by the Belize Chamber of Commerce, this facility sells a wide variety of handicrafts made by more than one hundred artisans. Prices are reasonable, and you may choose from among fine carvings, ceramics, paintings, sculptures, baskets, embroidery, T-shirts, maps, posters, cassette tapes, postcards, and even furniture.

Mom's Triangle Inn and Restaurant at 11 Handyside Street is one of the best places for breakfast and lunch in Belize City, as well as a good place to make travel arrangements or meet your boat skipper to the cayes. A Belizean institution, Mom's also serves as the communications center (via two-way radio) for the Belize Zoo and Tropical Education Center. Mom's can call ahead and make sure there will be someone to meet you at the zoo, which sometimes has flexible hours and staffing. Next door to Mom's you can dine on the best pizza in Belize City at Pearl's Pizza at 13 Handyside. Take-out is also available.

The Belize Guest House perches on the Caribbean sea and offers moderately priced lodging only footsteps from the water. For couples seeking romance and an ocean breeze, this small hotel at the corner of Hutson Street and Marine Parade has a lovely room overlooking the Belize City harbor. Watching the wooden sailing ships (known as "lighters") slip by as you sip a rum and orange juice on the Belize Guest House veranda is a recommended experience.

Macy's Café, 18 Bishop Street, serves Belize's inexpensive main dish of rice and beans, with extras ranging from stewed chicken to curried gibnut. Harrison Ford stopped here during the filming of *Mosquito Coast* several years ago, but even a movie star's presence has not affected the restaurant's laid-back atmosphere and humble furnishings.

G G's Café and Patio at 2B King Street features a pleasant, romantic patio atmosphere, friendly service, and very good food.

The Seaside Guest House at 3 Prince Street, just a few steps up from the Southern Foreshore, provides comfortable low-cost accommodations. Nature enthusiasts of all nationalities are especially welcome. The proprietors offer a healthy breakfast for visitors who request it and can share a lot of stories about conservation in Belize. This has literally been headquarters for many environmentalists over the years.

The Bellevue Hotel, located around the corner from the Seaside on the Southern Foreshore, has modern rooms and a lively upstairs bar decorated like an old oceanliner. This is a favorite among divers.

For some of the biggest portions of the best modestly priced Chinese food in Belize City, visit New Chon Saan Restaurant. The original is located at 55 Euphrates; their second location is at 184 North Front Street; and for a more formal, air-conditioned atmosphere, the New Chon Saan Palace at 1 Kelly Street is the place. All three locations, unfortunately, are local hangouts for panhandlers or even more dangerous folks. Go with a friend in a taxi. Other recommended restaurants include The Grill (164 Barracks Rd.) and Dit's (50 King St.), serving continental and Belizean cuisine, respectively.

Romac's Supermarket, at 27 Albert Street, and Brodie's, directly across the street at the corner of Albert and Regent, come in handy for all those provisions one needs to explore the tropical forest. The latter has a deli, pharmacy, produce section, and good selection of Belizean books and magazines. The nearby Mopan Hotel, at 55 Regent Street, is a moderately priced establishment run by Jean and Tom Shaw, longtime environmentalists who are creating the Shawfields Nature Reserve in the interior. Other options include the modern Ramada Royal Reef on Barracks Road and charming Colton House, at 9 Cork Street.

Belize City is also a good place to finalize travel arrangements and get those insider tips on special people and places to visit in this diverse country. We recommend, particularly for the ecology-minded visitor, Jal's Travl and S & L Travel Services. Lombardo "Bardy" Riverol runs Jal's Travl out of an air-conditioned office at 148 Front Street just west of the Swing Bridge (tel. 2-45407 or 2-73443). As an ardent conservationist, Riverol has excellent contacts within the Belize conservation community and can set up a complete package tour for the traveler interested in visiting protected areas such as the Cockscomb Basin Wildlife Sanctuary and Crooked Tree Wildlife Sanctuary. Jal's offers guided trips to see manatees: Riverol himself takes visitors by boat to the nearby Drowned Cayes or on a full-day trip through Burdon Canal and past Bird Caye to Gales Point. Jal's also specializes in cave tours, overnight visits to Belizean families, and trips to the Cayo District. Riverol and his friendly staff are proficient at booking flights within Belize—sometimes a tricky task. Remember that it is a good idea to double-check flight times for air travel in-country. The Tillet family's S & L Travel Services at 91 North Front Street (tel. 2-77593, fax 2-77594) offers recommended package tours to the following destinations: Crooked Tree and Altun Ha; Community Baboon Sanctuary and Altun Ha; Tikal, Guatemala; and any of Belize's offshore islands. For those interested in auto rental, we recommend Crystal at 1.5 Mile Northern Highway, which offers a wide variety of cars and vans at reasonable prices (all major credit cards accepted). They also arrange car transfers from the United States.

If You Go: From the Phillip Goldson International Airport, a 15-minute taxi ride into Belize City costs about $15. Less expensive and less reliable shuttle bus service is also available for about $3 (tel. 2-73977). (See Inside Belize for listings concerning other hotels, restaurants, and services in Belize City.)

Altun Ha and Crooked Tree Wildlife Sanctuary

One of several rewarding day trips from Belize City can combine a visit to a major ancient Mayan ceremonial center, Altun Ha, and one of the premier bird sanctuaries in Central America, Crooked Tree Wildlife Sanctuary. Of course, you may want to spend more time at either Altun Ha or Crooked Tree, but in a single morning and afternoon, it is perfectly feasible to visit both.

Stay alert on your way through the lowland pine savanna on the road to Altun Ha and Crooked Tree: the countryside along the Northern Highway is a rich habitat for many bird species. We once saw the Belizean "grand prize" for bird-watchers at Mile 11: a jabiru stork flew over the top of the vehicle, so close one could distinguish the bright red band on its neck. The jabiru is easy to identify since it is one of the largest birds of the Americas, with an adult wingspan of up to 10 feet. It is rare in Belize and an imperiled species in other parts of its range, such as southern Mexico. (See chap. 7 for a more thorough description of the majestic jabiru stork.)

Other birds you might encounter on the Northern Highway are the vigilant roadside hawk (often perched on the telephone wire awaiting an opportunity to swoop down and prey on an unwary rodent) or an energetic pair of vermilion flycatchers playing tag among low bushes bordering the drainage ditches. A great heron will likely greet you as it patiently stalks small fish in the many lagoons along the road. A large bird, the contrast of the heron's white plumage against the dull silver-green of palmetto palms and brown savanna grass makes it easy to spot.

Altun Ha

The ancient Mayan ruins of Altun Ha are 31 miles from Belize City on the *old* Northern Highway toward Maskall (the *new* Northern Highway continues in a more westerly direction toward Crooked Tree Lagoon). The site, 8 miles from the sea, was an important Mayan trading and ceremonial center. Here the sun was a focus of worship, and thus Mayan priests were buried within one of the tallest temples known as Temple of the Sun God. Altun Ha, named "stone water" in Maya after the nearby Rockstone Pond, also became a focal point for the sacrifice of such valuables as jade jewelry and carved pendants, as well as offerings of copal resin. The latter is a hardened saplike substance, probably used as incense by the original Maya as it still is by their descendants today. At the top of the Temple of the Masonry Altars, such precious items were smashed into small pieces and cast into an intense fire. Like many Mayan rituals, the origin and purpose of this sacrificial offering remain unclear.

Thirteen structures surround two main plazas at the site. The two tallest temples, Temple of the Sun God and Temple of the Masonry Altars, rise 60 feet above the grassy plaza floor. Altun Ha covers an area of 1.5 square miles and includes an extensive swamp north of the plazas.

Visitors interested in birds are also likely to be rewarded here. Brilliant green Aztec parakeets often streak by in tight formation, level with the tops of the temples. Ringed kingfishers rest on the summit of the Mayan structures before returning to the nearby swamp to fish. Tropical mockingbirds and brown jays squawk persistently at tourists. There are also trails into the bush for birders driven by a constant chorus of calls and songs that echoes around the plazas.

Altun Ha was first excavated by A. H. Anderson in 1957 and has undergone some of the most extensive fieldwork of any Belizean ruin. In 1961, W. R. Bullard worked at Altun Ha and examined portions of the site. This rich ceremonial center remained archaeologically quiet until 1963 when quarry workers unearthed an elaborately carved jade pendant. This discovery triggered a chain of events culminating in Belize's first long-term intensive archaeological excavation, from 1964 to 1971, spearheaded by David Pendergast with support from Canada's Royal Ontario Museum. Restoration work at the site was performed from 1971 to 1976 by Joseph Palacio and during 1978 by Elizabeth Graham. Altun Ha was the second Mayan ruin in the country, after Xunantunich, to be cleared and prepared for tourism. Crews from the Department of Archaeology now keep the grass neatly trimmed and groom some of the surrounding bush for visitors. Brochures and rest room facilities are also available.

Perhaps Altun Ha's most famous historical footnote is Pendergast's discovery of a huge jade head replica of Kinich Ahua, the Sun God, in one of the last tombs to be excavated. It was made in about A.D. 600 and owned by an elderly priest. This priceless relic was at that time the largest of its type ever recorded in the Mayan world: almost 6 inches tall and weighing nearly 10 pounds. This jade head is now in the Department of Archaeology's vault in Belmopan, where it can be viewed by appointment. On rare occasions it is taken on exhibition tours with other artifacts.

Because of its proximity to the sea and the lack of stelae and tombs, Altun Ha was probably more significant to the Maya as a trading center than as a ceremonial site. Jade found at Altun Ha probably came from Guatemala's Sierra de las Minas, since this stone does not occur naturally in Belize. Other goods found at the site have been traced to Teotihuacán, near Mexico City. Altun Ha's obviously important religious function as a sacrificial site remains unexplained.

Several phases of construction have occurred at Altun Ha, which was occupied from around 1000 B.C. until its abandonment in A.D. 900. You can easily detect this phased construction in the distinct sets of walls that are evident as you walk around the backsides of the plazas. One of the most distinguishing aspects of Altun Ha and a feature of paramount importance in the development—and possibly the fall—of the ancient Maya is the reservoir known as Rockstone Pond. A short trail leads there from the stone ruins. Like catchments at other Mayan sites, including Tikal in Guatemala, Rockstone was lined with clay to hold water. Recent scientific evidence suggests that, at least for lowland Mayan urban centers, spurts of population growth followed by temporary abandonment of sites may well have corresponded to fluctuations in annual rainfall and the availability of stored water. Researchers suggest that a lack of consistently available water supplies in times of drought may have had more to do with the permanent abandonment of lowland Mayan population centers than either political or military conflict.

Pendergast concluded, however, that Altun Ha fell into disuse as the result of social upheaval. He found unmistakable evidence of desecration at several of Altun Ha's tombs. The archaeologist concluded that modern-day looters were not responsible for the destruction of contents of tombs, burying of crypts with soil, and the displacement of roof slabs. Pendergast reasoned that such activity, accompanied by violence, may have involved some form of peasant revolt among the Maya around A.D. 1200.

The hypothesis that this kind of total collapse of the civilization occurred has been challenged. Other specialists have concluded that large-scale economic, political, and demographic rearrangements shifted the Maya Classic era from the southern to the northern low-lands. Perhaps a break in the continued availability of water brought down Altun Ha and other centers of Mayan civilization. The fall of the Maya remains an unsolved puzzle that should keep archaeologists debating for years.

If You Go: From Belize City, take the Northern Highway, and turn right at the junction of the old Northern Highway (the sign is marked Maskall and Orange Walk). Proceed 31 miles and turn left at the sign for the 2-mile connecting road to the Altun Ha parking lot. The drive from Belize City takes approximately 45 minutes, not counting numerous stops to identify and observe birds along the way. There is no regular bus service to the site, although it is possible to hire a taxi or hitch a ride with a truck that brings goods to market in Belize City from the village of Maskall just north of Altun Ha. A fee of $1.50 per person is collected at the open-air cabana registration center.

We recommend hiring a local guide for the day, such as Bardy Riverol at Jal's Travl and Tours. Bardy is particularly helpful in identifying birds, and he gives an informative tour of Altun Ha. Mayaland Tours (tel. 2-30515; fax 2-32242) in Belize City offers a reasonably priced package tour called "Northern Sights One" to both Altun Ha and Crooked Tree.

There are no accommodations at Altun Ha, but camping is allowed with permission from the caretaker. The only nearby rooms are at the attractive (and expensive) Maruba Resort at Mile Post 40.5 on the old Northern Highway (tel. 3-22199). Maruba Resort boasts a swimming pool, an open-air Japanese-style tub, and massages. The resort offers cabana-style accommodations and tours to Altun Ha and other nearby ruins, such as Lamanai. A few moderately priced guest houses are scattered through the nearby countryside. Try the Naga Bank Lodge near Bomba off the Maskall Road.

Crooked Tree Wildlife Sanctuary

Crooked Tree Wildlife Sanctuary is one of Belize's prime "natural destinations." Visitors from temperate zone countries can easily see more birds in a single day than they are likely to see back home in a year. Even before you cross the causeway that connects the freshwater island where Crooked Tree Village is situated with the outside world, you are liable to have spotted the American coot, northern jacana, snail kite, least grebe, white ibis, and rough-winged swallow. Hundreds of other different species have been recorded in Crooked Tree's lagoons and wetlands, but one could easily conclude from the richness and variety of habitats here that many more birds are waiting to be "discovered." Mexico Lagoon, Spanish River, and Black River are some of several excellent birding spots within the sanctuary's boundaries.

Not only is the variety of bird life tremendous, especially during the February-May dry season, but the sheer aggregate number of waterfowl is astonishing. Huge flocks of olivaceous cormorants, roseate spoonbills, egrets, and other species congregate here, taking advantage of the area's abundant food resources and safety as a resting spot on spring migration routes. The rare jabiru stork nests within the 3,000-acre sanctuary, and the limpkin, with its black body and strange-looking neck, is another frequently observed inhabitant. You may delight in identifying an elegant green-backed heron, sleek green-winged teal, ungainly wood stork, or brilliantly colored Yucatán jay.

Crooked Tree Wildlife Sanctuary was established by the area's 750 residents in November 1984 with substantial financial assistance from the Wild Wings Foundation. But the Belize Audubon Society has made the most significant contribution to the success of Crooked Tree. During the early years, Audubon management was accomplished exclusively by dedicated volunteers. Another group that has helped manage Crooked Tree's jabiru stork population is the New Mexico-based conservation organization LightHawk. Using light aircraft that carry sharp-eyed spotters, flight missions are designed to thoroughly survey the sanctuary to help perform an annual census for this imperiled species. Counts are made, locations of the giant birds are pinpointed, and nests are located. The collected data are then compared to information obtained from ground surveys, reports from villagers and visitors, and previous aerial surveys.

The sanctuary's well-maintained visitors' center and museum is located at the end of a 3-mile-long causeway, which runs between Crooked Tree Village and the paved road to Belize City. You must check in here before you explore the area. The center has informative displays that are designed to test your knowledge of birds that inhabit the sanctuary. The resident manager is happy to answer questions and assist in your explorations. Excellent maps are also available.

Donations to Crooked Tree Wildlife Sanctuary are encouraged and graciously accepted. This financial assistance keeps both the sanctuary and the Belize Audubon Society going. While no mandatory visitor fees are currently collected for this and other sanctuaries, monuments, and parks managed by Belize Audubon, plans to do so were being evaluated in mid-1993.

From sanctuary headquarters, you can follow several different nature trails. One is appropriately named after the northern jacana, a delicate bird that flashes yellow wings when it flies and is light enough to tread confidently on water hyacinth as it forages for small fish and mollusks.

Since 1993, an event has been held at Crooked Tree each May which exemplifies positive action by foreign-owned tour companies whose revenue is derived from nature-based tourism. Alabama-based International Expeditions co-sponsors the Crooked Tree Cashew Festival, a communitywide celebration that includes music, dancing, feasting, story-telling, folklore performances, and, of course, demonstrations of the harvesting and preparation of local cashew nuts. Cashew trees are native to the area, and their delicious fruits are used to make wine, jam, and sandwich spreads, as well as being sold in raw and roasted form. Mango products are also made and sold from the enormous centuries-old trees that dominate the village. During the festival, birding trips and tours of the local Mayan ruins of Chau Hiix are offered as well. The site is about 20 minutes by boat from the village and is now being excavated by an Indiana State University archaeological team.

International Expeditions has championed the extremely important concept that natural history or cultural tourism is not the only means to achieving effective, long-term conservation. Clearly, such tourism cannot do it all. By promoting the *combination* of the cashew harvest with tourism, the company is putting money into Crooked Tree through two means at once. And while tourism is the village's fastest-growing industry, its mostly Creole residents still engage in subsistence farming, livestock rearing, and fishing. The sale of cashew products throughout Belize and the rest of the world is an important boost to their economy.

For the best tour of Crooked Tree, we recommend that you inquire at the Belize Audubon Society office in Belize City. Have them radio as far in advance of your trip as possible to arrange for a hired boat to take you into the Crooked Tree Lagoon area, which is a very complex network of waterways. (In addition, the connecting causeway is sometimes underwater, making it necessary to reach Crooked Tree Village by boat.)

There are not very many boats in the village (the Belize Audubon brochure recommends Jex & Sons Boat Tours, based at Jax Store next to the visitors' center), and unless you arrange in advance, you will be stuck on the opposite shore. The sanctuary headquarters has a two-way radio, and its manager can help set up a boat tour. We recommend that you allow at least a half day and bring along a local guide. One rewarding boat trip takes you through Northern Lagoon to Spanish Creek. We also suggest that you ask your guide to periodically kill the engine and quietly float among the bird life.

The greatest amount of wildlife can be seen during April and May, when the water is low. Mornings and evenings are times of peak activity at all times of the year. As you travel along the shore of Crooked Tree Lagoon, you will see Belize's largest contiguous stand of remaining logwood. The village, one of the first ever in Belize's interior, was established because of the easy accessibility of this commercially valuable timber, still exported in small amounts. Logwood blossoms are lilac-shaped clusters of beautiful yellow flowers. On the way to Spanish Creek, your guide can also point out distinctively shaped bullet trees and dense stands of bamboo. Along this portion of the shoreline the master of hovering flight, the snail kite, searches with neck craned downward for the abundant snails that cling to logwood stems. The captured snails leave behind white, multichambered clusters of eggs, thus replenishing the food chain. Calabash

Pond, Revenge Lagoon, Western Lagoon, Southern Lagoon, Jones Lagoon, and Mexico Lagoon are some of the other wild places encompassed by the Crooked Tree Wildlife Sanctuary. Morelet's crocodiles and several species of turtles can be found here. You may spot a howler monkey or ocelot, both found in the Black River area. Indeed, there is so much to explore within this unique ecosystem that first-time visitors may quickly conclude that a half-day tour is, after all, entirely inadequate.

If You Go: Crooked Tree Wildlife Sanctuary is some 33 miles northwest of Belize City and 3.5 miles west of the new Northern Highway. We recommend that visitors arrange trips in advance through the Belize Audubon Society (tel. 2-77369) or International Expeditions (800-633-4734). Overnight accommodations are provided by several rustic lodges and at the homes of Crooked Tree Village residents. The latter are simple, inexpensive bed-and-breakfast arrangements in a rural atmosphere. Try the Raburn or Urrick family. Hotels include the Crooked Tree Resort (manager Sam Tillet offers guided boat trips), Paradise Inn, Crooked Tree Lodge (owner Rudy Crawford also operates a boat chartering service), Bird's-Eye View Lodge, or Maruba Resort (in Maskall). Meals, which may include local fish, are available at these hotels and at the Corner's Inn Restaurant. Accessible by boat up the Spanish River is the Chau Hiix Lodge, operated by American expatriate Robert Brooks and catering specifically to bird-watchers.

Buses from Belize City run daily to Crooked Tree. Check Venus Bus Lines (tel. 2-73354) or Batty Brothers Bus Service (tel. 2-72025 or 2-77146) for fares and schedules. Travel agencies arrange frequent tours. Taxis can also be arranged from Belize City or Orange Walk Town during the dry season. Expect to pay $75 and up for a round-trip from Belize City.

The Community Baboon Sanctuary

In Belize, black howler monkeys are called baboons; therefore, the "baboons" being protected here have little in common with their

African cousins of the same name. They are, in fact, Central American black howler monkeys, an endangered species found only in thick lowland forests from southern Mexico to Honduras.

Howlers—so named because adults (mostly males) emit a distinctive raspy, guttural growl that can be heard for a mile or more—are threatened in much of their rapidly shrinking range. The protected colony that can be seen by visitors on an easy day trip from Belize City numbers about 1,500 and is considered one of the few healthy-sized populations in the region. And, thanks to an innovative management scheme, the size of this group is increasing all the time.

What is most unusual about the Community Baboon Sanctuary and its interpretive museum is the fact that the project is voluntary, entirely reliant on the goodwill of interested subsistence farmers who work the lands immediately adjacent to the broadleaf jungle the howlers prefer. Although the sanctuary is both praised and admired by government officials, it is completely dependent on private lands and funding for its survival. Since the sanctuary's creation in 1985, the mostly Creole landowners have responded generously to the international scientific community's concern about the primate's dwindling habitat.

"You know, the baboons are so much like people that nobody around here wants to hurt them," explained Alvin Dawson, a lifelong resident of Bermudian Landing, when we asked him about his reasons for participating in the effort. As he was speaking, several howlers were noisily settling down for the night in a tall fig tree next to his rice field.

"How close," we asked, "do the animals get to your yard?"

Dawson grinned broadly and gestured toward a mature cashew tree just a few steps from the front door of his two-story clapboard farmhouse. "They climb that tree every year when the nuts are ripe," he said. "Since the sanctuary was started, they've become much more trusting of people. You can walk right up to them."

The current situation is a dramatic change from only fifteen years ago, when the howler monkeys were frequent targets of Mayan Indians and Guatemalan refugees (who killed them for meat) as well as unscrupulous poachers (who sold them as pets). Both practices are

"Caution—Baboon Bridge" sign alerts travelers along road at the Community Baboon Sanctuary (Photo by Richard Mahler)

now illegal throughout Belize, where only licensed hunters can stalk wild game. The howlers have also been hard hit over the years by hurricanes, which destroy their treetop aeries, and yellow fever, the same deadly disease that affects humans. But more significantly, they have been victims of deforestation. As arboreal vegetarians partial to wild fruits and flower blossoms, they need a thick forest canopy to survive.

To preserve this critical habitat along the Belize River, about 25 miles inland from the Caribbean Sea, nearly one hundred farmers in an 18-square-mile area agreed to maintain corridors of tall broadleaf jungle along the borders of their fields, to refrain from cutting such favored food trees as sapodilla, roseapple, fig, trumpet, and hogplum, and to protect 66-foot-wide strips of forest along the riverbank. These practices not only ensure that the monkeys will have a safe place to live, eat, and raise their families but also help reduce erosion, minimize river siltation, and allow more rapid regeneration of the soil after slash-and-burn agricultural clearing. The smaller plots of cultivated land are now hedged in by thick vegetation that will quickly invade the area once it loses its productivity.

Organizers began asking their neighbors to sign conservation pledges in the mid-1980s, and so far not a single farmer has turned them down or withdrawn from the sanctuary. Locals have found that visitors help them out financially by hiring guides, patronizing stores, and staying at informal bed and breakfasts that residents have set up in their homes. The women of the village often prepare hot meals for tourists, and the men take foreigners on leisurely canoe trips to observe the flora and fauna along the meandering Belize River. There also several small stores where drinks and food items can be purchased.

Like Bermudian Landing, seven other villages within the sanctuary are gradually attracting some tourism business. They bear the sort of colorful names encountered all over Belize: among them are Double Head Cabbage, Scotland Halfmoon, and Flowers Bank. The howler population has expanded so vigorously that the preserve's boundaries now may have expanded to include other villages.

"When I came here, I immediately noticed that the monkeys had a strong, viable community and the forest was relatively intact," recalls Robert Horwich, a zoologist from the University of Wisconsin who helped develop the plan for a voluntary wildlife sanctuary operated by local residents. "People seemed to genuinely like the howlers," notes Horwich, who still comes every spring to study the animals. "It struck me as logical to ask villagers to help preserve this habitat."

Backed by a disparate coalition that includes the Zoological Society of Greater Milwaukee, the World Wildlife Fund, the Lincoln Park Zoological Society, the International Primate Protection League, and the Belize Audubon Society, the Community Baboon Sanctuary now embraces a 20-mile stretch of Belize River watershed. The facility employs a full-time manager, two nature guides, and an education director. The latter takes the messages of conservation to classrooms throughout the country. Half the sanctuary's visitors are schoolchildren, most of whom had never seen a wild monkey before. (Since almost all of the reserve is on private land, visitors are asked not to stray from designated trails without a guide.)

Howler monkey troops, ranging from four to eight individuals, seem to appreciate the efforts being made to save them. Although the primates still spend most of their lives high in the tree boughs, they sometimes scamper along the ground within a few feet of lucky observers. The loud rasping call of the howler is most often used by dominant males to mark territorial boundaries between the troops they lead. The monkeys, including females, also howl when waking up in the morning and before going to sleep at night. Some locals swear that they also become vocal before the onset of a big rain storm. Howlers can reach up to 4 feet in length and weigh about 50 pounds when full-grown. Like other monkeys, they nurse their young, use their hands during feeding, and communicate with humanlike facial expressions.

This black howler is one of only two species of primate found in Belize. Their spider monkey cousins prefer wetter forests at higher elevations. In the entire world, there are only five other species of howler.

By 1992, the monkey colony along the Belize River was strong enough to withstand the transfer of some of its members to the Cockscomb Basin Wildlife Sanctuary, about 80 miles to the south. They may also be reintroduced to the Shipstern Nature Reserve and other protected areas. In these locations, a combination of hurricane damage, hunting, and yellow fever has wiped out indigenous troops of howlers during the past thirty years.

Another side benefit of the Community Baboon Sanctuary's success is the resurgence of other wildlife in the protected area. Nearly 200 bird species have been identified here, along with dozens of different mammals, including jaguars, ocelots, paca, and deer. Researchers are also coming here to study a highly endangered river turtle, the hickatee, which is now holding its own within the sanctuary's borders.

Though modified by centuries of selective logging and small-scale farming, local forests still support about 100 tree species and scores of varieties of vines, shrubs, flowers, and herbs. Many wild orchids and bromeliads can be seen clinging to the trunks of tall trees. A nursery is being established near Bermudian Landing to help alleviate Belize's deforestation problem and to reintroduce species like the mahogany that have become locally extinct. The sanctuary is the winter home of many migratory birds that fly to Belize every year from as far away as Canada. Colorful year-round residents include parakeets, parrots, toucans, and tanagers.

Besides a close-up look at Belize's flora and fauna, a visit to the sanctuary also affords an intimate view of life in a rural Creole village, where little has changed over the decades. Until only a few years ago, for example, these villages lacked all-weather roads, telephones, and electricity. Many still do without the latter two conveniences. The residents one meets are invariably gregarious and friendly, happy to share a funny story about their "baboons" over a glass of homemade whiskey or wine. "Baboon ya de fu we," is a favorite Creole slogan in the villages along the river, which means, "We're for the baboons!"

While some environmentalists still debate the wisdom of maintaining a wildlife refuge in a populated area, participants seem pleased with the results, and there is not even a whisper about discontinuing this grass-roots management plan. Indeed, plans have been put forward to adapt the Community Baboon Sanctuary model to projects in Mexico, Guatemala, Australia, and Sierra Leone. Already in the United States, box turtles and bald eagles are being protected in a similar fashion. And in Belize itself, the experiment is being imitated on Ambergris Caye by local residents who have volunteered to safeguard the nests of sea turtles and in Gales Point by villagers eager to guide visitors to local manatee and waterbird habitats.

If You Go: The Community Baboon Sanctuary is in north-central Belize and an easy day trip from Belize City. The site, whch is about 30 miles from Belize City, can be reached by car in about an hour via either the Northern or Western Highway. From either direction, take the Burrell Boom cutoff and follow the signs to Bermudian Landing. Note that there are only a few stores and no gasoline stations within 20 miles of the reserve. Several informal bed and breakfasts are available in the sanctuary and outlying villages.

Three independent buses are operated by local residents (Oswald McFadzean, Sydney Russell, and Valentine Young) on imprecise schedules. They generally leave Belize City around noon each day (except Sundays and holidays) and return from Bermudian Landing about 6:00 the following morning. On Fridays and Saturdays the buses fill up quickly. Taxi drivers from Belize City typically charge $70 and up for a round-trip to the baboon sanctuary.

Specific directions on how to get to the sanctuary by car or bus are available from the Belize Audubon Society's office at the old Customs House in Belize City (tel. 2-77369). Belize Audubon can also make arrangements for groups interested in touring the area, as well as for overnight accommodations. As of mid-1993, the only direct contact with sanctuary headquarters was by two-way radio, which is sometimes unreliable. It is possible, however, to simply stop at the Community Baboon Sanctuary office, pick up a field guide, tour the sanctuary on your own, and arrange to stay overnight with a local family (about $6 per person) and eat home-cooked meals ($2 and up). A Canadian-owned lodge planned to open in early 1994, and there is a two-room bed and breakfast, the Little Eden Guest House, in nearby Burrell Boom. Camping sites (on the museum grounds only) are $2 per tent per night. Meals cost around $3 each.

Guide fees are $2.50 an hour or $20 a day. Canoe trips are also about $20 per day. The free services of a local guide are included with the $15 purchase of a guidebook, which is recommended.

Because the jungle trails are often overgrown and muddy, rubber boots, long-sleeved shirts, trousers, hats, and insect repellent are advised. Always check in at the sanctuary headquarters and obtain a map before heading out. The natural history museum here is arguably the best in Belize.

Donations to the sanctuary's tax-deductible endowment fund are welcome. Checks should be made payable to Howlers Forever and sent in care of Robert "Baboon Man" Horwich, RD 1, Box 96, Gays Mills, WI 54631. Telephone (608) 735-4717. With a donation of $50 or more, a sanctuary-theme poster by artist Caroline Beckett is included, along with the group's quarterly newsletter, "Baboon Update."

The 420-page book, *A Belizean Rain Forest: The Community Baboon Sanctuary*, has been written by Robert Horwich and Jon Lyon for distribution to Belizean schools and interested individuals. It can be ordered from the Howlers Forever address above for $12, plus $2 postage and handling.

The Belize Zoo and Tropical Education Center

One place where you are guaranteed to see native animals in natural settings is the Belize Zoo. Most of us regard zoos as anything *but* a natural setting; however, as you know by now, things are done a bit differently in Belize. Instead of placing its animals behind bars in severe-looking cages, the zoo's managers have created an intimate, cozy atmosphere by putting their creatures in chicken-wire enclosures beneath a shady forest canopy. Each of the animals is referred to by its own pet name—from Sugar the purring ocelot to Rambo the keel-billed toucan—and all are well cared for.

The Belize Zoo is located about 30 miles west of Belize City and 14 miles east of Belmopan on the Western Highway. This is another easy day trip from Belize City or a good diversion en route to the Cayo District or Tikal.

The philosophy that permeates the zoo's exhibits is one of respect for all wildlife. There are many hand-lettered signs reminding visitors that such practices as poaching and live capturing are continuing to threaten the survival of several unusual Belizean natives, including cats, macaws, and monkeys. In fact, many of the creatures held by the zoo are "pets" that were abandoned by their owners after they became too big, too wild, or too unwanted. Guides at the zoo are closely involved in a conservation outreach program designed to teach visiting Belizean schoolchildren (as many as 300 a day) about the natural wonders of their homeland.

A particular favorite is Belize's national animal, the Baird's tapir, which thrives at the zoo. Throughout Central America, this large but shy creature is in trouble: its future survival as a species is threatened by habitat destruction and hunting. The tapir is the largest of all land animals native to the region, and adults may weigh up to 650 pounds. The zoo's female tapir, April, has endeared herself to thousands of Belizean children who have watched her frolic in her jungle paddock. April's recent pairing with a new mate reflects one of the major goals of the zoo—to give every animal a partner and thus ensure that in the future, visitors will always be able to view each species at close range. Captive breeding programs for such exotic creatures as the citreoline trogon and basilisk have also been carried out at the Belize Zoo.

At least 100 other animals can be seen here, including the endangered scarlet macaw, jaguarundi, margay, jaguar, anteater, and great curassow. The assembly includes some 18 mammal species, 12 bird species, 6 reptile species, and 2 insect species. All live within areas that are as large and as close to their natural habitats as could be achieved by the zoo personnel.

The Belize Zoo was founded in 1983 by its director, Sharon Matola, after wildlife filmmaker Richard Foster had his budget cut and was left with 17 animal "stars" that had no movies to appear in and no place to go. Matola, Foster's assistant, was told to disband the troupe of jaguars, coatimundis, pecarries, pumas, and other animals that had been trained to "act" in nature documentaries.

Instead of abandoning them, Matola boldly painted a description in front of each animal's enclosure and put up a "Belize Zoo" sign in front of the compound. Success came swiftly. Matola's credo is manifest in the way she has always run the zoo: public awareness and education are critical to wildlife conservation. Her nature-oriented storybooks have become favorites of Belizean children, who, in turn, are convincing their parents to adopt life-styles that protect the country's environment. The zoo's education director, Amy Bodwell, has organized countrywide lectures that have made a noticeable impact on prevailing attitudes toward native flora and fauna.

Matola has also organized and led scientific assessment teams to study the ecology of critical habitat areas in Belize such as the Raspaculo wilderness and the Columbia Forest Reserve. A 1990 expedition organized by the Belize Zoo to the latter, a subtropical moist forest in the southern part of the country, yielded such treasures as an unusual type of Mayan pottery, an amphibian of the genus *Eleutherodactylus* that was new to science, and a bird that had never before been recorded in Belize (the common woodnymph [*Thalurania furcata*]).

The Belize Zoo site incorporates approximately 1,700 acres of land, with an actual animal exhibit area of about 30 acres. Such Belize-loving celebrities as Harrison Ford and Jimmy Buffett made donations that enabled the zoo to move to expanded quarters in late 1991.

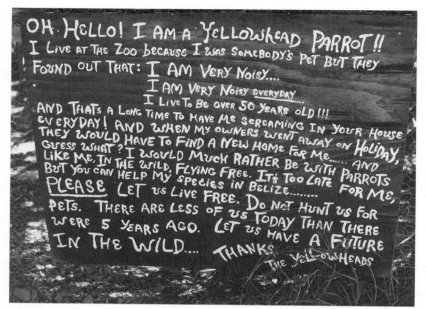

OH. HELLO! I AM A YELLOWHEAD PARROT!!
I LIVE AT THE ZOO because I was SOMEBODY'S PET BUT THEY
FOUND OUT THAT: I AM VERY NOISY....
I AM VERY NOISY EVERYDAY....
I LIVE TO BE OVER 50 YEARS OLD !!!
AND THATS A LONG TIME TO HAVE ME SCREAMING IN YOUR HOUSE
EVERYDAY! AND WHEN MY OWNERS WENT AWAY ON HOLIDAY,
THEY WOULD HAVE TO FIND A NEW HOME FOR ME..... AND
GUESS WHAT? I WOULD MUCH RATHER BE WITH PARROTS
LIKE ME, IN THE WILD, FLYING FREE. ITS TOO LATE FOR ME,
BUT YOU CAN HELP MY SPECIES IN BELIZE........
PLEASE LET US LIVE FREE. DO NOT HUNT US FOR
PETS. THERE ARE LESS OF US TODAY THAN THERE
WERE 5 YEARS AGO. LET US HAVE A FUTURE
IN THE WILD.... THANKS
THE YELLOWHEADS

This sign in front of the yellowhead parrot cage at the Belize Zoo illustrates the pro-conservation philosophy of its founders (Photo by Richard Mahler)

A large waterbird aviary was opened in 1993, and future plans include a butterfly exhibit, a freshwater aquarium (the famous Monterey Bay Aquarium is involved), and a reptile center. A biologist by training, Matola works constantly to improve the zoo and has taken advantage of Belize's thawed relations with Guatemala to acquire both a jaguarundi and a jaguar from that country.

The nearby Tropical Education Center is a sort of nature school for Belizeans, operated by University College of Belize and funded in part by Chicago's McArthur Foundation. The property was previously owned by Dora Weyer, one of Belize's first conservation leaders and a founding member of the Belize Audubon Society. Weyer retired to the United States in 1989, and her legacy is a 140-acre complex that has a self-guided nature trails, visitors' dormitory, lecture rooms, a library, and offices for its Belizean staff. Schoolchildren who have never spent a night in the bush come here to spend a few days surrounded by nature. Solar energy powers the entire compound.

If You Go: The Belize Zoo and Tropical Education Center are clearly marked on the Western Highway at about Mile Post 30. Going west from Belize City, you will encounter the Tropical Education Center first on your left, then the old zoo site on your right, and finally the new zoo a little farther along, also on the right. The visitor center, which includes an excellent gift shop and children's playground, is located about one-half mile off the highway on a dirt access road.

Taxis are easy to arrange from either Belize City or Belmopan. Many package tours also stop at the site. Expect to pay $60 and up for a round-trip.

Buses from Belize City run several times daily. Check Venus Bus Lines (tel. 2-73354) or Batty Brothers Bus Service (tel. 2-72025 or 2-77146) for fares and schedules. Drivers will be happy to pick you up and drop you off on the highway.

The Belize Zoo has no telephone but can be reached via two-way radio from its Belize City office on the second floor of Mom's Restaurant and Hotel on Haulover Street.

There are biting and stinging insects at the zoo, and a good repellent is strongly advised. We recommend that you keep your arms, legs, and ankles covered while observing the animals, since they tend to attract flying creatures that pester humans. Admission is $1 for Belizeans, $1.50 for military personnel, and $5 for foreign citizens. The zoo is open from 9:30 a.m. to 4:00 p.m. every day except Christmas and Good Friday. Zoo memberships (starting at $25) are available by writing to Box 1787, Belize City. Supporters receive a free newsletter about the Belize Zoo's ongoing activities.

Monkey Bay Wildlife Sanctuary and Nature Reserve

Located along the Western Highway only a few miles west of the Belize Zoo and Tropical Education Center, Monkey Bay Wildlife Sanctuary is a privately owned and operated nature reserve encompassing 1,070 acres of mostly pine and cohune palm savanna, tropical gallery forest, freshwater wetlands, and lagoons. In late 1992, the

Belize government created the 2,250-acre Monkey Bay Nature Reserve on land immediately adjacent to the private sanctuary, extending an important wildlands corridor along both sides of the Sibun River. The two parks now permanently protect this varied habitat for education and research, although casual visitors are welcome to certain areas of the sanctuary. Among the latter's attractions are rolling ridges of savanna as well as both traditional and broadleaf forest. Monkey Bay has nearly 2 miles of frontage along the Sibun River, including a secluded bathing beach and diverse riparian habitat.

Since its establishment in 1990 by an Arkansas conservationist, observers at Monkey Bay have reported seeing at least 250 species of birds within the reserve's borders, including parrots, toucans, storks, trogons, flycatchers, aplomado falcons, mottled owls, and cuckoos. Wildlife sightings include jaguar, puma, deer, peccary, crocodile, iguana, and coatimundi.

One goal of the sanctuary's founders is to reintroduce indigenous animals to the area by providing an attractive and well-protected habitat. With this is mind, many native fruits, such as pomegranate, sapodilla, sour orange, and baboon cap, have been planted. Seedlings of important hardwoods—among them, the majestic guanacaste—are also being planted to provide sites for nesting and breeding. The area was heavily logged during the past three hundred years and suffered the blows of several strong hurricanes; thus few tall specimens remain.

According to Monkey Bay's mission statement, the project's overall purpose "is to create a self-supporting economic entity so the sanctuary can, essentially, protect itself from conversion to another use," such as agriculture. Conservation organizations in the United States, Japan, and Belize are helping to develop Monkey Bay. Among the ventures they are supporting is an environmental outreach program for Belizean schoolchildren and an archaeological excavation of Mayan mounds along an old channel of the Sibun River. A field research station accommodates visiting scientists at the sanctuary, which has been a study site for the redstart warbler and orange-breasted falcon.

Monkey Bay is considered an ideal location for bird-watching and many other kinds of field research. This is also one of the few places in Belize where visitors are not only allowed but encouraged to camp. They are accommodated with four raised platforms covered by thatched roofs. Nature hiking, picnicking, swimming, and canoeing are also available. The classroom facility seats twenty students and includes over two hundred references on tropical natural history and anthropology. The sanctuary has solar-generated electricity, a radio-telephone, a small organic vegetable garden, and a fruit orchard. On-site arrangements should be made through co-founder Matthew Miller at 8-23180. In the United States, call (206) 324-7163 or write P.O. Box 4418, Seattle, WA 98104.

If You Go: The well-marked dirt road entrance to Monkey Bay Wildlife Sanctuary is at Mile 31 on the Western Highway, about one hour by car west of Belize City. Local buses will drop you off at the turnoff, and you can walk the short distance to the sanctuary's head-quarters. There is no admission fee to the sanctuary itself, although there is a small charge for camping. The mailing address is Monkey Bay Wildlife Sanctuary, P.O. Box 187, Belmopan.

Parrot Hill Farm

A short distance east of Monkey Bay along the Western Highway (at Mile 29.7) is Parrot Hill Farm, a private training center for farmland production and management as well as alternative technologies and rural income-generating enterprises. In 1992, the American-owned facility began hosting students and interns from Belize and around the world who are interested in sustainable tropical agriculture. Parrot Hill accepts overnight visitors at its moderately priced accommo-dations. Excellent meals are served and tours arranged. Call 92-3310 or 8-23180, or write Box 720, Belize City.

Stann Creek District

Until recently, the southern coast of Belize was all but ignored by vis-itors. Relatively isolated from the rest of the country by poor roads, rugged mountains, saltwater swamps, and an almost perpetually damp climate, many of the region's attractions were (and, for the most part, still are) seldom seen and little developed. This situation is changing, however, as a number of entrepreneurs have already targeted the region for developments ranging in scope from rugged rain forest treks (Belize's only true rain forests lie in the extreme southern part of the nation) to luxurious sportfishing resorts on palm-studded beaches. In the meantime, the most intriguing destinations in southern Belize continue to be its large tracts of unspoiled tropical jungle and long stretches of pristine coastline, plus an unusual mix of cultures that includes Mayan Indians, Garifuna (Black Caribs), Guatemalan refugees, and Creoles.

The easiest way to reach the far-flung coastal communities is by air (fast but comparatively expensive) or boat (slower but less costly). Other alternatives are private car or scheduled bus service. Daily buses ply the bumpy Hummingbird Highway that links Belmopan with Dangriga, continuing from Dangriga to Punta Gorda via the Southern Highway. (An unpaved shortcut, called the Lagoon Road, heads directly south from the Western Highway near Hattieville and rejoins the Hummingbird Highway near Dangriga.) The 52-mile Hummingbird Highway is scenic and uncrowded but notorious for its bone-jarring potholes and muddy bogs. Allow at least 2 hours for the drive from Belmopan to Dangriga. Along the way, you may wish to stop at the Blue Hole National Park, Five Blues National Park, or St. Herman's Cave (see Cayo District in chap. 6 for descriptions) or perhaps take photographs of the Hershey Chocolate Company's large cacao plantation. There are also a couple of large citrus plantations where, as at Hershey's, tours are available by appointment.

Midway along the Hummingbird Highway you will enter the Stann Creek District, the more populous of Belize's two southern districts. Although Dangriga is its administrative center and largest town, there are several other communities worth a visit.

Gales Point

At the culmination of a dead-end 15-mile dirt road that stretches through swampy terrain north of Dangriga, Gales Point offers visitors a refreshing dose of rural Creole hospitality and some unparalleled

Mayan children collecting firewood (Photo by Kevin Schafer)

nature attractions. Although it is not difficult to reach by road, the village is more frequently approached by chartered boat. Small craft can make an inland passage from Belize City (20 miles away) via the Burdon Canal and Boom's Creek in only a couple of hours, navigating a complex maze of waterways. An alternative is heading directly south along the Inner Channel in open water and then following a narrow estuary across Manatee Bar into Southern Lagoon, also called Manatee Lagoon. A limestone escarpment on the northwest bank of this lagoon is the location of several caves that can be explored as an interesting side trip. We also recommend a boat ride up Soldier (also called Plantation) Creek, which has especially abundant orchids.

The name Gales Point describes both a community of 350 souls and a narrow 2-mile finger of land jutting up from the south end of Southern Lagoon. The village was founded by logwood cutters many years before Belize became a British colony and is inhabited mostly by Creole farmers and fishermen. The lagoons and estuaries near the village are full of marine life and represent one of the world's last strongholds for the East Indian manatee. These shy mammals, which look somewhat like a walrus, feed on the thick grasses and other vegetation found in these lagoons. Local guides are happy to direct tourists to several breathing holes where the gentle beasts surface for air. (They must breathe every four or five minutes.) The nearest breathing hole is a few hundred yards from the village.

In 1992, residents created the Gales Point Manatee Community Sanctuary to protect the manatee and develop conservation-oriented tourism. This cooperative venture, a part of the government-mandated Manatee Special Development Area, pools local skills and resources to provide boat trips, wildlife observation, sportfishing, cave exploration, and protection of the hawksbill sea turtle, which nests in the area. About fifteen residents provide boating and/or guiding services, while twenty homes are open to overnight visitors. Other residents produce and sell handcrafted items such as tie-tie baskets and hats. Cashew and berry wines as well as mango and cashew preserves are made and sold locally. This activity is designed to enhance Gales Point's base of subsistence agriculture without jeopardizing the community's rural character and beautiful environment.

Boat excursions take visitors past small cayes in the various bodies of water—particularly Bird Island in Northern Lagoon—that are important breeding grounds for iguanas, crocodiles, and water birds, including the white ibis and boat-billed heron. Aquatic flora and fauna are very abundant here, since a tremendous amount of nutri-ent-rich runoff flows through these passageways en route from the Maya Mountains to the Caribbean Sea. The tangled mass of man-grove forests along the shoreline is an important nursery for young shrimp, crabs, lobster, and fish. Wildlife in the area includes deer, peccary, armadillo, gibnut, and various cats.

If You Go: Upscale accommodations are provided by the Gales Point Manatee Lodge (co-owned by the Hidden Valley Inn), orient-ed to sportfishermen and nature lovers. Remodeled in 1993, the 12-room facility offers boat tours to manatee breathing holes and a tur-tle nesting beach. Foreign anglers are attracted to the several species of gamefish that abound in these waters, notably tarpon, snook, and cubera.

Simple bed-and-breakfast accommodations and tent sites are available through the Gales Point Community Progressive Coopera-tive, with no advance reservations required. Call the community tele-phone at 5-22087 and ask for Alice or Josephine. Arrangements can also be made through the Seaside Guest House in Belize City (2-78339). A planned seven-room waterfront lodge, the Gales Point Cooperative Hotel, may be open by the time of your visit.

Tour operators arranging trips to the area include the recom-mended S & L Travel and Jal's Travl in Belize City, Pelican Beach Resort in Dangriga, and Ricardo's Beach Huts on Bluefield Range Caye. Competent local boatmen include Allen "Passo" Andrewin and his brother, Mose.

Dangriga

The name of this busy port town was changed from Stann Creek to Dangriga some years ago to honor the proud Garifuna people who make up the majority of its 9,000 residents. The name means "standing water" in the Garifuna language, a reference to the brack-ish pools that sometimes form here when the rain-swollen Stann Creek overflows its banks on the way through town. Dangriga was settled by European traders and farmers in the late seventeenth cen-tury, then became an important shipping center during colonial times.

The Garifuna (also known as Garinagu or Black Caribs) are a close-knit people of mixed West African and Caribbean Indian ancestry who arrived here in great numbers beginning in 1823, after civil unrest along the Honduran coast drove them north. The Garifuna history begins at least fifty years earlier, when shipwrecked slaves escaped to the British-controlled islands of Dominica and St. Vincent in the West Indies. These West Africans intermingled with aboriginal Red and Yellow Caribs, sharing many customs and rituals as the years progressed. Their mixed-blood offspring developed impressive skills in fishing, farming, and hunting. They also remained staunchly independent, refusing to bargain with the Europeans who tried to subdue them and take over their lands. For several decades they successfully resisted colonization. Finally, in 1795, the Garifuna chief was killed by an English soldier's bullet. His conquered people were rounded up and shipped off to the Bay Islands off Honduras, at that time a part of the British empire. Over the next twenty-five years, small bands of restless Garifuna wandered up and down the Central American coast, establishing settlements in what are now Belize, Guatemala, Costa Rica, and Nicaragua, as well as mainland Honduras.

On November 19, 1823, a large group of Garifuna from the Bay Islands joined about 200 others who had settled at the mouth of Stann Creek some twenty years earlier. Originally, a Puritan trading post had been built on this spot. The Puritans called these structures "stands." Over time, this term was locally corrupted into "stann," and the revised name stuck. The date of the mass Garifuna landing, November 19, is still celebrated each year as Settlement Day, a national holiday throughout Belize.

Because Dangriga is one of the largest Garifuna communities among the many now spread along the coastline of four Central American nations and the Windward Islands, a visit here provides an excellent opportunity to learn about a fascinating Afro-Indian subculture that is little known outside Belize. The ideal time to come is on Settlement Day and, if possible, the week leading up to the November 19 celebration. Hundreds of Garifuna from throughout Central America and the Caribbean flock to Dangriga for the festivities. The streets are alive with dancing, drumming, and impromptu music concerts. (At other times of the year, several nightclubs offer indigenous music and dancing.) Feasts and celebrations last far into the night. Scheduled events include a reenactment of the arrival of Alejo Beni and his boats from Honduras, plus a fascinating religious ceremony in the Catholic church which combines European, African, and Carib Indian rituals. (Most Garifuna—like most Belizeans—now consider themselves at least nominally Roman Catholic.) The ceremonies are performed in the Garifuna language, a unique mixture of West Indian, African, Spanish, English, and French words and grammar. The language structure is similar to Yoruba, a West African tongue.

Many outsiders, including Belize's early white colonists, have contended that the traditional spiritual beliefs of the Garifuna are akin to Haitian-style voodoo, which is only partly true. The central focus of Garifuna religion is the mysterious and magical practice of *obeah*, originating in West African traditions brought to the Americas during the 1600s. Through the use of fetishes, amulets, symbols, and rituals, it is believed that spiritual energy—both positive and negative—can be directed to individuals. Indigo blue crosses on the foreheads of small children, for example, are used to keep away bad spirits, and the blood of sacrificed animals (usually chickens or pigs) is used in ceremonies to ward off evil. A small cloth doll stuffed with black feathers, called a *puchinga*, may be buried under the doorsteps of an enemy to bring about tribulation, illness, or even death.

At the opposite end of the spectrum, a kind of white magic healing ceremony and feast of reconciliation known as the *dugu* is also used to rid the community of evil spirits. The ritual, rarely observed by outsiders, takes place over the course of a full week and is accompanied by animal sacrifices, hypnotic music, and nonstop dancing.

Through the intercession of a *byei*, or shaman, the Garifuna believe they can communicate with the dead, thereby tapping the power of their ancestors. Some expatriate Belizeans come from as far as the United States and Canada to attend such ceremonies, called *gubida*. It is believed that these healing rituals can cure sick relatives and avenge evildoers.

Practitioners of obeah believe they can make contact with the dead whenever certain ceremonies are performed with the accompaniment of monotonous, trancelike drumming, singing, and dancing. These performances may go on all night without a break, or even continue for days on end. Ethnomusicologists have noted that the rhythms and call-and-response patterns of the Garifuna are very similar to those used in the religious and social rituals of West Africa, where they presumably originated. The practice of playing with sticks is also African.

The devotion of the Garifuna to their culture has always set them apart from other Belizeans, particularly those of European descent. So fearful were the early colonials of Garifuna practices that traders from Dangriga and neighboring villages were officially barred from staying overnight in Belize City. Those bringing their produce and handicrafts to the public market were ordered to be out of town by sundown. As recently as the 1960s, Garifuna were afraid to hold dugu ceremonies in Dangriga for fear local magistrates might disapprove. The situation has changed dramatically, and the Garifuna now represent a large percentage of Belizean schoolteachers, civil servants, and physicians.

But it is in arts and crafts that the Garifuna particularly excel. Their drum makers are revered for a perceived ability to induce the obeah magic through the music of their instruments. Dances are performed to the beat of three drums of varying sizes. These are traditionally made out of carved cedar trees or sea turtle shells (despite the latter's endangered status). Some of the younger Garifuna have incorporated these ceremonial instruments into their modern reggae and calypso bands, giving birth to a distinctive style of music known as "punta rock." More traditional groups that often perform in Dangriga include the Turtle Shell Band and Warribaggabagga Dancers. A performance by the latter critically acclaimed group, which has toured throughout the world, should not be missed.

Although Dangriga itself is a rather drab town, full of clapboard houses perched on high stilts above the muddy ground, its citizens clearly love music, good food, laughter, and celebration. Even on an ordinary day, they like to dress in brightly patterned shirts reminiscent of the tie-dyed robes of West Africa. Young women consider it the height of fashion to decorate their hair with plastic Day-Glo curlers, a practice that has caught on throughout the country. On Settlement Day, the main street is closed to traffic so that musicians, costumed dancers, and revelers can parade with abandon. In the weeks leading up to Christmas, garishly painted and masked John-Canoe (also spelled Yan-kunu) dancers perform in the streets for gifts of rum, money, and candy. The dance is performed only by men, who imitate the strident movements of a slave master. At midnight on Christmas Eve, the town echoes with the deep blast of several hundred hollow conch shells blown simultaneously.

Such rituals are favored subjects of several well-known Garifuna painters living in Dangriga whose studios are open to visitors. Most have adopted a kind of folk-primitive realism recalling the simple artwork of Haiti. There is an emphasis on bright colors, a flat perspective, and festive or rural themes. The studio of Pen Cayetano closed in 1992, but fellow painter Benjamin Nicholas still welcomes visitors at 27 Oak Street. Accomplished drum maker Austin Rodriguez has a similar gallery at 32 Tubroos Street, where baskets, masks, and reed purses as well as fine drums (priced from $50 and up) can be purchased. Hours vary from place to place. Next door to Rodriguez is a boat builder who carves dories out of a single trunk. PJ's Gift Shop and the Treasure Shop on St. Vincent's Street are recommended for smaller handicrafts. Be sure to visit Melinda's Historical Museum at 21 St. Vincent's (5-22266), which displays Garifuna artifacts such as the mahogany *badaya* bowls used in making cassava flour. The museum is open ($1 admission) from 9:00 a.m. to noon and 2:00 to 5:00 p.m. daily except Thursday and Sunday.

Dangriga is also a good place to sample traditional Garifuna cuisine, which vaguely resembles "soul food" of the American South. Home-brew cashew wine and "local dynamite" (a mixture of raw coconut milk and Belizean rum) are popular lubricants, along with chicory-flavored coffee. Endless varieties of cassava bread—all delicious—can be purchased from the smiling housewives who make them in simple outdoor ovens. The preparation of such breads using a flour made from potatolike cassava roots that have been strained and ground by hand is a time-honored practice among the Garifuna which takes two days to accomplish. The cassava's importance to local people cannot be overestimated, and in fact the word "Garifuna" roughly translates as "the cassava-eating people."

Other popular dishes are hudut, masked plantain (also called plantain fu-fu), and boiled fish in coconut sauce (known as "fish sere"). Also not to be missed are the sweet oranges and juicy grapefruits grown on nearby citrus plantations for shipment to North America and Europe.

If You Go: Dangriga's hotels are generally modest and have few amenities. Travelers have recommended Pal's Guest House, the Río Mar Hotel (which arranges lodging and boats for Tobacco Caye visitors), Sofie's Hotel, and the Bonefish Hotel. There are several Chinese cafés and a handful of other restaurants (try Burger King, no relation to the franchise), plus some bars, gas stations, and general stores. Melinda's Historical Museum on St. Vincent's Street is definitely worth a visit. Punta rock can be heard at one of several nightclubs: the Wrong House, Son-Flo Disco, and Dada's Disco.

Nearby is the enormous citrus processing facility a short distance south of town, at Commerce Bight, where a large pipeline sends fruit concentrate directly to the holds of oceangoing vessels anchored offshore. Along this stretch of private beach are a few campsites that can be leased from either of the two owners, Mr. Williams and Mr. Sue, for a reasonable fee.

Because of its location and services, Dangriga is a good base for excursions to the southern cayes and atolls or to the nearby Gales Point Manatee Community Sanctuary, the Cockscomb Basin Wildlife Sanctuary, and the Mopan Indian village of Maya Center. Accommodations on Tobacco and South Water cayes, along with the nearby research stations on Carrie Bow and Wee Wee cayes, are easily reached from here. Inquire at the Río Mar Hotel, near where Stann Creek enters the sea. Several bus companies, notably the Z-Line, have daily departures to and from Dangriga via the Hummingbird and Southern highways. The town is about 35 miles by boat from Belize City, 105 miles via the Hummingbird Highway (through Belmopan), or 70 miles via the Lagoon Road cutoff.

The moderate-to-expensive Pelican Beach Resort Hotel is a favorite of many travelers. A two-story wooden colonial building with a wide veranda and high ceilings, this is a comfortable jumping-off point for excursions to the barrier reef or interior. Located on a sandy beach adjacent to the Dangriga airport, the Pelican's friendly staff also arranges trips to the Cockscomb Basin, various Mayan ruins, Gales Point, the Sittee River, Hopkins, and barrier reef. Local tours of Dangriga and area citrus plantations are also available. The hotel and restaurants are run by members of the Bowman family, a pioneering Belizean clan that has contributed to many of their nation's conservation achievements. Your hosts are Belize Audubon board member Therese Bowman Rath and her American husband, nature photographer Tony Rath, whose photographs and videotapes are on sale here. An excellent local guide is taxi driver Charles Neil (tel. 6-3389 or 6-3291), who offers tours of Dangriga, Hopkins, Sittee River, and the Cockscomb Basin.

Melinda Farm

A pleasant day trip from Dangriga is the 400-acre Melinda Farm, located in the foothills of the Maya Mountains. This verdant plantation is the home of Marie's Hot Pepper Sauce, a neon-orange condiment made from the spicy habanero chili pepper, formerly called Melinda's. (Products sold under the Melinda's label are now distributed by a Costa Rican competitor.) Praised by connoisseurs as nature's hottest pepper, the habanero only grows along the Yucatán peninsula and a few other subtropical locations.

Marie and Jerry Sharp began making their hot pepper sauce atop a kitchen stove in 1983, and now the fiery product is one of Belize's most popular exports, gracing tables throughout the world. Their farm also produces oranges, Surinam cherries, papayas, mangoes, guavas, pineapples, and passionfruit, most of which is used in the Sharp's extensive line of dried fruits, jams, and jellies. Their cottage-style factory relies on recipes personally developed by Marie and tested on discriminating Belizean palates. The farm, located on Stann Creek Valley Farm Road, is open to visitors by appointment. Call 6-22080.

Hopkins

Located on the inlet of a small bay some 8 miles south of Dangriga, Hopkins is a relaxed Garifuna fishing village of about 800 people. It can easily be reached by private boat or by following a 4-mile cutoff from the Southern Highway. This route crosses a marshy landscape that is particularly rich in bird life. Even the rare and majestic jabiru stork has been sighted here, so keep a sharp eye out as you head for the village.

In Hopkins, life is simple and unhurried. There is no electricity, no television, and hardly a single car. Women still tend the family garden plots and sing together as they weave red baskets or grate cassava roots on wooden slats. The men hand-carve their dugout canoes (called "dories" throughout Belize) and weave fishnets out of hemp cloth. The children chase each other on the broad beach, build sand castles, and splash about in the calm sky blue water.

At the end of each day, the fishermen of Hopkins haul their brightly painted dories beneath the coconut trees and join their families for the evening meal inside thatch-covered one-room houses. When a dispute arises, they repair to an open-air longhouse at one end of the village where decisions are made by consensus in community meetings.

Many homes in Hopkins, as in other villages along the south coast, are built in a pseudo-Mayan style, perched atop stilts with roofs made of long grasses or palm fronds. They are clustered close together, with marvelous views of a gently curving bay to the east and misty jungle mountains to the west.

Eager to see Hopkins remain a self-sufficient traditional village and at the same time provide employment for its young people, a group of women have formed a tourism cooperative that operates the Sandy Beach Lodge there. Several neotraditional cabanas, built with the assistance of the Caribbean Council of Churches, based in Barbados, have been open since 1987 and provide an important source of income to the friendly people of Hopkins.

Houses can also be rented for about $8 a night, and there is informal camping along the beach, with prior permission required. Local housewives are happy to fire up their oil-burning stoves for casual

Fishermen with dory, Hopkins (Photo by Peter Bylen)

and overnight visitors. Meals usually include fresh fish, rice, fruit, and the ubiquitous cassava bread. If the Sandy Beach Lodge is full, accommodations can be arranged at the Hopkins Tropical Paradise Hotel, providing cabana-style quarters over a drained swamp at the intersection of the Hopkins cutoff and the Southern Highway. Other small hotels, the Arrow and Caribbean View, opened in 1993.

Getting to Hopkins involves hopping aboard one of the daily supply trucks heading south from downtown Dangriga at 2:00 p.m. or arranging private transportation via the Southern Highway or by boat from Dangriga (about $25). Many tour operators will gladly make a side trip to Hopkins when traveling to or from either the Cockscomb Basin Wildlife Sanctuary or the Possum Point Biological Station.

Possum Point and Wee Wee Caye

About 5 miles south of Hopkins, on the banks of the Sittee River, is Possum Point Biological Research Station. The 22-acre, private nature reserve is owned by Paul and Mary Shave, American expatriates who lease government-owned Wee Wee Caye (9 miles east, its name is the local term for the leafcutter ants found in abundance on the island) for use as a marine laboratory. The couple also manage

Bocatura Bank Campground, located on a 4-acre plot about a mile from Possum Point on the Sittee River. Although these operations cater primarily to natural history study groups, individuals and groups of kayakers, fishermen, and birders are accommodated (by reservation only) on a space-available basis.

The research station is located in a lush setting, surrounded by broadleaf forest at a sharp bend in the river. It is named after the many opposum found here when the lab and surrounding cottages were being built in what was then thick bush. Wildlife still abounds, and bird-watchers will be especially rewarded: Possum Point has well over 100 species of "yard birds." The call of the jaguar can often be heard as the cat passes through the property at night. Possum Point and Wee Wee Caye embrace studies in coral reef ecology, botany, herpetology, entomology, ornithology, and mammalogy.

Up to thirty people can be accommodated in the dorms and bungalows of Possum Point, and there is room for another fifteen among the raised tent platforms and two cottages of Bocatura, 5 miles from the river's mouth. Wee Wee Caye has seven cottages, and the tiny island is a wonderful place to snorkel, swim, and relax. The Shaves have taken great pains to preserve the mangroves, where a number of boa constrictors (locally called *wowlas*) make their home, feeding on lizards, iguanas, and small birds. Paul Shave, a marine biologist, has counted 46 species of coral and 10 species of crab in the immediate area of Wee Wee Caye. Bring plenty of insect repellent as the no-see-ums here can be fierce.

The Creole village of Sittee River makes an interesting side trip, and there are several places to stay (see Inside Belize). The ruins of the nineteenth-century Serdon sugar mill are preserved as a park not far from the Southern Highway. Nearby Sapodilla Lagoon has an abundance of orchids, and howler monkeys have been spotted near False Sittee Point. Trips from Possum Point can be arranged to these destinations as well as Boom Creek, a jungle tributary of the Sittee River.

Seine Bight Village

Even smaller and more laid-back than Hopkins, the Garifuna community of Seine Bight is about 30 miles south of Dangriga on the remote and idyllic Placencia Peninsula. Until the mid-1980s, the village could only by reached by boat (a 4-hour trip from Dangriga by dugout canoe). Since then, daily buses and private auto traffic have dimmed its status as one of Belize's most isolated coastal communities.

Seine Bight is said to have been founded by pirates in 1629 and later inhabited by French fishermen deported by the British from Newfoundland when the latter took control. Like Hopkins, the residents occupy small thatched houses atop high stilts (to keep away insects, rodents, snakes, and floodwaters). They follow the traditional Garifuna patterns dictating that women will take care of children and subsistence vegetable gardens while the men hunt and fish. Less accustomed to outsiders than their coastal neighbors, the people of Seine Bight are shy about having their pictures taken, and permission should be requested before wandering around their village. The location is very picturesque, tucked along a narrow beach about 5 miles north of the Creole/Garifuna community of Placencia. The only accommodations here are in private homes. There is one bar called the Wesebahari.

Seine Bight can be reached either by way of the daily bus shuttling between Placencia and Dangriga or by private car or bicycle. It is a pleasant 2-hour walk (3 miles) up the beach or dirt road from Placencia. A small (and expensive) cabana-style lodge, the Singing Sands Inn, operates at Maya Beach a few miles north of Seine Bight.

Placencia

Straddling a sandy, palm-forested spit of land at the tip of an 11-mile peninsula, Placencia (also spelled Placentia) is one of the oldest continuously inhabited villages in Belize. Its several hundred proud residents brag that their small settlement was founded by English buccaneers in the early 1600s, and artifacts discovered beneath their homes suggest this was the location of several fierce battles between British and Spanish sailors. There is also ample evidence that Placencia was a Mayan fishing camp long before the Europeans arrived. For the last few centuries, it has been home to a close-knit cluster of mostly Creole families whose ancestry includes Garifuna warriors, freed African slaves, and Scottish pirates. A new land development north of the village, Playas de Piratas, draws attention to the latter.

Chapter 5

Much of Placencia's considerable charm can be attributed to its scenic locale. A long and gently curving beach—arguably the finest in Belize—graces the village's windward side. A few hundred yards opposite this wide strip of talcum-powder sand is Placencia Lagoon, a placid waterway harboring abundant marine life. And since the southernmost tip of the settlement borders the Caribbean, one has the illusion of being on a tropical island. Before a road was completed through the swampy jungle north of Placencia, it might as well have been an island, since the only access was by boat.

One unusual feature of Placencia is its main "street," which happens to be an 18-inch-wide concrete sidewalk through the center of town. Most vehicles discharge their passengers and cargo at the only grocery store, on the sidewalk's north end. The ambience is reminiscent of Caye Caulker, with smiles and friendly exchanges the norm among locals and visitors alike. One of the friendlier restaurants along the walkway is Jene's, opposite the Seaspray Guest House, where a hearty breakfast and lunch are available for a good price. Another recommended choice for an afternoon snack is Miss Lilly, who sells delicious homemade cassava and coconut bread from her front door. Baker John Whylie makes excellent pastries.

Along the 3-mile Placencia beachfront, dozens of guest houses and lodges snuggle beneath the palm trees. The azure water is surprisingly deep here, and dolphins occasionally frolic very close to shore. (The depth and tricky currents can make swimming hazardous.)

Up the coast a short distance are several upscale resorts offering rooms, meals, tours, and equipment for snorkeling, diving, or fishing. They can also arrange nature trips to nearby Lark and Laughingbird cayes or such far-off destinations as the Sapodilla Cayes. Recommended full-service hotels here include Placencia Cove Resort, Turtle Inn, Kitty's Place (which also accommodates campers), and the Rum Point Inn, 2 miles north on a secluded stretch of beach. The latter is operated by Carol and George Bevier, early supporters of the Belizean environmental movement and knowledgeable tour guides. Their compound includes a gourmet restaurant, a well-stocked library, and Mayan-style garden cottages.

The outside world is slowly but surely making its way to Placencia. A diesel generator drones in the background most of the time, providing electricity for the fishing co-op's refrigerator as well as various homes and businesses. Telephones and television sets are no longer a rarity, and the spillover from Ambergris Caye has boosted prices in recent years. Sportfishermen have also discovered Placencia, with good reason: the tarpon and bonefish opportunities here are superb. Several resorts and businesses now cater exclusively to anglers, and there are a number of topnotch fishing guides based in Placencia. Some foreigners have decided to build holiday or retirement homes here, and real estate speculation is rampant.

There are several popular night spots in the village, where a $3 bottle of local rum goes a long way. Favorites include the Cozy Corner Bar, Thatch Bar, Sonny's, and the Crab Shell Restaurant.

By and large, Placencia is a sleepy, tranquil, and informal place where one can easily fit in by doing nothing. If you change your mind, this is an excellent departure point for the lesser-known southern cayes or the interior nature parks and Mayan ruins. Bird-watching and beachcombing are especially rewarding here, and the nearby lagoon is an important breeding area for saltwater crocodiles, marine turtles, and the elusive manatee.

The hub of activity in Placencia—such as it is—can be found at the very tip of the peninsula, where the pier, marina, gas station, bus stop, and fishing co-op are all located. Boats leave here frequently for nearby Big Creek (a half-hour trip), from which there are daily airline flights to Dangriga and Punta Gorda as well as bus connections to both towns. Placencia's one-room post office, just a stone's throw from the pier, dispenses airline and bus tickets. The postmistress will happily place phone calls and find you a camping spot on the nearby beach. If you want to charter a boat, reserve a hotel room, or sample some cassava bread, this is a good place to do so. You can also accomplish such tasks at just about any of the friendly bars and restaurants found along the cement pathway that heads north of the post office from one end of Placencia to the other.

The boat ride to Big Creek costs between $5 and $15, depending on the number of passengers; boats are on hand to meet every plane.

Rides on the mail boat are free on a space-available basis. Buses run between Placencia and Dangriga every Monday, Wednesday, Friday, and Saturday at 6:00 a.m., returning the same day (call 6-23152). A Z-Line bus passes through nearby Independence daily.

Laughingbird Caye National Park

A small, coconut-studded island about 12 miles southeast of Placencia, Laughingbird gets its name from the large number of laughing gulls that once used it as a rookery. Overuse by humans caused the gulls to abandon the island completely, although a few have been sighted here since 1990, along with brown pelicans, green herons, and melodious blackbirds. In recent years this has been a popular destination for picnickers, campers, and sea kayakers, who placed Laughingbird on their regular route. The government has taken steps to minimize this disruption, and in the interest of conservation you may wish to drop anchor elsewhere. Laughbird Caye is the southernmost island in the Inner Channel and is about 120 yards long by 10 yards wide. Its unusual shape, an angular atoll on a continental shelf, is called a faro formation. Like true atolls, faroes are steep-sided and widely separated from other land formations. Trips to Laughingbird and the nearby (and equally idyllic) Silk, Bugle, Colson, and Lark cayes can be arranged easily in Placencia. Whiprey Caye, Little Water Caye, and Ranguana Caye have overnight accommodations; a lodge on Hatchet Caye was scheduled to open in 1993. Many of the cayes on the southern part of the reef have fishing camps frequented by Guatemalans and Hondurans as well as Belizeans.

Big Creek, Independence and Mango Creek

The small towns of Big Creek, Mango Creek, and Independence dot a 7-mile branch of the Southern Highway directly across the lagoon from Placencia. They are about 40 miles by road south of Dangriga and slightly father north of Punta Gorda.

Big Creek has been developed as an important port servicing the deep-water cargo ships that anchor a short distance offshore for the loading of bananas, mangoes, citrus fruits, and other cash crops. Until the late 1980s, shallow-draft boats and barges had to shuttle small loads of these exports to Puerto Barrios in neighboring Guatemala.

Big Creek is home to the Toucan Inn, a remodeled barracks for employees of Big Creek's largest banana company now known for its Irish food and the English pub atmosphere of its Tipsy Toucan bar. The Toucan also houses a small bank that is open one day a week.

Just north of Big Creek is the tiny settlement of Independence, and a short distance beyond that is Mango Creek (some would argue that these two villages are one and the same). This community consists of only a few houses and the moderately priced Hello Hotel. The latter is owned by Antonio and Beth Zabaneh, operators of the Zabaneh Grocery Store, who are very knowledgeable about boat trips that can be arranged here to Glover's Reef, Guatemala, and Honduras. (For those leaving Belize from Mango Creek, the necessary passport exit stamp can be obtained from the village police station.) There is a basic hotel above the People's Restaurant, also in Mango Creek.

Monkey River Town

Monkey River Town has not been visited by the authors but is said to be an interesting side trip for travelers based in the area. This sleepy Creole/Garifuna fishing village is about 10 miles by boat south of Mango Creek, tucked behind mangrove forests at the mouth of the Monkey River. This lowland waterway drains the Bladen and Swasey watersheds, which now enjoy protected status as important sources of irrigation water and sanctuaries for wildlife. The Paynes Creek/Monkey River Wildlife Sanctuary encompasses 28,000 acres south of the village and north of Punta Ycacos. This area is gradually being developed for natural history research and tourism. An overgrown dirt road (impassable in wet weather) also connects Monkey River Town with the Southern Highway, about 15 miles to the north.

For a prearranged fee, guides from Placencia or Big Creek will turn a visitor loose in the Monkey River estuary with a tent and canoe, returning in a day or two for the trip by powerboat back to home base. Some of these guides will also be happy to take visitors up the river itself, where many species of birds and, yes, even monkeys (Geoffroy's spider monkeys) can be seen.

Recent visitors describe the village itself as something of a ghost town, its population drained by a lack of jobs and the desire to live in a less isolated community. The few remaining residents struggle along through subsistence farming, fishing, and hunting. Over the years, Monkey River Town has been hard hit by natural disasters: a blight destroyed the local banana industry, and trappers sold most of the crocodiles for their skins.

During April, the village briefly comes alive again with a celebration centered around the iguana egg-laying season. People from throughout the area descend on Monkey River Town to eat freshly killed iguanas and their eggs, which are considered a tasty delicacy. Efforts are now under way to develop forms of low-impact tourism that would provide more jobs for local residents while preserving the environment.

Toledo District

Heading south from the citrus and banana plantations of the Stann Creek District, travelers enter the most sparsely populated and undeveloped region in the country. The Toledo District is (barely) connected to the rest of Belize by one dirt road—the Southern Highway—and a single airstrip at Punta Gorda. Public transportation consists of one daily bus (the Z-Line) and a couple of domestic airline flights. Much of the area is still without electricity, indoor plumbing, and hot water. In fact, the majority of its residents are subsistence farmers living in wooden, thatched-roof huts. The per capita annual income here is estimated at less than $500. Obviously, a trip to the Toledo District is not for everyone. Although there are a growing number of accommodations with modern amenities, most lodges and guest houses are decidedly rustic.

Travel within the area is manageable during the dry season but problematic the rest of the year. This part of Belize averages over 165 inches of rain annually; therefore, its many rivers and creeks can be difficult to ford during a downpour. There are few gas stations, grocery stores, or restaurants. In short, the infrastructure of tourist-related services is minimal.

Yet a visit to the Toledo District is a must for those who wish to get a firsthand look at the Kekchí, Mopan, and Garifuna cultures and to experience small-scale tourism as a strategy for ecosystem conservation. The district also features Belize's only true rain forest and some of its most unusual Mayan ruins and caves.

Punta Gorda

Even in the Toledo District capital of Punta Gorda, some 200 miles south of Belize City, the pace is slow. In the middle of this light and airy town (pop. 3,000), chickens roam freely between clapboard houses and patches of uncut vegetation. There is virtually no automobile traffic to dodge, and the silence at night can be deafening. Uniformed schoolchildren play in front of unpretentious churches; adults gossip on street corners as they go about their errands. A spectacular view of the Caribbean and, on clear days, the mountains of Guatemala greet you as you walk from the airport to the center of town, which happens to be only a few steps away. The five streets of "P.G.," as the town is known locally, run parallel to the coast and are unpaved.

This tranquil facade belies a colorful and sometimes violent history. Punta Gorda is believed to have been founded by Puritan traders in the seventeenth century, then occupied off and on by English pirates and Spanish soldiers (who gave it a name that translates as "large point"). Throughout most of the colonial era, it was primarily a fishing village. In 1867, a group of disaffected Confederate army veterans and their families settled on unoccupied land nearby and tried to re-create their Deep South life-style around a group of sugarcane plantations. Chinese, Creole, and East Indian laborers were brought in to cut the cane and clear the forest. A dozen sugar mills were built. By 1910, the Toledo Settlement, as it was known, had failed and most of the Americans returned to the United States. But the name and townsite (plus many descendants of the conscripted laborers) remain. Although Punta Gorda is still an important fishing port (especially for foreign anglers), it has been converted into a market town and service center by the gradual construction of roads and the influx of peasant farmers from nearby Guatemala. There are also many traditional Garifuna and Creole farms along the coast, primarily growing beans, maize, and rice. The town itself has an interesting ethnic mix that includes Maya, Garifuna, Creole, East Indians, Chinese, Europeans, and Lebanese (an important merchant class throughout Belize). There are also some British forces stationed here and the Voice of America has a large radio transmitter south of the town which beams programming throughout Central America.

Punta Gorda is a good base for trips to Toledo's Mayan villages and ruins, jungle rivers, caves, and sportfishing grounds. Excursions can also be made to the southern end of the barrier reef, particularly such recommended destinations as the Ranguana and Sapodilla cayes, but these islands are so far offshore here that it is sometimes easier to head for them from Placencia or Dangriga. Recommended interior destinations include the Maya's sacred Hokeb Ha Cave (also called Blue Creek Cave), the awesome opening of a 5-mile-long underground river. The water flowing from this passageway is crystal clear and perfectly suited to a refreshing swim on a hot day. Access is by a well-marked riverside trail from Blue Creek Village, about 20 miles northwest of Punta Gorda. Local guides Bobby Polonio and Alfredo Romero also offer treks to sugar mill ruins and chicle camps. Timeless Tours runs 7- to 12-day camping excursions to cayes and jungle rivers aboard its 38-foot schooner *Juanita,* based in P.G. harbor. The sailboat goes as far as Wild Cane Caye (site of a Mayan ruin), the Snake Cayes, and Livingston, Guatemala.

We recommend spending at least a day or two in the Toledo District to experience this seldom-seen corner of Belize. Saturday is market day in P.G., and this is a good time to inspect the wares of Mayan artisans from local villages and Guatemala.

One of the greatest challenges facing Belizeans is the need to ensure that local people—mostly Kekchí Maya, Mopan Maya, Garifuna, and Creole—benefit from an increase in Toledo District tourism and are given incentives to protect the natural and cultural resources of the region. Complicating the matter are some daunting environmental problems facing the area's subsistence farmers. Natural habitat degradation has been especially heavy here, mainly because of new road construction and the collective impact of forest destruction by the kind of slash-and-burn agriculture practiced by a growing Indian population and Guatemalan immigrants. However, in mid-1993, there were at least three noteworthy locally initiated projects under way here seeking to combine tourism, sustainable agriculture, cultural revitalization, and environmental conservation: the Punta Gorda Nature Trail and Greenbelt; the Garifuna Village Project; and the Toledo District Mayan Guest Houses.

Punta Gorda Nature Trail

Punta Gorda residents are hoping to create a 4-mile trail and maintain a greenbelt around their town for the benefit of locals and foreign visitors. Be sure to check with local travel agents about its status before setting out, since development of the trail has been subject to repeated delays. The trail is designed to help achieve a sustainable agricultural base for local farmers through the participation and education of tourists interested in Punta Gorda's forest and marine resources. It showcases local Garifuna and Mayan culture as well as homesite farming.

The trail begins at the end of Main Street, on Punta Gorda's outskirts, from a bluff overlooking the ocean. It then penetrates coastal and mangrove swamps, the flora and fauna of which are described by a local guide accompanying the visitor. The plan is to visit a traditional Mopan or Kekchí home so visitors can learn about Mayan traditions and culture. In addition, a demonstration permaculture homesite farm is planned. This approach involves, among other things, planting nitrogen-fixing shrubs around a plot of cultivated land and recycling all farm wastes back into the soil. Such models are critical in the Toledo District because rain forest destruction here is proceeding virtually unchecked. Next along the trail will be a small zoo with parrots, iguanas, crocodiles, wild pecarries, armadillos, swamp deer, and other animals that inhabit the region. As envisioned, the trail will also feature an East Indian farm where descendants of people conscripted from India to work in the sugarcane industry will describe their ethnic life-style and history.

When fully operational, the trail will provide income for many local people through employment as trail guides, rangers, artists, and service providers. Profits for a homesite farmer's fund will be used to develop sustainable agricultural techniques designed to replace the traditional slash-and-burn system.

Creole and Garifuna culture are represented on this multifaceted trail in the town of Punta Gorda itself and at the Toledo Community College, where students will be trained to operate and maintain the project. The trail ends on the north end of P.G.; a canoe trip down a quarter mile strip of Joe Taylor Creek completes the journey.

The Garifuna Village Project

The Garifuna Village Project at St. Vincent Block is one of the final stops on the Punta Gorda Nature Trail. It is an example of cultural revival that a visitor will not experience anywhere else in Belize.

According to a 1980 census, almost 50 percent of Punta Gorda's population is Garifuna. These people have had a difficult time keeping their unique culture alive, and the modern world provides few financial and social incentives for them to do so. Their rich and varied language is not taught in the schools, and the difficulty of finding steady employment is ever-present. Farming once was a part of the Garifuna culture in the Toledo District, but today such traditions as the baking of cassava bread are practiced by only a few families. In spite of these challenges, a group of Garifuna are using about 40 acres of a 960-acre block of land passed on by their forefathers in an ethnically oriented tourism venture. The site is below a forest-carpeted mountain called Cerro just outside Punta Gorda. "This is a conservation of culture project," organizer Emma Martinez told us, as she stood next to a fine clear spring that bubbles up on one side of the property. "This land is very rich and very important, and I would never want to see it converted to houses."

By the time you read this, Martinez and her group may already have completed construction of a museum at St. Vincent Block which will display Garifuna artifacts of everyday life such as *nadu* (mattresses), washing bowls, drums, and tools. There will be a restaurant serving traditional Garifuna meals, an entertainment center (*debase*) and an arts and crafts shop selling souvenirs. An 80-foot-long debase was under construction in 1993.

Mayan Guest Houses and Homestays

What is possibly Belize's most promising program for ecologically minded and culturally engaged travelers is under way in several small Kekchí and Mopan Maya villages west of Punta Gorda. This venture is designed to help feed growing families, provide incentives for milpa farmers to preserve Belize's rain forests, and promote tourism at remote Mayan ruins.

Several villages have constructed small guest houses, designed and marked nature trails, and started introducing travelers to Mayan customs. As of mid-1993, guest houses were completed and operational in six communities: San Pedro Columbia, San Miguel, Santa Cruz, San José, Laguna, and Barranco. The accommodations are very basic, but the overall experience cannot be duplicated.

Visits to local Mayan villages are being coordinated by two rival Punta Gorda companies: Dem Dats Doin/The Toledo Visitors Information Center, operated by Alfredo and Yvonne Villoria; and Nature's Way Guest House/Belize Adventure Travel, operated by William "Chet" Schmidt. Both firms offer similar packages, although we have heard more positive reports about the latter. Schmidt has spent seventeen years working with his partners and local villagers to devise a system that integrates ecosystem conservation, appropriate-scale tourism, and sustainable agriculture. The project is also designed to minimize stress levels on the natural and cultural resources, while employing the maximum number of villagers. Profits are used to support sustainable agriculture, a community fund, and the local government. Rates are about $20 a night, plus about $3 for each meal and $10 for guided tours. (Visitors are strongly encouraged to fill out a written evaluation of the program before they leave.)

The first guest house, constructed in 1991, is located in Laguna Village, a progressive Kekchí Maya agricultural center located about 10 miles from Punta Gorda. The population is descended from immigrants who originated in the Alta Verapaz highlands of Guatemala and came to Belize to escape brutal oppression at the hands of German coffee barons. Kekchí people have a strong tradition of cooperation, particularly in farming and building endeavors. Many Kekchí have memorized the myths and folktales conceived over 2,000 years ago during the Classic Mayan empire.

The residents of Laguna have built, on the outskirts of their village, an eight-person guest lodge with a veranda, a separate bathhouse, and outhouses. Guests are treated to a spectacular view of the rain forest-covered limestone karst hills nearby. The villagers take interested visitors to ancient Maya cave paintings that are a vigorous 2-hour hike into the surrounding hills. Since the thatched-roofed guest lodge does not have a kitchen, visitors eat in small groups at different households. Village guides take guests on carefully tended footpaths where the native medicinal plants are marked in various languages. Another recommended stop is the arts and crafts center, where tourists are strongly encouraged to buy handmade baskets and other Mayan craftwork directly from the village cooperative. Potential cultural erosion and the acceleration of an unnatural competition are important concerns in the Toledo District, where the Maya have only recently formed such cooperatives.

The Toledo District Mayan Guest House project was originally designed to incorporate an important but controversial strategy—controlling access of tourists. In an attempt to minimize stress levels on the natural environment and not overburden local people with massive infusions of outsiders, a main office in Punta Gorda maintains radio contact with each village to monitor how many foreigners are there at any given time. This way organizers can arrange for other small groups to be cycled in and out on a rotating basis. Each village thus gets its share of tourists, but the overall demands on local people and resources are kept low.

Chet Schmidt believes that in order for this innovative kind of natural history and cultural tourism to work, visitors themselves must participate. In other words, certain guidelines and behavior must be accepted and practiced, such as respecting the cooperatives and showing flexibility with regard to which village one visits. In addition, a fixed fee is collected, and these monies are spread out to benefit many Belizeans. The plan also specifies that a portion of all proceeds

▲ Pelicans roosting at sunrise
▼ Conservation education at the Belize Zoo

Mayan children

▲ Mayan pots discovered in Vaca Plateau cave
▼ Iguana hunters   ▼ Tropical forest destruction

▲ Scarlet macaw
▼ Baird's tapir

▲ Black howler monkey
▼ Jaguar

▲ West Indian manatee
▼ Calliandra flower

▲ Heliconia flower

▲ Barrier reef of Belize from the air
▼ Rendezvous Caye from the air

▲ Keel-billed toucan ▲ Black orchid and toad
▼ Creole children along the Northern Highway

▲ The Blue Hole, Lighthouse Reef
▼ Snorkeling at Lighthouse Reef

Don Chama entertains visitors at the Nature's Way Guest House in Punta Gorda (Photo by Steele Wotkyns)

will go into a village fund that will eventually make possible services such as a new medical clinic and training in "homesite farming" techniques that will benefit all villagers.

In many ways, says Schmidt, permanent forest reserves are the most important goal of the project. "We're going to develop a system of sustainable forestry and harvest forest products without destroying the forest," he points out. Production of crucial genetic seed banks for commercial tree species such as mahogany and cedar (now rare in Belize) are part of this program. Corridors of intact forest surrounding and—with luck and comprehensive planning—connecting each village are now being designed. A collective known as the Toledo Ecotourism Association has recently been successful in convincing government leaders to declare a 100-acre site known as Río Blanco Falls a nature reserve. This area was protected because of the express wish of Mayan villagers at Santa Elena and Santa Cruz, who sought to protect a national corridor between their two communities.

The "Mayan Village Indigenous Experience" offered by Alfredo and Yvonne Villoria of Dem Dats Doin maintains a "host family network" whereby travelers stay in Mayan homes, sharing food, conversation, and such daily activities as corn preparation and tilling land. Accommodations include a large hammock with sheet. Guided trips are made to nearby ruins, caves, and nature trails. Rates are about $5 a night, plus $2 for each meal. The Villorias also offer tours of their own "low-impact" farm and nursery, one mile from the San Pedro Columbia village (about 3 miles from P.G.). Using biogas generators, photovoltaics, permaculture, and other "appropriate technology," the couple has approached energy self-sufficiency and grow most of their own food. Guided tours are $5. Guests may stay overnight for a modest fee.

Temash River

If you are interested in seeing some of the tallest and oldest mangrove forests in all of Central America, a trip up the Río Temash fills the prescription. This river is one of four major watercourses that drain into the Caribbean from the Toledo District. In 1992, the progressive minister of natural resources in Belize, Florencio Marin, created the 41,000-acre Temash and Sarstoon Delta Wildlife Sanctuary.

As you speed from Punta Gorda in a hired boat through the Gulf of Honduras, you will pass such scenic coastal destinations as Orange Point, the Moho River, and Mother Point. The tall forest canopy along the coast contrasts with brighter green cascades of mangrove and forest stands that have been disturbed by periodic hurricanes that batter the mainland.

We recommend that you hire an experienced boatman and guide for this adventure. The need becomes apparent as you negotiate past dangerous sandbars and tangled mangrove thickets. A local is also extremely helpful to the amateur naturalist once past the verdant tunnel entrance of the Temash's delta. Comfrey palm swamp is found around the estuary of the Temash River, possibly the only place in the country where the habitat type exists in such abundance. This entire area is officially classified as a tropical wet-transition to subtropical forest and harbors much wildlife. Even the usually short pal-

Temash River, southern Belize (Photo by Steele Wotkyns)

metto palms tower overhead here. The deeper you penetrate this wide river, passing Conejos and Sunday Wood creeks, the bigger the trees become. The tangle of vines and understory is almost completely impenetrable. Dense stands of Santa María and sapodilla trees are broken by swampy mazes of red mangrove. And then you begin to see the main feature: black mangrove trees tower above the Río Temash, sometimes reaching over 100 feet.

The Temash is among the most remote and unspoiled places in Belize, but it is not completely untrammeled by man. The hunting of wildlife goes largely unregulated here. Species like the Morelet's crocodile, quite rare in neighboring countries, are listed in Belize as game species and taken (mostly) in season by local hunters. A few boats occasionally shatter the tropical silence of the river. Possibly most threatening is the practice of selective logging along the riverbanks. One encounters downed sapodilla trees that smash a wide path through the forest as they fall. Generally milled on site, this dense wood is valued both by lumbermen and chicle harvesters, who tap its white, sticky sap.

The presence of many fish-eating birds and local anglers attest to the Temash's richness as a fishing area. Large snook and tarpon cruise in the river, which reportedly reaches a depth of 100 feet. Sportfishing guides in Punta Gorda and other coastal towns can arrange excursions to this rich aquaculture environment.

Farther north, the Columbia branch of the Río Grande drains the nearly 103,000 acres of uninhabited wilderness known as the Columbia Forest Reserve, one of the last remaining large tracts of intact forest in Central America. Recent explorations of the reserve have revealed sinkholes up to 800 feet deep and one-quarter-mile wide, plus many sacred Mayan caves containing ancient artifacts. Access is extremely difficult, however, and prior permission from the Department of Forestry is required.

If You Go: Maya and Tropic airlines have regular flights from Belize City's municipal and international airports to Punta Gorda. Buses run from Dangriga and Belize City (check Z-Line Bus Service, 53 Main St., tel. 2-73937 or 2-21650; in Punta Gorda, tel. 7-22165), but this trip takes 10 to 12 hours from Belize City along the rough Southern Highway. A number of buses and supply trucks carry passengers on semiweekly schedules to surrounding villages.

A passenger ferry provides regular twice-weekly (2:00 p.m., Tuesday and Friday) service from Punta Gorda to Puerto Barrios,

Guatemala, with connections from there to interior Guatemala and Honduras. (The boat no longer stops in Livingston.) The crossing takes 3 to 4 hours and you must have documents in order before embarking. Tickets for the *Indita Maya* are about $6 one way ($3 returning) and should definitely be purchased in advance at Godoy's Shop in Punta Gorda (tel. 7-2065, 24 Middle St.). Bring your own food and water on board. *Quetzales* can be obtained at the ticket office or on board, but Guatemalan visas are not available here or in Puerto Barrios.

A place to stay that provides the most tour options and information about the Toledo District is the Nature's Way Guest House. It is located at the south end of town along the waterfront at 65 Front Street (tel. 7-22119). Sleeping quarters are basic, clean rooms with bunks and shared baths. Proprietor Chet Schmidt can arrange visits to the Toledo District's many attractions. Schmidt has a reliable boat for trips to the Temash River and the Sapodilla Cayes. The Toledo Visitors Information Center (open daily from 9:00 a.m. to 1:00 p.m., except Thursday and Sunday), operated by Alfredo and Yvonne Villoria near the main pier, also offers tours and boat charters. The information center maintains a message center, bulletin board, and paperback book exchange as well. The Villorias have an overnight "homestay" at their farm. Charter by Land/Sea schedules boat and interior trips from 12 Front Street (tel. 7-2070).

Other accommodations in Punta Gorda that have been recommended include the Mira Mar Hotel (95 Front St.), Mahung's (11 Main St.), and the Saint Charles Inn (23 King St.). Campgrounds and guest houses are planned along the Punta Gorda Nature Trail and may be in place by the time you visit.

Restaurant choices are rather limited, but there are several good Chinese cafés, and the larger hotels serve a variety of cuisines. Man Man's is an authentic and highly recommended Garifuna restaurant at the corner of King and Far West streets. There is also a bakery and grocery store. Nightlife is limited to a handful of bars, which tend to be frequented by off-duty British soldiers stationed at the nearby Rideau military camp.

6
The Interior

It used to be that few of Belize's visitors ventured west of the Belize Zoo unless they were heading across the Guatemalan border to Tikal. The conventional wisdom was that, except for the capital of Belmopan and the roadside Mayan ruins of Xunantunich, there was not much to see in the country's interior. We have talked to some travelers whose only memory along the Western Highway is of the unsightly Belize City garbage dump, since closed down. Fortunately, the infrastructure of the interior has improved to the point where many rewarding destinations can (and should) be added to any visitor's itinerary. Besides the country's most extensive collection of Mayan ruins and a growing number of comfortable lodges, Belize's interior offers the best opportunity to encounter the marvelous flora and fauna of a relatively undisturbed subtropical forest. Although some of the nation's newest sanctuaries and reserves offer virtually no access to the casual tourist, others provide an "up close and personal" experience one is not likely to forget. In addition, there are caves, rivers, horse paths, waterfalls, ruins, nature trails, and campsites galore, just waiting to be discovered—in some cases quite literally, since much of the interior remains virtually untouched by humans.

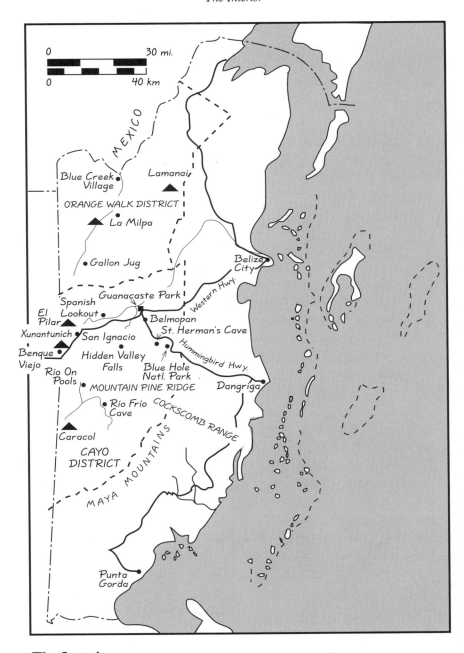

The Interior

Cayo District

With an estimated 1993 population of 38,000, Cayo (Spanish for "small island") is the second-largest and fastest-growing district of Belize. The capital city of Belmopan—the Belizean equivalent of Brazil's Brasilia—lies at the district's eastern edge, and Benque Viejo anchors its western border with Guatemala. In between these two towns, a visitor will find some of the nation's richest farmland, at times so carefully manicured by Mennonites that it looks more like the rolling hills of rural Pennsylvania than Central America. Besides cattle and pigs, Cayo farmers raise corn, sorghum, beans, fruit, and various vegetables for both domestic consumption and export. Significant amounts of pine, rosewood, Santa María, cedar, and mahogany are harvested by local lumber interests.

One of the district's most important industries is tourism. Travelers have much to choose from here: Mayan ruins, jungle trails, horseback rides, wild rivers, bird-watching, canoe trips, and such natural wonders as cascading waterfalls and limestone caves. The flora and fauna of Cayo are varied and plentiful. Such attractions have been enhanced in recent years by development of a tourism infrastructure that caters to the needs and interests of even the most discriminating visitor.

With 8,000 residents, San Ignacio, which is 22 miles west of Belmopan and 9 miles from the Guatemala border, is the largest town in the Cayo District and a fine place to have a meal, fill the gas tank, exchange currency, and load up on supplies. A colorful public produce market takes place every Saturday morning on the town square, and there are many pleasant hotels in San Ignacio. The town is laid out on a series of bluffs alongside the Macal River. The area is high enough in elevation to be noticeably cooler and less humid than the coastal plain. The people are friendly and happy-go-lucky, pointing with pride at their Hawkesworth bridge: a scaled down version of the Brooklyn Bridge and the only suspension span in the country. Until 1992, the one-way bridge had the only traffic signal in Belize. Locals will also steer you to the restored Mayan ruin of Cahal Pech, just up Main Street at the crest of a hill, and to Serendib, a Sri Lankan

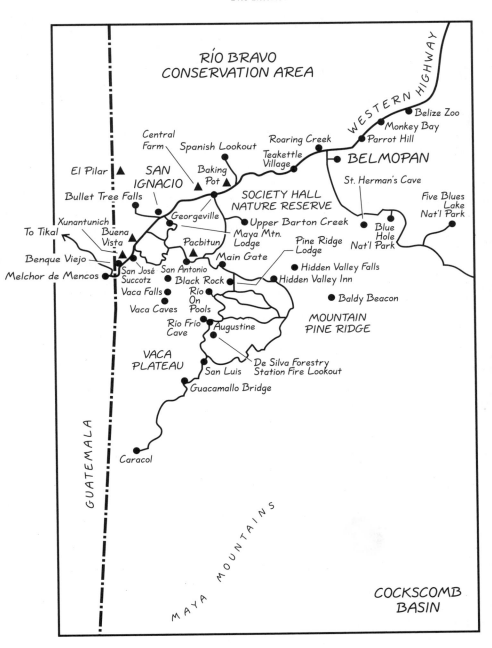

Cayo District

restaurant justifiably revered for its spicy curry. Another good dining spot is Eva's Restaurant, just across the road from Serendib, run by English expatriate Bob Jones and his Belizean wife, Nestora. Travel tips and assistance are cheerfully dispensed at Eva's, the unofficial tourist information center for western Belize. Among other noteworthy stops are Belize Arts & Crafts, a well-stocked souvenir shop next to the bus station; the Bel-Brit Bar, an English-style pub on Burns Avenue; Blue Angel Club, a justifiably popular nightclub on Hutson Street and Farmer's Emporium, a rustic grocery at 24 Burns Avenue.

Other Cayo District towns include Santa Elena, San Ignacio's sister city across the suspension bridge, and Benque Viejo, which practically straddles the Guatemalan border. Both communities are largely Spanish-speaking, and you are likely to encounter marimbas, fiestas, and colorful social customs centered around Catholic holidays and the rituals of baptism, confirmation, and marriage. Many inhabitants are descended from Guatemalan immigrants who crossed the border into Belize to escape political persecution and economic exploitation.

Until the late 1980s, the Western Highway was unpaved beyond San Ignacio, and rural residents here were very isolated. Many still make do without electricity, telephone, and indoor plumbing.

Tucked in the folds of the lush green hills are a dozen or more "cottage" resorts, ranging from luxurious to rustic but catering to the visitor who wants to get as far away as possible from urban distractions. Some of these charming retreats are located on working farms or ranches, while others are exclusively dedicated to a kind of gracious, low-key jungle tourism that brings to mind images of E. M. Forster's British India.

Each cottage resort is slightly different in style and character, with its own set of advantages and disadvantages. Some specialize in horseback riding or canoeing; others cater to jungle trekkers and bird-watchers. Still others can arrange strenuous camping trips in the unexplored forest or investigations of little-known caverns. All, however, supply meals and other basic amenities to their guests, and most can set up tours of the nearby Mayan ruins at Xunantunich,

Caracol, and Tikal. A few even have reciprocal agreements with resorts on the coast or cayes that allow visitors to package a "surf and turf" holiday. Rates and accommodations vary widely, from budget to five-star, depending on such variables as location, meals, services, and transportation costs.

The friendly resort operators take individual preferences into account, making breakfast at 5:00 a.m. for eager bird-watchers, for example, or eliminating the meal entirely for late risers who wish to sleep in. If you want to be chauffeured, they will pick you up at the Belize City airport. Charters can now be made to the Cayo airport at Central Farm, a few miles east of San Ignacio. If you have your own transportation, operators will be just as happy to give you detailed instructions and maps to any destination that pleases you.

Some of the more established cottage resorts with good reputations among experienced travelers include the Maya Mountain Lodge (encompassing a farm and forest preserve on the Cristo Rey road); Chaa Creek Cottages (offering Mayan-style cabanas on a bluff above the Macal River and specializing in "adventure tours"); Mountain Equestrian Trails (a 150-acre, 20-horse ranch catering to nature lovers); Nabitunich (a family-run farm near the Xunantunich ruins where you can simply relax and watch the Mopan River flow by); Banana Bank Ranch (operated by former Montana cowboy John Carr and his artist wife Carolyn); Parrot's Nest (a collection of tree-houses built above the river near Bullet Tree Falls Village); Crystal Paradise Resort (operated by a Mayan-Creole family and offering horseback riding or boat trips from Cristo Rey Village); and Las Casitas (a cluster of rustic bungalows at the confluence of the Belize and Mopan rivers).

Several of the Cayo resorts have become actively involved in projects that combine conservation and sustainable economic development. Mountain Equestrian Trails, for example, has joined with neighboring private landowners to establish the Slate Creek Preserve, a limestone karst area covered with moist broadleaf forest and home to such endangered fauna as the keel-billed motmot and Baird's tapir. The preserve is a vital link in establishing a biological corridor between the Río Bravo wilderness, Society Hall, and Mountain Pine

Ridge. Mountain Equestrian Trails owners Jim and Marguerite Bevis are involving local residents in handicraft production and nature-oriented tourism as an alternative to slash-and-burn agriculture, which threatens the Slate Creek watershed and other tracts of unspoiled wilderness. A Belizean of American descent, Jim Bevis hires well-informed local guides to lead visitors on horseback to remote area caves, waterfalls, and ruins. These highly recommended trips are tailored to equestrians of all abilities, including novices. Visitors may camp out or stay in beautifully appointed bungalows at the ranch. Other MET expeditions, conducted in association with The Divide Ltd. (Neil Rogers), combine camping and hiking to such unusual destinations as Puente Natural and Las Cuevas, deep in the Chiquibul forest.

The operators of Maya Mountain Lodge, located a short distance south of Santa Elena, also show genuine concern for the future of Cayo and its people. Owners Bart and Suzi Mickler are developing a ceramic handicraft industry using local artisans and materials. They began holding ceramics classes in 1993 with the goal of more evenly distributing the economic rewards of tourism among all Belizeans. Besides the usual sightseeing trips, Maya Mountain offers guided horseback trips, canoe rides, mountain biking, birding, Mennonite visits, and nature treks (with accompanying guidebooks prepared by biologist Bruce Miller and Suzi Mickler, who holds a master of science degree in education). The facility maintains an educational field station and reference library for cultural, archaeological, and wildlife studies. Acclaimed local naturalist Fermin Tzil is a consultant and tour guide here, often appearing during the resort's Friday "Belize Night" slide shows. Maya Mountain grows much of its own food and has established a private nature reserve that includes a small Mayan ceremonial site.

A favorite of many travelers is Chaa Creek Cottages, established many years ago by British expatriate Mick Fleming and his American wife, Lucy. Guests stay in Mayan-style cottages set beneath tall tropical trees. You are serenaded by exotic birds every morning: there is no glass in the windows because Chaa Creek has almost no biting insects. Interior accents are Guatemalan tapestries and carvings. International

Expeditions often brings its tours here because of the resort's high standards and commitment to environmental awareness.

Three Mountain Pine Ridge lodges specialize in natural history tourism. The Blanquano Lodge, owned by movie director Francis Ford Coppola, reopened in 1993 in an area surrounded by nature trails. The more moderately priced Pine Ridge Lodge specializes in cave exploration (including three rediscovered Mayan caves 3 miles away), hiking, river trips, birding, and archaeology. The cabana-style hotel also operates a small restaurant. An unusual combination of options is offered by the Hidden Valley Inn, maintained by the Georgia family that owns 18,000 acres of the pine ridge and adjacent subtropical jungle. Visitors can either stay in comfortable cottages or camp under the stars in the orchid-scented forest. Carefully maintained trails lead to Central America's highest waterfall, several caves, and a small lake. A large section of the property constitutes the Hidden Valley Reserve and Institute for Environmental Studies, where biologists recently found a new toad species and a rare nesting pair of orange-breasted falcons. Tours are arranged to Caracol, the Chiquibul rain forest, and other nearby attractions.

More budget-priced accommodations catering to nature lovers include the Belizean-owned Crystal Paradise Resort, offering horseback riding, boat trips, and bird-watching on a 71-acre parcel along the Macal River in Cristo Rey. Mida's Resort, operated by a British-Belizean family, offers thatched roof cabins on the banks of the Macal downstream from San Ignacio, with canoeing and nature treks available. Near Xunantunich is a 400-acre working ranch called Nabintunich ("stone cottage") with 11 cabins and lots of horses. Bridal trails extend through miles of dense bush. On a sharp bend in the Belize River, near Bullet Tree Falls, the Parrot's Nest accommodates visitors in rustic treehouses. Swimming and birding are excellent; horseback tours are offered to the nearby ruin of El Pilar and a jungle chicle camp.

There are at least two dozen other lodges and hotels in the Cayo to suit every taste and pocketbook. Check with travel agencies or the Belize Tourist Board for a complete rundown. For those heading off the beaten path, we highly recommend The Divide Ltd. (92-3452).

Chapter 6

If You Go: The Cayo District is easily reached by private or rental car on the Western Highway, or by the same route via the Batty, Novelo, Piache, and Shaw bus lines. Check with local agents for schedules and fares. The drive from Belize City to San Ignacio takes just under two hours, the bus somewhat longer. There is a taxi stand at Columbus Park (the traffic circle by the bridge) in San Ignacio and Market Plaza in Belmopan. Small airstrips near Belmopan and Central Farm (east of San Ignacio) are used by private and chartered aircraft. Most lodges can arrange pick-up at Belize's international airport.

Ix Chel Farm and the Panti Medicinal Trail

A few miles west of San Ignacio, a dirt side road follows a Macal River tributary called Chaa Creek which has become one of the centers of laid-back Cayo District tourism. The Chaa Creek Road first winds through a series of barren cattle pastures before bisecting verdant farmland—vast Mennonite plantations on one side, small Indian fields on the other. About 4 miles from the Western Highway the road splits, with one branch heading toward DuPlooy's Resort and the other to Chaa Creek Cottages. Both lodges perch on cliffs above the swift Macal River and are surrounded by thick second-growth subtropical vegetation. The forest setting is tranquil and shady, a perfect setting for a slow canoe trip or unhurried horseback ride. A maze of pathways penetrate the foliage, including the remarkable Panti Medicinal Trail located about 100 yards away from Chaa Creek Cottages on the grounds of Ix Chel Farm, an unusual research facility specializing in the healing properties of plants.

During the summer rainy season, when visitors from other parts of Belize complain about bug bites, Ix Chel founder Rosita Arvigo walks out the back door of her farmhouse and snaps a small branch off a red gumbo-limbo tree. The bark, she informs them, produces a natural insect repellent. It can also be made into a tonic for treating urinary tract infections and provides an antidote to the itchy rashes caused by contact with the poisonwood tree, which invariably grows nearby. There are many other local trees, shrubs, and vines that have proven equally useful.

166

Typical cabana-stlye bungalow of Cayo District cottage resort, this one at Chaa Creek (Photo by Richard Mahler)

A dedicated herbalist and botanical field practitioner from Chicago, Arvigo is in a race against time. She and her colleagues at this remote encampment are scouring the Central American forests in search of tropical plants that may help win the war against a number of deadly diseases. With her husband, Greg Shropshire, Arvigo works at the place where the timeless wisdom of venerable native healers intersects with the untested theories of Western medicine.

"Much of what I have learned is from Don Eligio Panti," she explains, referring to the Mayan healer who began—albeit reluctantly at first—sharing his secrets (beginning at age 86) with Arvigo. This Mayan *yerbero*, or herbalist, has provided Arvigo's Ix Chel Tropical Research Center with vital information about hundreds of plants that have traditionally been used in Belize to treat everything from heart attacks to snakebites.

Arvigo's ultimate goal is not only to preserve the encyclopedic herbal lore Don Eligio has memorized during his long lifetime but also to determine the healing properties—if any—of hundreds of other native plants that may have never been ingested by humans and thus have unknown biochemical effects.

The U.S. government's National Cancer Institute is funding the New York Botanical Garden's Institute of Ethnobotany in support of Ix Chel as part of a thirteen-country, five-year search for little-known flora that could be used in the successful treatment of incurable diseases such as AIDS. The effort underscores a deepening alliance between native healers and modern scientists in a bid to find and study potentially useful plants before they are wiped off the face of the earth by deforestation and industrialization.

The World Health Organization, among other international agencies, is now requesting samples of such plants from Ix Chel Farm. The materials are dried in a specially made oven in Arvigo's botanical workshop, then labeled and packaged before being sent to a laboratory for analysis. All this work is carried out in an isolated setting that has only solar electricity, minimal hot water, and no telephone.

The campaign is spurred by the knowledge that the world's forests have already yielded such medicines as quinine (antimalarial), vinblastine (used to treat Hodgkin's disease), and taxol (a treatment for ovarian cancer). Many so-called miracle drugs are plant-derived compounds from tropical forests. Examples include Tubocurarine (commonly called curare), used in operating rooms to relax muscles and prevent spasm, and Pilocarpine, used in opthalmology for the treatment of glaucoma. An estimated 25 percent of all prescription drugs were derived from the plant kingdom.

At Ix Chel Farm, the Panti Medicinal Trail winds through a living display of arboreal and herbal remedies in the second-growth forest. The treasures of nature seem overwhelming as one strolls along the path, along which signs describe one plant after another, many bearing unusually descriptive names. The "tres puntos" plant, distinguished by its large three-pointed leaves, yields jackass bitters, a tonic used to treat upset stomachs, diabetes, salmonella poisoning, and malaria. A few steps farther is the skunk root, effective in purging the body of toxins, and wild grapevine, filled with an antiseptic used to wash newborn infants. Nearby grows the fiddlewood tree. Its bark is used in an herbal bath to kill the parasite known to cause a painful

Rosita Arvigo and jackass bitters (Photo by Richard Mahler)

condition called leishmaniasis. When a Western physician was unable
to cure her of this ailment, Arvigo used a fiddlewood tree bark bath
to eliminate the parasite from her own body. Other medicinal plants
gathered here include the billy web, balsam, allspice, contribo, and
guaco. Also here is the wild yam, which is effective in preventing
pregnancy and which led directly to the synthesizing of cortisone, the
powerful muscle relaxant. When brewed as a tea, it does wonders for
rheumatism and anemia.

As practiced by Panti and other Mayan shaman, herbal medicine
is religious as well as physical. Natural and supernatural forces are
seen in every aspect of daily life. Traditionally, a Mayan healer was
called a *h'men*, or doctor/priest. Every one of his patients receives a
series of nine prayers to the nine principal Mayan spirits. And before
Panti cuts any plant with his machete, he always pauses to murmur a

prayer: "In the name of God, I take the life of this plant to heal the sick and I give thanks to its spirit."

Much of the information that Panti has passed on to Arvigo in tape-recorded meetings and early morning field trips is also being fed into a computer, to be shared with scientists and medical researchers around the globe. Arvigo and Michael Balick of the New York Botanical Garden have published a book about their findings, *One Hundred Healing Herbs of Belize*.

By cooperating with the wise elders of a community, ethno-botanists have been able to collect samples of many unusual plant specimens, and new kinds of nontraditional medicine are now being used to treat the sick and injured. "We're teaching health care workers in village clinics how to use medicinal plants," says Arvigo, who welcomes more than 3,000 visitors a year to Ix Chel Farm and sees patients privately for specialized forms of acupuncture, chiropractics, and other health treatments. Her husband is a homeopathic doctor with his own practice as well.

The facilities at Ix Chel Farm have been expanded to accommo-date conferences where Arvigo and Shropshire, residents of Belize since 1983, share their knowledge of natural healing practices. The couple also sell a variety of teas and ointments directly to the public (mail orders carry a 10% surcharge).

If You Go: Open during daylight hours every day except Monday, the Panti Medicinal Trail and Ix Chel Farm are located at the end of Chaa Creek Road, next door to Chaa Creek Cottages. The site can be reached by car (4-wheel drive recommended during wet season) or taxi. Turn south off the Western Highway 6 miles west of San Ignacio (watch for Chaa Creek signs). An alternative is to take a boat 5 miles upstream from the Hawkesworth Bridge and put in at the Chaa Creek Cottages dock.

Call 9-23310 or write Ix Chel Farm, General Delivery, San Igna-cio. Visits by groups can also be arranged through the Belize Center for Environmental Studies, telephone 2-45545 in Belize City.

A self-guided tour of the mile-long Panti Medicinal Trail is $5 per person, including an explanatory booklet. Fresh fruit and spearmint tea are available. A guided one-hour tour and lecture by an Ix Chel staffer is $30, $50 if given by Arvigo. There is an additional charge for meals and canoe trips.

Ix Chel Farm sells many herbal elixirs and potions, with names like Belly Be Good and Female Tonic. Prices are around $10. Some of these items are also available in gift shops and groceries in other parts of the country; look for the Rainforest Remedies label. Ten percent of all sales goes to traditional healers and educational programs in Belize.

Arvigo and Shropshire welcome tax-deductible donations to support their research, either sent directly to Ix Chel Farm or in care of Michael J. Balick, Director of the Institute of Economic Botany, New York Botanical Garden, Bronx, NY 10458, or call (212) 220-8763. Checks sent to the latter address should be made out to the New York Botanical Garden with an accompanying letter specifying use by the Belize Ethnobotany Project.

The Mountain Pine Ridge

An unnerving sight for many travelers is their first glimpse of stately pine forests carpeting the steep hillsides of the Cayo District's subtropical Maya Mountains. After winding through impenetrable, moist broadleaf jungle en route to this highland ecosystem, one is suddenly confronted with a landscape straight out of red-dirt Georgia. As far as the eye can see, tall pine trees reach to the deep blue sky. The sandy terrain is covered with rust-colored pine needles interspersed by maidenhair ferns, sparse grasses, and delicate wildflowers. In some areas, clusters of gnarled oak trees grip the thin, fragile topsoil.

The Mountain Pine Ridge—in Belize, the term "ridge" refers to a forest type and not a geographic formation—is an unusual natural phenomenon covering nearly 300 square miles. Located in the foothills southeast of San Ignacio, the pine ridge is a Central American anomaly. Its nutrient-poor soils and subsurface rocks are of a type found only here, in the Brazilian highlands, and in America's southern Appalachians. The prevailing geologic theory holds that these old mountains are the last vestiges of a large formation that was split off from what is now the southeastern United States and pushed over millions of years against the Central American peninsula. This

The Mountain Pine Ridge (Photo by Richard Mahler)

might explain why the vegetation and wildlife here is so out of sync with its surroundings but not Georgia.

The ancient Maya chose not to settle here, apparently concluding that seasonal droughts and shallow soils made the area unsuitable for farming. Many well-maintained logging roads and nature trails criss-cross the forest reserve, and the terrain is especially suited for hiking and horseback riding. Birds are plentiful, and butterflies are particularly numerous. Travelers will spy many unusual varieties of bromeliads and other air plants in the pine branches.

Along the edges of the pine ridge are limestone caves, waterfalls, white water rivers, hardwood forests, and sharp escarpments with sweeping views. The almost total lack of human habitation means that much of this wilderness is in virgin condition, just the way it might have looked when Mayan hunters traversed its footpaths 2,000 years ago.

If You Go: The easiest way to see the Mountain Pine Ridge is by signing up for a minivan tour through a hotel or travel agency. This can be done easily through one of the three lodges within the forest reserve or those that are located in the rest of the Cayo District. During the dry season several vehicles a day explore the area, and overnight camping and equestrian trips can be arranged. Camping is allowed in certain areas with permission of the Department of Forestry (check with officials in Belmopan or the guard at the main entrance). There is no public transportation into the Mountain Pine Ridge beyond taxis and rental cars. Those driving their own vehicles are advised that the region's dirt roads are sometimes a challenge during rainy periods.

Hidden Valley (Thousand-Foot) Falls

Hidden Valley Falls, also known as Thousand-Foot Falls, is one of the Mountain Pine Ridge's primary attractions. This is the tallest waterfall in Central America, plunging almost one quarter of a mile over a granite precipice into a deep jungle canyon. The distance is so great that the bottom of the waterfall becomes lost in mist and green foliage.

To see the falls, follow the Baldy Beacon Road east of the forest reserve's main entrance for about 5 miles. Then proceed as directed by the well-marked signs for a couple of miles to an overlook area where a $1 admission fee will be collected by the resident caretaker (the attraction is on private land). This is a good place to take photographs, savor a picnic, and observe bird life. The rare king vulture and orange-breasted falcon are sometimes seen riding the thermal air currents here. The latter predator nests near the waterfall. Dozens of orchids and bromeliads cling to nearby tree branches, and steep trails wind through the underbrush. On a clear day, the capital buildings of Belmopan shimmer on the horizon.

Across from the caretaker's cabin is the Hidden Valley Institute for Environmental Studies, a privately funded research facility that conducts field research and develops much-needed conservation education materials for local schools. Wooden bungalows accommodate visiting naturalists and a small natural history museum. Just below the institute is a rugged 4-mile track to the base of the waterfall. The trail is not well maintained, and a round-trip may take all day. The reward is a deep, wide pool at the bottom of the cataract which is perfect for swimming. Along the way, hikers make a dramatic transition from the relatively cool and spare pine forest ecosystem to an almost impenetrable, steamy lowland jungle. Visitors may spy a jaguar or tapir en route. Guests of the nearby Hidden Valley Lodge have access to three other magnificent falls: King Vulture, Tiger Creek, and Butterfly.

Río On Pools

About 10 miles southwest of the Hidden Valley Falls overlook, the forest reserve's main road crosses the Río On, a cascading upland tributary of the Belize River. As it makes its way down from the Mountain Pine Ridge, the Río On swirls and splashes through a maze of giant granite boulders. The warm, deep pools formed by these enormous rocks are as much as 15 feet deep and make delightful swimming holes, especially after a long day of hiking or horseback riding. The smooth stones make natural water slides, and many visitors like to stretch out and sunbathe on them in the warm tropical sun. There are outhouses (doubling as changing rooms) and picnic tables nearby, plus a freshwater tap. The parking lot accommodates a growing number of visitors, which may swell to several dozen on weekends and holidays.

Río Frío Cave and Nature Trail

Not much farther south, a few miles past the village of Augustine and the forest reserve headquarters, visitors descend into subtropical vegetation and one of Belize's best-known cave districts. Several small caves lie within sight of the roadway and are well marked. At the parking area for these caves, the Río Frío Nature Trail makes its way through dense forest to the largest and most spectacular of the group. (The Río Frío Cave can also be easily reached by driving a couple of miles down the same road to a picnic area outside the cavern entrance.) The nature trail takes about 45 minutes to negotiate (longer in wet weather) and displays a wide variety of subtropical trees, each carefully labeled. The common names of many of these species are rather whimsical and include the give-and-take palm, quamwood, boy job, poisonwood, and gumbo-limbo. There are even naturally occurring rubber, mahogany, and sapodilla trees (the latter is the source of chicle, a chewing gum base: look for scarring of the bark). Wildlife in the area is abundant.

The Río Frío Cave is the largest known river cave in Belize, extending for one-half mile through a solid limestone mountain. Centuries ago the tunnel was used as a ceremonial center by local Maya, but all artifacts have long since been removed or washed away.

There are enormous arched entryways at either end of the cave, which narrows midway to a height and width of about 40 feet. Because the fast-moving Río Frío cuts a broad channel through the underground passage, it is impossible to traverse the cave during rainy months. Even during the dry season, visitors will probably find it necessary to at least get their feet wet. The inside of the cave is musty and cool but not entirely dark. Enough daylight filters through from either end to make flashlights unnecessary. Footholds can be slippery, however, and some rock climbing is required.

The cave's interior displays some unusual striations and colors that are the result of erosion and mineral deposits. Some of the rock surfaces have an odd spongy texture; others resemble rice paddy terraces or water fountains. Many stalactites hang from the ceiling, and a small colony of bats dwells in the darkest crevices. There are other, equally scenic caves in the Chiquibul wilderness, including the Domingo Ruíz Cave about 5 miles away, but they are much less accessible, little explored, and in some cases dangerous to visit without a well-trained guide. The latter can be engaged through hotels, travel agencies, or conservation organizations (see Inside Belize for suggestions).

Augustine Village and Beyond

The headquarters for the Mountain Pine Ridge Forest Reserve is in a large and impressive-looking wooden building in the settlement of Augustine, renamed Douglas DiSilva in 1990 after a politician's grandfather (who happened to be the area's first forest ranger). Only about 100 people—all forestry employees—live here, and the place has the look and feel of a run-down summer camp. Many of the houses are in disrepair, and others are being used to store pine seeds for reforestation projects. Worth visiting are the self-guided nature trail on the headquarters grounds and the small store (source of the only beer and picnic supplies for many miles around). Thatch-shaded tables are available to picnickers, but there is no restaurant or gas station. Inquire at the headquarters about camping and overnight rental of government-owned guest houses. You may reportedly also gain permission to camp at the Pincherichito Gate near San Antonio. If you are continuing to the Mayan ruin at Caracol (see description below), you will need to secure a permit from the Forestry Department officer on duty here. Permits are not granted when the road is judged to be in such poor condition that travel will be hazardous (both to visitors and the road surface itself). When the surface is dry, you can reach Caracol from here in about 45 minutes. Heading the other direction, Georgeville on the Western Highway is between 90 minutes and 2 hours.

San Antonio Village

The more westerly of the two routes leading into (and out of) the Mountain Pine Ridge passes through the small and mostly Indian farming village of San Antonio. This is one of the few remaining communities in Belize where the modern version of the Mayan language is still spoken; in this instance, the Mopan dialect. (Note that there is a second San Antonio, populated by Kekchí-speaking Maya, in the Toledo District near Punta Gorda.)

The Cayo's San Antonio village is situated in a picturesque valley where beautifully terraced fields of beans and corn have been carved out of the leafy jungle. Agriculture has persisted here for thousands of years. Recently, a few small shops and restaurants have been opened in an attempt to diversify the local economy.

Among the several attractions that are especially worth visiting in the San Antonio area are the García Sisters Museum, the Itzamna' (Magaña Family) Gallery and Gift Shop, and the Pacbitun archaeological site. Pacbitun (meaning "stones set in the earth") is one of the oldest middle Pre-Classic Mayan ruins in the country, first occupied

SUPPORT THE GARCIA SISTERS·A $1·00 FEE·TO VISIT THEIR·ARTS COLLECTIONS LET US SUPPORT YOUNG ARTISTS AND LET THEM·BE AN OUTSTANDING EXAMPLE FOR YOUTHS AND FUTURE GENERATIONS.Thank You

María García, one of five Mayan sisters who own and operate this combination museum/gift shop in San Antonio Village (Photo by Richard Mahler)

in 1000 B.C. and abandoned around A.D. 900. The location was known for many years by local residents but not registered by the Belize Department of Archaeology until 1971. Canada's Trent University excavated and partially reconstructed this major ceremonial site during the 1980s. Findings include a number of Mayan altar stones and ball courts as well as ancient musical instruments such as ocarinas fashioned out of carved and molded pottery. There are at least twenty-four temple pyramids at Pacbitun, the largest standing 60 feet tall. Two thousand years ago this was apparently a wealthy trading center with fancy homes, elevated walkways, a ball court, and raised irrigation causeways up to a half-mile long.

The Pacbitun site is on private farmland, but the owner, Fidencio Tzul, welcomes visitors for a $1 fee. His family home is at the well-marked turnoff to Pacbitun one-half mile east of San Antonio. The ruins are about 3 miles farther down the side road. Mr. Tzul will be happy to give you a tour and answer any questions.

Just north of San Antonio on the main road to Cristo Rey and Santa Elena is the García Sisters Museum—a combination crafts shop, herbal medicine pharmacy, and Mayan shrine. The five lovely García sisters, at least one of whom is always on hand, make and sell slate carvings that depict traditional Mayan masks, gods, and history. Although the art form has been practiced by the modern Maya for years in neighboring Guatemala, this is believed to be the only place in Belize that makes and sells such carvings. (There is a $5 admission charge to the museum itself.) The women were taught by their father, Aureliano, who also carves much of what is sold here. Aureliano García spent thirty years roaming the nearby jungle as a *chiclero* (tapper of chicle gum base), and at one time he trapped crocodiles for a living. The García sisters' uncle on their mother's side is Don Eligio Panti, the famous Mayan herbalist healer. In mid-1993, the legendary *curandero* was still sharing his one hundred years of accumulated wisdom, and one of his nieces, Aurora, was serving as his apprentice. The forest medicines, teas, and potions for sale at the museum are prepared under Panti's supervision.

At one end of the museum building is a round structure built in the shape of a traditional Mayan hut, where explanations of the various masks and symbols seen in the carvings can be found. There are also some large pieces of carved slate that emulate the sacred altar stones of ancient times.

Another group of local artisans, the Magaña family, has recently opened a San Antonio art gallery and gift shop of their own, which sells carvings of wood and stone. The Magañas produce wood and limestone carvings that incorporate traditional Mayan themes. Glyphs from the Mayan calander are also hand-painted by family members on the same type of cloth supposedly used by ancient royalty.

Vaca Falls and Caves

The upper stretches of the Macal River extend into a remote and seldom seen area that drains the Vaca Plateau watershed. Access has improved in recent years through grading of a new road being used in the construction of a large dam and hydroelectric plant, which will eventually flood much of the upper Macal basin above the confluence of the Mollejon River. The Belize government, working with a Chinese contractor, hopes to begin generating electricity here by the end of the 1990s. In the meantime, you are strongly urged to see the area's natural wonders while you still can.

A highly recommended destination is a privately owned cave complex not far from the Vaca Falls, a scenic and rocky plunge on the Macal River. This location can be reached by a one-hour boat trip from San Ignacio or a two-hour hike from the Negroman Farms Road. The Antonio Morales family provides bungalow-style accommodations and delicious meals as well as guided tours of the Chechen Ha Caves (also called Vaca Falls Caves), which are located on their property. The caves are well worth seeing and contain many Mayan artifacts, such as ancient pottery vessels used for holy water. These have been left undisturbed for at least 1,200 years, and iron grates now protect them from looters and vandals. The interior of these caves is very slippery, and one should not attempt to explore them without the help of an experienced guide. The Morales compound may be reached by local VHF radio (try Bob Jones at Eva's Restaurant in San Ignacio) or through Chaa Creek Cottages, which arranges tours.

Another conservation-oriented lodge in the same area is Ek' Tun (Mayan for "black rock"), the home of American expatriates Ken and Phyllis Dart, who maintain a rustic cottage, dining pavilion, and several nature trails for visitors. The 200-acre facility is on the Macal River, a few miles downstream from Vaca Falls. Over 150 species of birds have been sighted here, including the spectacled owl and orange-breasted falcon, along with jaguar, howler monkey, tapir, tayra, peccary, and brocket deer. Mayan artifacts have been found in nearby caves, and there are many house mounds, causeways, and even a hand-dug well. It is believed that the Ek' Tun site was once a Mayan village and, much later, a chicle camp. The Darts provide guided hiking tours of up to four days duration and will pick up guests by boat in San Ignacio or vehicle in Belize City for a fee. Other than by boat, Ek' Tun is only accessible by foot or horseback. An optional jungle survival training course teaches the basics of identifying edible plants, locating water, making a shelter, and finding one's way in the wilderness. Other activities include canoeing, swimming, and fishing. Rates are high but include all meals. Up to six people can be accommodated if bookings are made at least 45 days in advance.

A few miles downstream from Ek' Tun (8 miles upstream from San Ignacio) is the Guacamallo Ruins Campground, which rents tent sites and treehouses in a riverbank setting. There are many unexcavated Mayan ruins in this area as well as dense subtropical forests now maintained as a private nature reserve. In the same area is the solar-powered Black Rock Resort, owned by the operator of Caesar's Place, a restaurant and hotel on the Western Highway a few miles east of San Ignacio. Black Rock provides cabana-style accommodations as well as hiking, boating, swimming, fishing, horesback riding, and nature treks. It is most easily reached by private launch from San Ignacio. Call 92-2341 to arrange transport.

If You Go: Take the Negroman Farms Road south off the Western Highway between San Ignacio and San José Succotz. You will reach the upper Macal River within an hour if the road is in good condition. Ask Antonio Morales at his riverbank farm for permission to visit the nearby caves and obtain a guide. Boats can be hired in San Ignacio below the Hawkesworth Bridge for trips up the Macal, or inquire at local lodges. Remo at Float Belize (92-3213) also offers river trips on this and other Belize River tributaries, even a week-long float to Belize City. Tour guide Chris Heckert of San Ignacio offers tours of the Vaca Falls area at reasonable prices in his Uni-Mog, a sturdy vehicle with very large tires and a high clearance. Inquire at Eva's Restaurant.

The Chiquibul Wilderness

Rather than loop through the Mountain Pine Ridge in only a day or two, some travelers continue south beyond the Río Frío Cave into some of the wildest areas of Belize. Only a handful of people live full-time in this area, mostly chicle tappers, poachers, and looters. The British military forces maintain a training camp in the inner reaches of the forest, but most of the territory is left alone.

The enormous Mayan ruin of Caracol, currently being excavated, is about 30 miles south of Augustine on a part of the Chiquibul wilderness called the Vaca Plateau. This broad tableland consists of hundreds of square miles of intact forest, the last stronghold of many wildlife and plant species that are endangered elsewhere in Central

America and southern Mexico. The plateau is crisscrossed by old logging and chiclero trails, but over the years, many have been almost reclaimed by the jungle. A detailed map of the Vaca Plateau might suggest that there are a number of villages in the area, but in reality these are abandoned lumbering camps established long ago when mahogany and other hardwoods were being selectively harvested and skidded, then floated, downriver to Belize City. Travel in this area is now limited to horseback and high-clearance, four-wheel-drive vehicle. Overnight trips can be arranged through local operators to such spectacular destinations as Puente Natural, an arch cave similar to Río Frío through which a small river flows. Highly recommended for such rugged adventures is Mountain Equestrian Trails; contact Neil Rogers or Jim Bevis there for details.

Several other local tour operators, notably Chaa Creek and Maya Mountain, also run overnight or daylong mule/horse trips into this area. Destinations include remote Mayan ruins, caves, waterfalls, rivers, and chiclero camps. Because of the rough terrain and the absence of freshwater streams during the dry season, overland trips to the area are only recommended for travelers who are healthy and fit. The scenery, however, is some of the best in Belize.

Blue Hole and Five Blues Lake National Parks, St. Herman's and Other Caves

For experienced spelunkers—the technical term for cave explorers—Belize can be a dream come true. Underlying most of the country (with the notable exception of the Maya Mountains) are the kinds of limestone platforms and uplifts that almost guarantee the formation of extensive cavern networks. Unlike the western rim of the Americas, which is part of the so-called Ring of Fire circling the Pacific Ocean, there is virtually no volcanic activity in Belize. The nation's only known hot springs, for example, is a small pool in the Toledo District.

Because of their isolation, many Belizean caves have not been fully explored, and it is likely that many entrances have not even been discovered. The Chiquibul complex of the Vaca Plateau, for example, is perhaps one of the largest underground labyrinths in Central America. No one knows for certain, since many branches have yet to be explored by modern man. In fact, no systematic scientific exploration of any kind occurred until the late 1970s. Since then, researchers have found fossilized insects and crustaceans in some of the Vaca Plateau caves which have been extinct for many centuries. A large number of the caves show signs of ceremonial usage by the ancient Maya, whose abandoned belongings are often found in dusty yet pristine condition.

According to Logan McNatt, a former Department of Archaeology employee who has spent many years exploring the caves of Belize, most of these sites are and should remain closed to the general public. "There are two main problems," McNatt told us. "First, most of the caves are important archaeological sites that have not yet been evaluated or protected. Second, most cavern systems of Belize are subject to sudden, unexpected flooding that can make them very dangerous. In addition, few maps of the inner passageways exist."

McNatt points out that many of the caves are actually part of underground river courses that form a massive aquifer. A spelunker may descend under a clear blue sky, only to find a rapid surge in water elevation caused by a far-off thunderstorm. For these reasons, only experienced and well-equipped persons should attempt to explore the wilder, lesser-known caves of Belize and then only with permission from the government. Knowledgeable and experienced guides should also be engaged for every journey, except for such small and well-traveled caves as Río Frío, St. Herman's, and Ben Lomond. These latter caves have an eerie kind of beauty, punctuated as they often are by occasional streams of light from ceiling cracks and side entrances. Some of the underground chambers are a hundred or more feet high, adorned with majestic stalactites and stalagmites. They provide an unusual habitat favored by bats, sightless fish, and other small creatures, plus mosses and ferns that adapt well to filtered light and cool, humid microclimates.

A well-marked sign guides visitors to the entrance trail of Blue Hole National Park, a federally protected area administered by the Belize Audubon Society and located 12 miles southeast of Belmopan on the Hummingbird Highway. Down a flight of wooden steps, one comes upon an amazing sight—a deep pool of churning sapphire-colored water formed after the collapse of an underground river channel. The Caves Branch Creek tributary wells up from an unseen cave and travels for about 100 yards before plunging mysteriously down a siphon that carries it into yet another cave beneath the mountainside. The dome-shaped chamber where the water is sucked underground creates an unusual echo chamber effect as liquid swirls beneath it. This idyllic blue hole, not to be confused with the offshore destination of the same name near Half Moon Caye, is a good spot for swimming, picnicking, and bird-watching. There are no overnight camping facilities. The sparkling pool is about 25 feet deep and fast moving, so bathers should be careful.

The same Caves Branch Creek travels through nearby St. Herman's Cave and Mountain Cow Cave, which are accessible from the Blue Hole via a well-maintained forest pathway called the Nature Trail. Fauna recorded in this area include jaguar, ocelot, jaguarundi, tapir, peccary, anteater, gibnut, coatimundi, deer, and kinkajou. Once you arrive at the cave, a flashlight or torch is handy in exploration, along with a good pair of waterproof boots such as Wellingtons. A smaller cave in the area not connected to St. Herman's or Mountain Cow is Petroglyph Cave, named after the ancient rock drawings left inside it by Indians many centuries ago. Permission from the Department of Archaeology must be obtained to enter either Mountain Cow or Petroglyph Cave, which are beyond the borders of Blue Hole National Park. The park itself is open from 8:00 a.m. to 4:00 p.m. daily.

The hike to St. Herman's Cave from the Blue Hole is about 1.5 miles and takes about 45 minutes. An alternative route involves driving one mile north along the Hummingbird Highway, where it is possible to join the Nature Trail only 10 minutes from the cave's entrance. Look for the Blue Hole National Park sign next to a citrus orchard at about Mile 11 on the Hummingbird Highway. The trail to St. Herman's begins immediately behind the sign and curves to the right along a dirt road next to the citrus plantation.

St. Herman's was used by the Maya during the Classic period, A.D. 100 to 900, and the concrete steps leading into its mouth are laid over stone steps carved over a thousand years ago. Ancient pots used to collect "virgin water" from cave drippings, along with spears and torches, have been removed by archaeologists for study.

Besides caves and underground rivers, attractions in the area include a majestic hardwood forest that is full of ferns, orchids, bromeliads, vines, and shrubs, as well as an impressive number of birds (at least 100 species have been confirmed here). Food and drinks are available at the Oasis Bar and Restaurant, located farther south next to a Texaco gas station.

Down the road from the Oasis is St. Margaret's Village, located near the crest of ridge on the Belize and Stann Creek District borders. A poorly marked turnoff indicates the unpaved road heading north several miles to Five Blues Lake National Park. The small, 200-foot-deep lake surrounded by steep limestone hills that is the centerpiece of this attraction is so named because of the various shades of blue reflected by the sky during the course of several days, or even hours. There are hiking trails and an unimproved picnic area but no services. Orchid Island, located close to one bank of the lake, is renowned for its impressive array of wild orchids and bromeliads. Access to the heavily forested island is possible by wading across a shallow ledge. A steady flow of water from the marshy end of Five Blues Lake becomes Indian Creek, along which is a small cavern network.

Another fairly large cave that is open to the public but not as accessible as St. Herman's is Ben Lomond Cave, located in the limestone hills fringing Southern Lagoon, about 25 miles southwest of Belize City and not far from Five Blues Lake. An excellent choice for a beginner, Ben Lomond is full of ruined artifacts, and its surroundings offer a perfect example of habitat transition from savanna to tropical forest. It can only be reached by taking a boat to the lagoon and then hiking through dense coastal bush. A stream flows from the cavern's wide mouth. We recommend hiring a local guide in Gales Point or Dangriga for the trip. Bardy Riverol of Jal's Travl in Belize City offers excellent tours to destinations in this area, including Ben Lomond Cave, as does the Pelican Beach Resort in Dangriga. The seldom seen Manatee River Caves, located in the same limestone karst area, are considered extremely dangerous and should only be explored by serious cavers. At least one of these rugged caves, which vary in length from a few hundred yards to perhaps a mile or more, can be entered only by boat and is full of unstable log jams.

Belmopan

The capital city of Belize has yet to find its way onto the itinerary of most foreign visitors. This is not surprising, considering the community's meager attractions. Looking more like a second-rate college campus than a national seat of government, Belmopan's concrete and stucco buildings are spread out over a wide expanse of manicured lawns and empty lots. The main complex is clustered around a central plaza that features a lively market, several unremarkable restaurants, and a bus depot. The architecture and layout are designed to evoke a Mayan feeling: the name Belmopan combines the "Bel" of Belize with the name of the country's indigenous people, the Mopan Maya. Despite warnings that another big hurricane could level Belize City, as Hattie did in 1961, only about 6,000 Belizeans have heeded the call to relocate here.

The main attraction for travelers in Belmopan is the Archaeology Vault of the Department of Archaeology. While the vast majority of Belize's Mayan treasures have been hauled off to foreign museums and private collections, enough fine pieces remain to make a stop here worthwhile. The department staff take reservations for tours (two days notice is required) at 8-22106. The vault is only open from 1:30 to 4:30 p.m. on Mondays, Wednesdays, and Fridays. Permission from the Department of Archaeology is also required to visit Caracol and certain other Mayan ruins.

The Belize government plans to construct a national museum in Belmopan that will eventually house the Archaeology Vault collection, as well as many other historic and cultural artifacts. Projected to cost at least $3.5 million, the facility is unlikely to open before 1995.

If You Go: Belmopan is located a short distance south of the intersection of the Western and Hummingbird highways, about 35 miles in either direction from San Ignacio and Belize City. There is frequent, inexpensive bus service to Belmopan from Belize City, San Ignacio, and Dangriga. Buses run about once every 90 minutes between these communities from 8:00 a.m. to 5:00 p.m., less often on weekends and holidays.

Services in Belmopan include a bank, a post office, and several restaurants. There are no inexpensive accommodations, although the Bull Frog Inn and Circle "A" Lodge (both on Halfmoon Ave.) are moderately priced.

Guanacaste National Park

On Earth Day (April 22), 1990, the Belizean government officially created 52-acre Guanacaste National Park in a lush parcel of forest alongside the Belize River. Located only 2 miles from Belmopan, at the intersection of the Hummingbird and Western highways, the park is named after a huge guanacaste tree growing near the reserve's southwestern boundary. Also known as the tubroos or monkey's ear tree, the guanacaste is a highly prized hardwood known for its resistance to insects and decay. Guanacaste lumber is the material of choice for construction of dugout canoes, feeding troughs, and rice-hulling mortars. Cattle and monkeys love to nibble on guanacaste fruit, which appear as shiny brown pods during the dry season after an explosion of small white flowers.

This particular giant (the species is one of the largest in Central America) towers more than 120 feet above the jungle and was only spared the woodcutter's ax because splits in its massive trunk make it unusable as timber (all other guanacaste in the park have been harvested). The tree's broad, sky-seeking branches support hundreds of epiphytes, including many brilliant species of orchid and bromeliad.

A short trail leads through the forest to the guanacaste tree from a visitors' center operated by the Belize Audubon Society. Other large trees seen along the way include the mammee apple, bookut, ramon, quamwood, silk cotton, and raintree. Several mahogany trees have been planted near the park's visitor center as part of a reforestation program.

Despite Guanacaste's diminutive size, it harbors an abundant wildlife population. Species observed here include jaguarundi, kinkajou, paca, armadillo, iguana, deer, and opossum. Resident birds include the blue-crowned motmot, black-faced ant thrush, smoky-brown woodpecker, red-lored parrot, black-headed trogon, and squirrel cuckoo, among more than 50 confirmed species.

Guanacaste National Park is just past the Cayo District boundary and easily accessible by bus, taxi, private car, or package tour. Rest rooms, drinking water, and picnic facilities are available. Cooking and camping are not permitted, however. The Chicago-based MacArthur Foundation has helped fund construction of a well-maintained trail network throughout the park which follows a graceful curve of the Belize River at the confluence of Roaring Creek. If you are new to Belize, this is an excellent place to become acquainted with the country's native flora and fauna.

Río Bravo Conservation and Management Area

A nonprofit group called Programme for Belize has, since its formation in 1988, achieved remarkable success in protecting a major portion of the northwest corner of Belize as a pristine lowland jungle. Thanks to their intervention, this forest remains one of the largest tracts of undisturbed subtropical habitat in the region. From its inception, the sponsoring group's primary objectives have been to create a model of appropriate economic development and to provide funding for conservation, education, and scientific and management training throughout the country for the lasting preservation of Belize's natural heritage and biological diversity.

Programme for Belize has acquired about 110,000 acres of its own in the Río Bravo Conservation and Management Area, in what the organization describes as "a vast tropical forest held in trust for the people of Belize." Another large tract of land, 42,000 acres, was donated by Coca-Cola Foods. Finally, in a cooperative agreement with landowners, an additional 125,000 acres owned by Belizean entrepreneur Barry Bowen are now being managed in a remarkable coordinated fashion to achieve the Programme's objectives.

This organization has raised over $6 million dollars to administer these wildlife-rich lands, which in 1991 totaled over 280,000 acres. Programme for Belize intends to be financially self-sufficient from

1995 but is still entirely dependent on outside funding by organizations, corporations, and individuals that share the long-term goals of this project. Private contributors are invited to donate $50 to protect an acre of tropical forest, something many schoolchildren have done as class projects throughout the United States and Europe. (Certificates are sent verifying the protection made possible by these $50 donations.)

Most of the Río Bravo area is a nearly untouched subtropical haven where howler monkeys, spider monkeys, king vultures, gray foxes, over 80 species of bats, and 110 species of orchids now enjoy a permanent refuge. Some 200 species of trees have been identified here so far. All 5 Belizean species of cats naturally occur here: margay, jaguarundi, jaguar, puma, and ocelot. And nearly 400 species of birds have been identified as either year-round residents or migrant species that frequent the area.

The government-approved management plan for the Río Bravo Conservation Area allows for the development of low-impact tourism based on archaeology and natural history tourism, plus some agricultural projects as well as limited and sustained-yield use of forest resources. Programme for Belize is hopeful that this multiple-use scheme can serve as a model as Belize weighs the benefits and costs in seeking United Nations Biosphere Reserve designation for other regions of the country. The entire area could one day become part of a multinational El Mundo Maya Park, combined with Mexico's Calakmul Biosphere Reserve and Guatemala's Maya Biosphere Reserve.

The Río Bravo Conservation and Management Area covers the northeastern part of the Petén Region, a large biogeographically distinct expanse that extends into southeastern Mexico and northern Guatemala. Río Bravo is now mostly undisturbed by human activities; however, parts of the area were once occupied by the Maya. Remains of their once-flourishing cities and homesites dot the entire region, and it is virtually impossible to walk in the forest without coming across evidence of their occupation.

Several levels of escarpments have developed over time near Río Bravo's eastern border. These dramatic terraces, which can easily be seen from the air, dissect the Río Bravo from northeast to southwest and are the only variation in an otherwise gently undulating forest carpeted terrain. Visitors who fly into the Río Bravo wilderness might spot majestic king vultures as they circle high over the escarpments, constantly searching for signs of their next carrion meal.

Nick Brokaw and Elizabeth Mallory, arguably two of the most qualified scientists currently working in Belize, have identified more than a dozen floristically distinct vegetation types in Río Bravo. Their research focuses on five general types: upland forest, palm forest, swamp forest, riparian forest, and second growth. A new research facility has been constructed by Belizeans deep within the forest and strategically located for easy access to these distinct habitat types. This facility provides training in archaeology, forest management, and ecology while concurrently monitoring the reserve's biological diversity.

Part of the motivation for Programme for Belize's sponsorship of scientific research is to determine the best "uses" for the area's forests, whether ecologically sensitive tourism or low-impact timber harvesting. The Programme and its scientists are actively studying forest types and the region's overall ecology to correlate this data to various sustainable timber harvest, agricultural, and agroforestry experiments currently under way. For example, to the south of the Río Bravo Conservation Area are 125,000 acres owned by Gallon Jug Agroindustry, Ltd. The center of this enterprise is located at Gallon Jug, once a major logging town and now a tiny residential center. Many families find employment here and in nearby Sylvesterville, since approximately 1,800 acres of this forest have been cleared for agriculture. The plan is to expand these clearings to make way for more agroforestry experiments. Río Bravo is the only place in Belize where coordination between large-scale habitat conservation and sustainable development is occurring.

A large tract of land farther south of Río Bravo, covering about 200,000 acres, is still heavily forested. The western portion of this Yalbac Ranch and Cattle Company-owned jungle is scheduled to be logged for mahogany and other tropical hardwoods. Other land, adjacent to the northern and northwestern borders of the reserve, is owned by Mennonite farmers and an American family, who are

Cabanas at Chan Chich Jungle Lodge (Photo by Kevin Schafer)

engaged in logging and other agricultural activity. A large tract south of the Mexican border has been almost completely turned over to cattle ranching and farming.

Although difficult for some environmentalists to embrace, Programme for Belize is taking a realistic approach to conservation and sustainable development. Preserving wildlife and the forest is one primary objective at Río Bravo, but there is recognition that conservation must generate income and cannot lock up resources forever. The Programme's goal is for people to benefit from the land and its resources, without destroying them for future generations.

Visitors wishing to see the Programme for Belize lands for themselves are best off staying in the jungle lodge near Gallon Jug called Chan Chich, meaning "little bird" in Mayan. This is a luxurious grouping of elegant cabanas set in the middle of a Classic period Mayan ruin. The accommodations were constructed for Belizean businessman Barry Bowen (the lodge's owner) by Tom and Josie Harding. Ancient Mayan monuments border the resort's grounds on all sides, giving the impression, when viewed from the outside, that the cabanas are original Mayan homes. Their plush insides, however, give a different impression. Polished and oiled woodwork, colorful drapes, a full bar, and a fine dining room combine to make Chan Chich one of the Belize's finest lodges. Indeed, it has received a top ranking in at least one world survey of jungle accommodations.

By prior arrangement with Programme for Belize, tourists can visit the nearby La Milpa archaeological site. (See chap. 6 for more details.) Other activities around Chan Chich and the Río Bravo wilderness include superb bird-watching (visitors may identify 200 species in a week and hear 20 others), jungle walks, canoeing, horseback riding, guided nature and archaeological tours, and simply relaxing. The Chan Chich motto sums up the experience well: "It's a jungle out there!"

If You Go: Book a stay at Chan Chich Lodge well in advance by contacting Programme for Belize in Belize City at 1 King Street (2-75616 or 2-75634). In the United States, call (800) 343-8009. Until the weather has been dry, it is best to fly to Gallon Jug rather than attempt the rough dirt roads to the area on your own. Javier's Flying Service, Ltd. (tel. 2-45332) is one of the best charter companies and flies frequently to the area. Expect to pay at least $150 round-trip from Belize City. Javier's offers a day trip to Chan Chich for about the same price which includes a forest tour with a naturalist and lunch at the Chan Chich Lodge.

It is possible to drive to Gallon Jug by turning north at Orange Walk Village (not to be confused with Orange Walk Town) near Belmopan and following the Iguana Creek Bridge road or by turning south from just west of Blue Creek Village near the Mexican border. The latter route is shorter (about 4 hours from Belize City) and better maintained than the former. Be sure to inquire locally about road conditions, especially when the ground is wet. A four-wheel-drive vehicle is recommended during any season. By the time you read this, a fleet of vans may be in place to take registered guests to the site from Belize City.

Programme for Belize also can accommodate up to 22 guests in a dormitory-style education and research facility in Gallon Jug. Individuals can stay here for about $45 per night by making arrangements through Rene Nuñez, senior project coordinator, in Belize City at 2-75616 (fax 2-75635).

Excellent educational resources for visitors to this area include cassette tapes of bird songs and calls made by Wildlife Conservation International research fellow Bruce Miller. Miller and his wife, Carolyn, also a WCI field scientist, wrote *Exploring the Rainforest*, a 64-page trail and natural history guide to the Chan Chich area that includes an exhaustive flora and fauna checklist for all of Belize. The Millers live in Gallon Jug and guide occasional tours through the Río Bravo lands.

Society Hall Nature Reserve

Wedged between Roaring Creek and Upper Barton Creek in the northern foothills of the Mountain Pine Ridge, not far from the capital city of Belmopan, the 6,741-acre Society Hall Nature Reserve is an intact block of tropical forest and home to all manner of flora and fauna. It has been kept this way because of the determination and foresight of its conservation-minded landowner.

Svea Dietrich-Ward had for many years sought a way to permanently save Society Hall, located between Hidden Valley Falls and the Western Highway in the Cayo District. Finally, in November 1986, the German conservationist (who now raises Arabian horses near San Ignacio) entered a long-term lease agreement with the government of Belize on the condition that the property's natural resources would be protected. Soon after, officials proclaimed it a "nature reserve." (In Belize, this label is a subcategory of the 1981 National Parks System Act specifying that such lands be preserved for scientific research and education only.)

The nature reserve designation means that Society Hall is not a destination for the casual tourist; researchers with specific scientific objectives who seek prior permission and groups of students with competent leaders who do the same are the only visitors legally allowed here. In addition, the qualifications list of the Belize Audubon Society is longer still, since that organization has also been entrusted with management duties for Society Hall.

Perhaps the greatest threat to the Society Hall Nature Reserve is from encroachment into the reserve by slash-and-burn agriculture. A growing number of Guatemalan and Salvadoran refugees are practicing this traditional form of agriculture very near its boundaries. There have even been reports of this forest-destroying practice actually occurring within Society Hall's borders, apparently taking advantage of the fact that the area is so remote. This is compounded by the lack of access for land managers to monitor and help prevent such deforestation. At Dietrich-Ward's requests, the conservation flying group, LightHawk, has monitored and shown law enforcement officers these incursions from the air for several years.

The whole area consists of undulating limestone karst topography dotted with sinkholes, exposed rock outcrops, small streams, and even a bubbling spring. Middens—the garbage heaps of the Mayans consisting mostly of shells, pot shards, and bones—are concealed by a dense forest of lianas (climbing vines), cohune palms, and scores of other tree species. In some of the valleys and low-lying portions of this reserve, the forest canopy crests at nearly 100 feet. Massive brown termite nests envelop tree trunks here and there, while leaf-cutter ants march past brilliant red and yellow giant heliconias, methodically going about the rigorous business of collecting and transporting food for their vast colonies. Once the leaves are collected, they are masticated and regurgitated by the ants, who subsequently consume the fungus-covered results.

Like much of Belize, Society Hall has probably been selectively logged for tree species such as mahogany, santa maría, and Spanish cedar. This species-specific logging has left the rest of the reserve's tropical broadleaf moist forest practically untouched.

If You Go: Because of its highly protected status, access to the Society Hall Nature Reserve is strictly limited to scientists and other researchers. Contact the Belize Audubon Society in Belize City for information about qualifications and procedures.

Chapter 6

Cockscomb Basin Wildlife Sanctuary

Standing at the entrance to the Cockscomb Basin Wildlife Sanctuary, with a modest sign wired to the pendulum gate and lush tropical forest as a backdrop, visitors may sense that beyond lies an exotic domain rich in history and wildlife. And, as one enters, this intuition will unquestionably be proven correct.

The huge tract of Stann Creek District wilderness locally referred to as "the Cockscomb," situated in a sweeping mountainside basin about 25 miles southwest of Dangriga, is the world's first-ever reserve established to protect the jaguar. It is steeped in a dynamic evolution of nature's wonders, scientific research, and conservation prowess.

The Cockscomb Basin Wildlife Sanctuary is highly recommended as a rewarding destination for the traveler who wants to actively support Belizean conservation while simultaneously reaping its benefits. This is one of the least expensive and most impressive locales for exploring Belize's lush tropical forest interior. Wildlife and plant life are abundant, and the patient visitor will probably see some truly exotic creatures.

From the combination registration hut and craft shop in the village of Maya Center (a mandatory check-in stop), just off the Southern Highway, you travel about 7 miles on a rough dirt road to arrive at the Cockscomb visitor's center, campground, and guest huts. Stay alert as you proceed up this road. You may be fortunate enough to see a tayra, a small weasel-like animal. A turkey-sized crested guan or a flock of toucans may also catch your eye in the forest canopy.

There is a small parking lot at the sanctuary's headquarters, located at the site of an abandoned lumber camp that is littered with some of the iron cages used by zoologist Alan Rabinowitz in his pioneering studies of the jaguar here during the mid-1980s. Nearby is a campground and rustic cabins available for overnight travelers. From the visitor's center and museum, one can head out for a self-guided tour along a number of well-maintained forest trails. Brochures, maps, and signposts help identify the various tree and plant species seen along the way, which include vibrant wild orchids and enormous naturally buttressed hardwoods. These pathways vary considerably in their length and ruggedness, so check with the resident manager before heading out. Fortunately, there are some fine swimming holes not far from the visitor's center where you can cool off after a strenuous trek.

Within minutes of arrival, one realizes why the Cockscomb Basin has a reputation as a bird-watcher's paradise. At least 290 species have been recorded here, including the endangered and dazzling scarlet macaw, chestnut-brown Montezuma oropendola (with bright yellow tail), Agami heron, collared aracari, keel-billed toucan, and king vulture.

In addition, the basin provides habitat for many amphibians, lizards, and snakes. Recent observations by a team of Belizean conservation leaders and scientists identified over 35 species that included 9 snakes, 12 lizards, 14 amphibians, and a frog known as *Smilisca phaeota*, not previously recorded in Belize. The red-eyed tree frog was also identified, and a major breeding area for it was located. The team estimated that the Cockscomb provides habitat for roughly 70 percent of Belize's nonmarine reptiles.

Among the main attractions for any visitor, of course, are the cats of Cockscomb. Because of their mostly nocturnal habits, however, the odds are that you will not actually see one. Still, your chances are better here than perhaps anyplace else. Besides embracing one of the highest concentrations of jaguars anywhere in the world, the sanctuary is home to many ocelots, margays, jaguarundis, and pumas. Best bets for a sighting are along the roads and riverbanks of the Cockscomb, where the felines like to hunt. Try not to be disappointed if you never see one of these creatures. Some researchers have waited weeks and months during their intensive field studies here only to catch brief glimpses of the elusive animals.

The Cockscomb Basin's human history dates back to the ancient Maya, who left a Classic era ceremonial site called Chucil Baalum deep within the forest. Pockets of fertile soil helped support their milpa agriculture for many generations. The last of the Maya's descendants were relocated during the late 1980s in the interest of wildlife habitat preservation.

Cockscomb also has survived its share of logging. Selective harvesting of such commercial tree species as mahogany and cedar was carried on for years in the area. The massive logs were cut and skidded from the forest, then floated the length of South Stann Creek to the coast, where they were loaded on tugboats and taken to market in Belize City. Logging camps with painfully descriptive names like Sale Si Puede (Leave If You Can) and Go To Hell have been reclaimed by the basin's subtropical wet forest, which attains a canopy height of between 40 and 120 feet.

The Cockscomb's powers of forest regeneration are among its most intriguing qualities. When you consider the hurricane damage inflicted on many of its tall trees and the collective insults of slash-and-burn agriculture and timber cutting over long periods of time, the lush character of the area is startling. Tree species found within the Cockscomb watershed include banak, cohune palm, ceiba, negrito, quamwood, yemeri, ironwood, Santa María, barba jolote, and mahogany. Bromeliads, tree ferns, giant heliconias, bamboo groves, climbing vines, and scores of other plants add to the density of the forest.

If you hike along the entrance road, you will need an experienced local guide to distinguish what is left of an airstrip that was last used in 1984 to facilitate radio tracking during Rabinowitz's studies of the jaguar. In a few short years, the tropical forest has almost completely taken over what was once a completely bare piece of land. At one end of the runway a narrow trail leads to a crash site, where a small plane still hangs from the forest canopy. The passengers (Rabinowitz, a pilot, and cameraman) were only slightly injured.

Back at the Cockscomb visitor's center, you can see Victoria Peak jutting up from the back of the basin. At 3,675 feet, this is Belize's most spectacular mountain. Sheathed in verdant forest, the rocky summit is capped by dark quartzite. At four million years, Victoria Peak may be part of the oldest geologic formation in Central America.

Victoria Peak and the Cockscomb Range have been sailors' landmarks for centuries. If you visit South Water Caye (or any of the other islands off Dangriga) and are blessed with clear weather, the sunset behind the pinnacle of Victoria Peak will long persist in your memory.

The most recent—and perhaps the most relevant—sequence of human involvement in the Cockscomb Basin is the effort to protect

it. This campaign initially focused on preserving the jaguar, a predatory "indicator species" that can serve as a good index of an ecosystem's health. The chain of events leading up to Prime Minister
Price's designation of this area as a permanent wildlife haven began
in 1983 with a two-year jaguar study sponsored by Wildlife Conservation International, a division of the New York Zoological Society.
Living in what is now a restricted-access warden's building, Rabinowitz carried out an intensive field study of the jaguar's range, diet,
habits, and general ecology. The American scientist trapped several
jaguars, recorded their vital statistics, and fitted them with radio collars. This enabled him to track the felines and thus determine the size
and location of their territorial ranges. Rabinowitz lived among the
Mayan Indians, employed several of them during his studies, and
chronicled his many adventures, with certain embellishments, in a
book entitled *Jaguar*.

With strong backing from Wildlife Conservation International and
important in-country political assistance from the Belize Audubon
Society, Rabinowitz recommended the area become an official jaguar
sanctuary. In late 1984, the Cockscomb Basin was declared a national forest reserve with a "no hunting" clause to protect the jaguar. The
World Wildlife Fund then provided crucial financial assistance to
support the establishment, protection, and maintenance of the basin
as a protected area.

After much deliberation about the trade-offs involved, in 1986, the
Belize government declared 3,000 acres of the 108,000-acre area as
the Cockscomb Basin Wildlife Sanctuary/Forest Reserve. This made
it the first country to protect an area specifically for jaguars.

Several Mayan families were required to move down the road to
Maya Center, where they have made the transition from milpa agriculture to craftwork. Their crafts cooperative now sells the work of
local artisans at the Maya Center visitors' registration booth. Some of
the men transplanted from sanctuary lands are employed there as
managers, caretakers, and guides. The Mayan-descended Belizean
now in charge of the reserve, Ernesto Saqui, is one of the best trained
and most knowledgeable natural area managers in Central America.

In November 1990, the Cockscomb Basin Wildlife Sanctuary was
expanded to include 102,000 acres of the Cockscomb Basin. This

feat was accomplished through the joint efforts of the Belize Audubon Society, World Wildlife Fund, and other conservation groups. Ongoing management by the Belize Audubon Society has made it possible for the Cockscomb to emerge as a successful model of ecosystem conservation that integrates low-impact tourism. In addition, wildlife habitat and ecosystem field studies, such as a 1990 expedition sponsored by the Belize Center for Environmental Studies, are crucial to continued success and refinements in the Cockscomb's management.

The most royal creatures of today's Cockscomb Basin, as in the Mayan era, are its many jaguars. This cat is the third largest of its genus in the world and the most powerful land predator in Central and South America. The jaguar is called tiger by many Belizeans, *tigre* by local Spanish-speakers, and *balum* by the Maya. Its diet includes the white-lipped peccaries, armadillos, agoutis, Virginia opossums, iguanas, coatis, and kinkajous that inhabit the area. Even if they cannot see them, Cockscomb visitors sometimes swear they can feel the presence of these elegant and graceful creatures, particularly when taking a nighttime walk along the sanctuary's main road. The croaking of thousands of frogs in the shallow ponds outside the guest huts takes on heightened meaning during such a stroll.

Incidentally, jaguars are not known to attack humans, except when provoked. It is not as if they are incapable of succeeding in such a foray, however. They are believed to sometimes prey on the Baird's tapir, an endangered relative of the horse (locally called the "mountain cow") that may attain 650 pounds when fully grown. You can sometimes see the tapir's skidding tracks in the muddy banks of South Stann Creek. Like the jaguar, the tapir is very shy, so these tracks may be your closest encounter.

During hikes through the Cockscomb, one may also come across the Central American river otter, a playful mammal that epitomizes a carpe diem, exuberant life-style. Seeing one frolic or fish in the perfectly clear waters of Cockscomb's rivers is a real thrill.

In the wake of Rabinowitz's studies of the jaguar, several other scientists have also used the Cockscomb as a field research base. One often-overlooked researcher is Michael J. Konecny, who lived in the Cockscomb from 1984 to 1986 and studied other carnivores that inhabit the sanctuary. Konecny was then affiliated with the University of Florida. The National Geographic Society supported the bulk of his work, and he received additional financial assistance from the National Wildlife Federation.

Like Rabinowitz, Konecny trapped the animals he was studying and affixed them with radio collars. This allowed him to determine their ranges and habits, as he monitored their movements from aircraft. During his eighteen months of fieldwork, Konecny collected an enormous amount of data about these seldom-studied mammals. He confirmed, for instance, that the jaguarundi and tayra are active during the day, while the ocelot and margay are nocturnal.

This was the first attempt to study the ecology of some of these species, including the house cat-sized margay. Although the density of margay in the Cockscomb appeared rather low at the time, Konecny was able to gather some fascinating facts about the arboreal feline, known to jump more than 8 feet straight up into an overhanging branch. Based on information collected from several captured ocelots, the scientist concluded that these graceful creatures were having trouble reproducing fast enough to keep up with losses to human hunters and deforestation.

Konecny also shed early light on the ecology of the relatively unknown tayra, a weasel-like species whose hind legs are longer than its front legs, giving it an advantage for climbing. Called "bushdog" by Creoles and *cabeza de viejo* (head of an old man) by Spanish-speakers, the tayra is a fierce-looking omnivore that thrives on fruit, insects, and small vertebrates. Konecny encountered this unusual creature on fifteen separate occasions, suggesting it may be one of the easiest of Cockscomb's mammals to see. We saw a tayra cross the entrance road on our first trip to the sanctuary.

Visitors interested in the ecology of the many animals roaming the Cockscomb Basin Wildlife Sanctuary owe much to the work of Michael Konecny, Alan Rabinowitz, Ben Nottingham (Rabinowitz's partner), and others who have turned the basin into a living laboratory. A major step in this direction took place in 1992 when Fred Koontz of the Bronx Zoo helped supervise the successful reintroduction of howler monkeys to the Cockscomb after an absence of many years, due to disease and hurricane damage. Much more work remains to be done, however. None of the carnivore studies, for example, gathered any data about the puma (or mountain lion). Although they are suspected to inhabit the area, the puma's place in the field community remains a mystery.

As you make your way along the Cockscomb's pathways, keep your eyes open for the creatures that make this their home. Even fleeting sightings of discreet animals like the puma (which should be reported to the sanctuary manager) are valued by the scientific community. And nowhere else in Belize will you find such an organized system of well-maintained trails. They are quite wide, and most are short and level enough that they do not involve difficult hiking. A complete trail map is posted in front of the visitor's center and guest huts.

The Ben's Bluff Trail takes the more ambitious walker, willing to endure a strenuous but short trek, to a ridgetop from which can be seen a good part of the entire Cockscomb Basin. This high point has been frequently used to track jaguar via radiowaves. Picture a researcher slowly sweep the antennae back and forth across the dense jungle that stretches for miles before him. Or envision the wily cat, resting in the shade of a tall tropical hardwood (probably one you are unwittingly staring at) or stalking its prey along the bank of a bubbling stream.

A much easier trail takes you to a bank of South Stann Creek for a refreshing plunge into clear, swiftly flowing water. This swimming hole also has a picnic area beneath a shady tree. Yet another trail heads in a westerly direction from the visitor's center, past the camping area and in the direction of Victoria's Peak. It is cut through a bamboo grove that is a remarkable sight for visitors who have never encountered such a dense and sticky thicket. A side trail on the left, past the bamboo thicket, takes you well into the forest, over a picturesque suspension bridge, and past a swampy area that is a fascinating observation ground for the Cockscomb's many amphibians (provided you can endure the millions of mosquitoes).

If You Go: There is only one road in and out of the Cockscomb Basin. It is well marked and intersects the Southern Highway at the Mopan village of Maya Center, about 25 miles south of Dangriga.

The Cockscomb's headquarters are about 7 miles up the dirt road. It is possible to walk there from the Southern Highway, but no services exist en route, and it can get very hot and dusty. The road has been improved in recent years but is sometimes impassable during very wet weather, even for those on foot.

All tourists must register at the visitors' booth in Maya Center before heading into the Cockscomb. Cold drinks and Mayan crafts are also sold here.

There are rustic, dorm-style cabins (about $8 a night) and camp-sites ($2) for rent near the Cockscomb reserve manager's headquarters. Reservations are strongly recommended, especially from November through April; contact the Belize Audubon Society office in Belize City or Pelican Beach Resort in Dangriga. There is fresh water, but you must bring your own food and other provisions (a stove is available). Those who do not wish to spend the night can easily find accommodations in Dangriga, Placencia, and Big Creek. Tours can be arranged from these locations, or you can get dropped off by one of the buses heading by the entrance and walk in (ask to be let off at Maya Center). Trail maps are available at the headquarters. Guides can be hired on site for about $14 with a two-visitor minimum.

There are fine swimming holes in the Cockscomb along South Stann Creek, so you may wish to bring a swimsuit, a towel, and sunscreen. Long-sleeved shirts, trousers, and hats are advisable. Tuck your pant legs into your socks to repel chiggers. Without such preparations, plus insect repellent, a visit can become very uncomfortable.

Bladen Nature Reserve

The 1990 designation of the Bladen Branch (of the Monkey River) watershed area as a nature reserve set a significant benchmark in the race to protect the earth's most biologically diverse ecosystems— tropical forests—before humanity destroys them. Protection of this 92,000-acre Toledo District wilderness, sprawling across the rugged foothills of the Maya Mountains, set the stage for an even grander vision in which Bladen may become the heart of a vast sanctuary that would be unique in Central America because of its size (a large percentage of the entire country of Belize) and scope (incorporating some of the least-disturbed forest in the hemisphere).

The Bladen Nature Reserve provides refuge for at least 194 bird species and several hundred plant species, in addition to such environmentally significant creatures as the Baird's tapir, white-lipped peccary, mountain lion, iguana, jaguar, southern river otter, white-tailed deer, brocket deer, and Geoffroy's spider monkey. Some of the Bladen's important birds include the king vulture, mealy parrot, slaty-breasted tinamou, and rufous-capped warbler. The area contains uninvestigated Mayan ruins amid its steep mountains, conical limestone outcrops, sinkholes, caves, underground streams, and waterfalls. Within the reserve's boundaries is Richardson Peak, second-highest mountain in Belize.

Local conservation leaders such as Dora Weyer had long recognized Bladen's significance as an unspoiled, remote haven for wildlife. As early as 1984, the upper Bladen watershed appeared first on a "wish list" of proposed protected areas. The Belize Country Environmental Profile characterized the upper Bladen Branch as almost completely undisturbed by man. It collects water from a series of almost parallel creeks that drain the main divide of the Maya Mountains over approximately 135 square miles. The lower watershed is subtropical wet forest, while higher areas include subtropical lower montane wet forest, with cloud elfin forest on the higher peaks. Reports from the few early expeditions to the upper Bladen include sightings of tapirs, spider monkeys, the great curassow, and the crested guan.

A 1987 biological survey of the upper Bladen Branch watershed by scientists from the Manomet Bird Observatory and the Missouri Botanical Garden (sponsored by the Brehm Fund of West Germany) yielded a special report that remains the most in-depth biological analysis of the Bladen's flora and fauna. It was then that the conservation group LightHawk joined with Victor Gonzalez (then the Belize Audubon Society's president, now the permanent secretary for the Ministry of Tourism and Environment) to convince Belize authorities to protect the Bladen.

Over a period of three years, LightHawk flew government leaders over the rugged Bladen area, providing many with their first look at the watershed. Early proposals to allow logging were thus thwarted, and the value of preserving this vast freshwater catchment became clear. At this time the area was part of the Maya Mountain Forest Reserve (a multiple-use designation in Belize that allows selective logging), so significant justification was needed for the government to set it aside. In a position paper prepared by LightHawk and Gonzalez justifying protection of the Bladen, it was argued that the region's protection would "preserve an important sample of Belize's heritage of wildlife and forest," as well as help ensure a steady stream of pure water to many downstream users. "The problems of accessibility and ruggedness of the terrain," the report concluded, "make the Bladen watershed undesirable for logging."

Finally, with the help of the World Parks Endowment and a financial commitment from the Frank Weeden Foundation, the moment arrived. On World Environment Day (June 5) in 1990, Deputy Prime Minister Marin signed a document creating the Bladen Nature Reserve. As a nature reserve, only educational activities and scientific research are allowed within the Bladen's boundaries. Like the Society Hall Nature Reserve, special permission is required for scientists and educators to visit the Bladen reserve. The primary motivation is to protect the integrity of the watershed and the abundant wildlife that inhabits it. The Bladen reserve was not set aside for the benefit of tourists, although low-impact tourism may be considered in the future as a means of generating income for residents of the area.

The upper Bladen Branch watershed shows traces of the past presence of ancient Maya. An alluvial valley in the area called Quebrada de Oro (Spanish for "the passageway of gold") contains Mayan ruins that have never been excavated by archaeologists. Participants in the Missouri Botanical Garden/Manomet Bird Observatory field study found eighteen roughly rectangular mounds here, now overgrown by vegetation. The block-style construction of these structures indicates they were Mayan houses that were subsequently used as tombs for their inhabitants. An abundance of breadfruit trees suggests that the Mayan inhabitants cultivated this species, as they did at Tikal. West of the first grouping, the team also located an integrated arrangement of ruins in many different shapes and sizes, including a raised avenue and courts. There appeared to be some looting of the Mayan ruins at Quebrada de Oro and at this more western site in the Bladen.

Specialists on the same field expedition identified about 90 tree species in the Bladen, including cramtree, copal, white gumbo-limbo, banak, ironwood, breadnut, and mammee apple. The most abundant woody plant was the spiny understory palm. This species, much shorter than trees reaching the forest's canopy, commands even greater respect than the giants of the forest. Its long sturdy spines treat anyone coming into contact with it to a painful ordeal that is not soon forgotten. Less common trees identified by the Manomet team included the bullhoof, ceiba, hogplum, mapola, mylady, ormiga, red gumbo-limbo, waika chewstick mahogany, Spanish cedar, and wild mammee.

Using a technique called "mist netting," visiting scientists catch birds in fine mesh nets stretched between trees. They are then banded and recorded by age, sex, wing length, weight, breeding condition, and other features. Thirty species of migrants, most of which nest far to the north in the temperate zone, have been seen in the Bladen. The barred forest-falcon, vermiculated screech owl, white-necked jacobin, keel-billed motmot, barred antshrike, eye-ringed flatbill, royal flycatcher, rose-throated becard, prothonotary warbler, yellow-throated euphonia, blue grosbeak, and yellow-billed cacique are among birds seen less frequently here. Birds that remain in the canopy or feed on the wing—such as parrots, toucans, hawks, and swifts—do not generally get caught in the mist nets and could only be identified through a censusing technique whereby researchers fan out at given times and locations to seek them out. Such strategies have yielded 2 species found elsewhere in Central America but not previously recorded in the Maya Mountains: the magnificent hummingbird and Audubon's oriole.

As of mid-1993, there was still a pressing need for on-the-ground management of the Bladen Nature Reserve. Illegal hunting, looting of archaeological resources, and unregulated visitation have created an urgent demand for full-time reserve wardens.

As you read this, the Bladen may have become the core of a much larger protected area through its possible designation as a United Nations (UNESCO) Man and the Biosphere Reserve. The government has considered linking, through protective declarations, the

Chiquibul National Park east to the Maya Mountain Divide, including the rugged Trio watershed that is sandwiched between the Bladen Nature Reserve and the Cockscomb Basin Wildlife Sanctuary.

If interconnected as a Biosphere Reserve, this Chiquibul-Bladen-Trio-Cockscomb combination would likely become one of the most biologically diverse and significant natural areas under protective designation in Central America. While ecologically sensitive development in the form of low-impact tourism and sustainable harvest of forest products might continue in appropriate parts of the reserve, such core areas as the Bladen should remain fully protected.

These types of vast and biologically diverse habitat corridors can continue to support viable populations of large predators like the jaguar. An abundance of such fauna at the top of nature's food chain serves as an indicator of the health of the entire ecosystem. Whatever the outcome, two things are certain: the government of Belize has set an international standard in protecting the existing pristine watershed. As one Belizean put it, "The Bladen is a little gem, and it shines."

If You Go: Access to the Bladen Nature Reserve is limited to qualified scientists, archaeologists, and other designated researchers. Permission must be obtained in advance from the Belize Audubon Society and government officials.

Mayan Ruins

Neither archaeologists nor government officials know exactly how many ancient Mayan sites there are in Belize, but certainly the number is in the thousands. The remnants of Mayan occupation, ranging from microscopic vegetable pollen found in the dust of pottery shards to sky-scraping temples poking through the jungle canopy, are found from border to border. They are even commonplace on the offshore islands. It is now widely conceded that Belize was at one time at the very heart of Mayan civilization. Experts speculate that this relatively small territory may have easily supported as many as a million or more Maya, five times the present population.

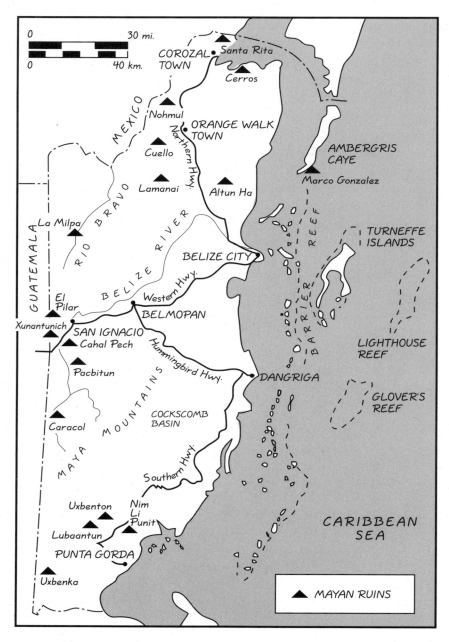

Belize's Major Mayan Sites

Within the map:

0   30 mi.
0   40 km.

COROZAL TOWN   Santa Rita

Cerros

MEXICO

Nohmul

ORANGE WALK TOWN

Cuello

Northern Hwy.

AMBERGRIS CAYE

Lamanai

Altun Ha

Marco Gonzalez

RIO BRAVO

La Milpa

BELIZE RIVER

BELIZE CITY

TURNEFFE ISLANDS

GUATEMALA

El Pilar

BELIZE RIVER

Western Hwy.

BELMOPAN

BARRIER REEF

Xunantunich

SAN IGNACIO
Cahal Pech

LIGHTHOUSE REEF

Pacbitun

Hummingbird Hwy.

DANGRIGA

GLOVER'S REEF

MAYA MOUNTAINS

COCKSCOMB BASIN

Caracol

Southern Hwy.

Uxbenton   Nim Li Punit

CARIBBEAN SEA

Lubaantun

PUNTA GORDA

Uxbenka

▲ MAYAN RUINS

Yet despite their clear domination of the area for hundreds of years, precious little is known about these early residents. Formal excavation of the largest ruins is relatively recent, and much of the early archaeological work is now regarded as amateurish and slipshod. Many important sites have remained virtually untouched, and others have been the object of only cursory field research. Even Caracol, the country's biggest Mayan complex, had seen no serious investigation until the mid-1980s.

Although many foreign agencies and universities are now helping the Belizeans study and preserve their Mayan relics, many precious artifacts have already been lost forever to looters, farmers, adventurers, and the vagaries of nature. A great threat continues to exist, as the impoverished and unscrupulous plunder sites anew in the hope of finding valuables that can be sold to collectors for starting prices of about $300 per pot. In some areas, the limestone ruins are also still being carted away piece by piece, to be ground up by local residents for the ingredients of cement or used as building blocks.

Unlike Mexico and Guatemala, Belize has lacked sufficient funds to restore its ancient Mayan cities, and only a handful of caretakers are looking after them. Informed guides are rare; literature on the individual sites is hard to come by. Access to many locations is difficult. In some cases, the ruins are on private property. Even during the peak tourist season, it is not uncommon to find oneself entirely alone at one of these Mayan ruins, or in the company of a single resident manager.

For travelers with an interest in the Mayan history of Belize, we suggest some background reading before setting out (see Appendix for suggested books). Once you are in-country, by far the best local guidebook is *Warlords and Maize Men: A Guide to the Maya Sites of Belize*, which contains detailed travel instructions and maps, plus photographs and archaeological histories for each location. Another good resource is *The Belizean Bullet*, an infrequent publication of the Department of Archaeology that provides detailed information about ongoing research.

Keep in mind that under Belize law, all "ancient monuments" (structures over 100 years old) and "antiquities" (man-made articles crafted more than 150 years ago) are the property of the state. Their removal, destruction, or possession is expressly forbidden without the permission of federal authorities. The collecting, buying, and selling of such artifacts is also illegal, and anyone seen engaged in such activity should be reported at once. Looting continues to be the single biggest threat to the integrity of Belize's Mayan sites.

Beware also that a thriving business exists in imitation artifacts, and many travelers spend good money on cheap fakes. Trading in these items is not illegal, but without proper documentation, the items may be seized by customs officials when departing the country.

Because of the varying degrees of isolation of the sites, it is best to visit during the drier months (February through May). Remember, however, that it can rain at any time and place, and waterproof boots or shoes are advisable. Lightweight, comfortable clothing should be worn, and a hat or raincoat may be useful. It is also a good idea to bring along insect repellent and drinking water.

Few of the Mayan sites allow overnight visits, and only a handful have sanitation facilities. Admission fees are about $1.50 per person. Children under 12 are admitted free, as are all Belizean nationals on Sundays. For permissions or further information, contact the Department of Archaeology in Belmopan at 8-2106.

Note that all of Belize's major Mayan sites are described in this section *except* for Altun Ha, which is included as a day trip from Belize City in chapter 5, and Pacbitun, discussed earlier in this chapter.

Caracol (Cayo District)

The largest Mayan site in Belize was until 1992 one of the most difficult to reach. Located in the Cayo District's rugged backcountry, Caracol is on the edge of the remote Chiquibul wilderness only 7 miles east of the Guatemalan border. Caracol is a bumpy three-hour journey (in good weather) by four-wheel-drive vehicle from San Ignacio via the Mountain Pine Ridge village of Augustine (also called Douglas DiSilva), about 30 miles distant.

The most extensive known Mayan ceremonial center in the country, the central core of Caracol covers 5 square miles of thick, high-canopy forest and comprises a Classic period complex that includes many pyramids, five plazas, and an astronomical observatory. The

Excavations at Mayan ruin of Caracol (Photo by Kevin Schafer)

main plaza is linked by causeways to a number of outlier ruins. Overall, the network of structures is at least three times denser and 85 percent larger (at 55 square miles) than nearby Tikal, although estimates
of Caracol's size are being revised upward every year. It is now
believed that 180,000 or more people lived in this area at the city-
state's peak, around A.D. 500 to 600. The site has ruins of an estimated 35,000 buildings.

Remarkably, Caracol (Spanish for "snail," a reference to the numerous land snail shells found here) remained unknown to the outside world until the early 1930s, when a local woodcutter stumbled upon its mysterious mounds while searching for mahogany and chicle. Loggers subsequently cut timber in the area over the next two decades, and it was not until 1950 that archaeologists began mapping it. The ruin was mistakenly considered a small site and left to loggers and looters (plus a few army patrols) for some time. It began receiving considerable academic attention in 1985, after the husband-and-wife team of Diane and Arlen Chase began making annual pilgrimages from the University of Central Florida that are ongoing.

In 1986, the archaeologists were poking around a Mayan ball court when, by chance, one of their Belizean workers made a major discovery: a well-preserved circular white altar stone that contained a hieroglyphic record of a military victory by an underdog Mayan leader known as Lord Water of Caracol over the mighty warlords of Tikal, some 60 miles to the northwest. This A.D. 562 conquest was the culmination of many years of fierce fighting between the two powers. The altar was significant because it documented Caracol's domination of the area throughout most of the so-called Middle Classic Hiatus, a period between A.D. 534 and 690 when Tikal built no carved monuments and buried even its holiest priests in tombs better suited to impoverished peasants. Caracol did its best to humiliate the royalty of Tikal and the neighboring Guatemalan city-state of Naranjo (conquered in A.D. 631) during Caracol's 150 years of domination, possibly even sacrificing its high-ranking captives in demeaning public executions.

The glyphic record shows a change in warfare strategies that left conquered city-states spared but shattered the power of the ruling elites. This allowed Caracol, much smaller than Tikal at the time of its victory, to divert the larger community's riches (and perhaps many of its citizens as slaves) to expand its own boundaries. Excavations at the outskirts of Caracol suggest that even the middle-class Maya had access to jade, polychrome pottery, ritual vessels, and fancy burial tombs. We know that Caracol grew rapidly for quite a while before suffering an inexplicable period of decline, possibly caused in part by an equalization in social power that destroyed the influence of Mayan royalty. Clues contained in the hieroglyphics of several circular stone altars now unearthed at Caracol may eventually help the Chases determine why the Maya fled. "We know that when they finally left, they left fast," Diane Chase told an Associated Press reporter in 1993, noting that buildings were burned and the body of a child was abandoned on the floor of a palace.

Another riddle not yet solved is why a city as large as Caracol was built on a plateau that has almost no reliable water supply during the four or five months of dry weather each spring. Mayan engineers managed to overcome the limitations of nature by building effective reservoirs, aqueducts, and gardening terraces that made clever use of rainfall. Nevertheless, their ingenuity does not explain the reason for locating such a large population here in the first place. It is speculated that Caracol may have been a good location for trading with other Mayan communities spread throughout Guatemala, Honduras, and Mexico, or that prized plants such as cacao grew here. Even today, 2,000 years after Caracol's founding, visitors are advised to bring with them all the water they will need during their stay. (A Mayan reservoir fulfills the needs of the research team during its February-to-June encampment.)

Another major discovery at Caracol were the bones of a woman in a royal tomb at the top of the highest pyramid. The find suggests that, in the absence of a male heir, females may have periodically ruled Mayan city-states.

The most visually striking structure at the site is Caana ("sky palace"), a temple towering 136 feet above the plaza floor. It is 2 meters higher than El Castillo at Xunantunich, previously regarded as the tallest man-made structure in Belize. Visitors can climb to the summit of Caana and enjoy a sweeping view of tall deciduous and evergreen hardwood forests for as far as the eye can see. Looking west and southwest from the temple, dozens of unevaluated building mounds up to 70 feet in height are evident all the way to the horizon.

Much of Caracol is still to be excavated, although in recent years as many as 100 people at a time have worked here—digging, mapping, measuring, photographing, cataloging, and analyzing. Laser technology is now being applied to eroded hieroglyphics taken from underground tombs, and experts are brought in to read them on-site. A solar collector electrical system has been donated by a Florida firm, and a sophisticated subsurface radar unit is used to find the most promising areas for excavation.

In the first four years of digging, Caracol yielded fifty-four burial tombs, twice as many as have been found in all the decades of searching at Tikal. The project's directors estimate there are as many as 4,500 structures at the central core of Caracol, compared to 2,300 mapped in the center of Tikal. The archaeological richness of this site, one of the five largest Mayan cities anywhere, is expected to eventually result in a much better understanding of the civilization's social structure, particularly since many of the Caracol tombs and monuments were clearly dated at the time of their initial construction.

The Belizean government has expanded the Caracol Archaeology Reserve to the borders of the much larger Chiquibul National Park. This high-canopy forest, much of it in pristine condition, is an important habitat for several species of cat and the endangered howler monkey, plus such rare birds as the keel-billed motmot, thought to be extinct in Guatemala, Mexico, and Honduras. Ocellated turkeys and other large birds walk through the ruins with impunity, whereas they have completely vanished from almost all of the rest of Belize. A wide variety of orchids, vines, and trees (many as tall as 120 feet) are found in the area. One enormous ceiba tree, at least 700 years old, towers above the epicenter of Caracol.

The vast Chiquibul cavern system (believed to be the longest in Central America) begins about 8 miles south of the site. The three largest caves in the complex measure a total of at least 20 miles in length and have yielded several invertebrates that were new to science as well as many ancient Maya ceremonial artifacts. A chamber in one of the Chiquibul caves is believed to be the fourth-largest in the world.

En route to Caracol, visitors will pass through the deserted logging town of San Luis and cross the Guacamallo Bridge (*guacamallo* is the local name for the scarlet macaw) spanning the upper Macal River. The contrast between pine forest and subtropical hardwoods is like night and day here, owing to sharp alignments in geology. Farther along the road to the ruins are one or more chicle camps that have been revived in recent years as Japanese companies buy more and more of this natural chewing gum base from Belizean tappers.

Following Guatemala's example with its famous Tikal National Park, Belize is eager to turn Caracol into a major tourism attraction some day in a manner that will preserve present-day flora and fauna as well as ancient history. In a 1990 interview, the Chases told a *Smithsonian* magazine reporter that they are looking forward to Caracol's ultimate status as an important archaeological park. "But," Diane Chase cautioned, "it will take years [of excavation] to get to the point where visitors can get a sense of what it once was."

If You Go: Permission must be obtained from the Belizean government's Department of Archaeology in Belmopan and the Forestry Department's western division in Augustine prior to any visits to Caracol. As of mid-1993, there was no fee for either permit, although this situation may have changed. The Department of Archaeology permit is valid only for a specific day and number of visitors. It is not transferable. Forestry officials grant their permits based on road conditions, since the last 30 miles between Augustine and Caracol are rough, especially during or after wet weather. High-clearance four-wheel-drive vehicles are recommended. The nearest gas station and mechanic are in San Ignacio, about 60 miles away. There is no public transportation to Caracol, and few taxis will make the trip. Rather than attempt a visit on one's own, we recommend checking with local resorts for guided tours to the site. Since road improvements were made in 1992, few operators run horseback trips to the site.

There are no overnight accommodations at Caracol, and camping is no longer allowed. Remember to bring your own food and water. A solar-powered telephone is available for emergency use only.

There is a $1.50 visitor's fee, payable on registration at an open-air kitchen used by Caracol's Mayan caretakers. These workers are fairly knowledgeable about the archaeology of the area and will provide guided tours if they are not busy. Fluency in Spanish is helpful.

Xunantunich (Cayo District)

In contrast to Caracol, Xunantunich (the Mayan "X" is pronounced like a cross between an English "S" and "Z") is one of the most accessible ancient Mayan sites in Belize. The ruins are located near the confluence of the Belize and Mopan rivers.

This is a Classic period ceremonial center of impressive height but relatively small size. It is just across the river from the Western Highway and only a few miles east of the Guatemalan border. The temple complex, occupied until about A.D. 850, is surrounded by thick bush that is gradually being whittled away by local farmers.

Because of its commanding presence and proximity to populated areas (high on a limestone bluff above the Mopan River village of San José Succotz), Xunantunich has been visited by a lengthy parade of archaeologists stretching back to 1894. Sadly, several of these investigators botched their work and in one instance lost an irreplaceable set of altar hieroglyphics. Other inept researchers freely dispersed the burial goods and ceremonial offerings to museums in England and Germany. No serious archaeological work was done until 1938, and the tallest structures were not stabilized until 1960.

Perhaps the most amazing fact is that no systematic large-scale excavation has *ever* been carried out here, even though Xunantunich may hold valuable clues about the stormy years in which it thrived, roughly A.D. 150 to 850. In 1959, it was determined that the site had been partially destroyed in an earthquake during the Late Classic era. Some experts feel this incident may have shaken the faith Mayans had in their leaders, who claimed an intimate relationship with the gods.

Xunantunich is now surrounded by a protective fence. A modest admission fee of $1.50 is charged by resident caretaker Elfego Panti, himself of Mayan descent and very knowledgeable about the history of Xunantunich. He is happy to point out structures of interest and is familiar with local wildlife and plants. Drinking water is also available near his office.

About 100 yards away from Panti's quarters and dominating the entire topography of Xunantunich (variously translated from the Mayan as "stone woman" or "maiden of the rock") is a spectacular 135-foot monolith known as El Castillo (The Castle). In typical Mayan fashion, the corbel-vaulted temple at the summit is actually built on the rubble of several earlier temples constructed one on the

El Castillo at Xunantunich (Photo by Richard Mahler)

other over the centuries. Visitors can climb nearly to the top of this impressive tower, which affords a wonderful view of the green steamy jungle and overlooks the three adjacent plazas of Xunantunich. Visible on the east side of El Castillo's lower temple is an unusual stucco frieze, restored in 1972, showing symbols of the sun, moon, Venus, and days of the week. Also included is a headless man, apparently decapitated for some long-forgotten transgression against the royal rulers. Originally the frieze continued all the way around the structure, and its highest point was probably topped by a roof comb. An excavated stairway continues to a small chamber in the upper temple of El Castillo, now exposed to the elements. Near the structure's base is a wide terrace that once supported several smaller temples.

In the plaza below El Castillo there is a thatched pavilion where visitors can picnic, rest, or listen to archaeological lectures. On one side, protected by corrugated roofing and palm fronds, are three ceremonial offering stones containing intricate carvings that refer to the powers of fertility and the victories of the warlords.

The grass-covered mounds surrounding the three primary plazas are the remains of ancient residential buildings that might have been something like modern condominiums. On the west side, near the rest rooms, is a flat narrow rectangle believed to be a ball court, used in a complicated and deadly form of basketball developed by the Mayan hierarchy. Also visible is a room with a built-in stone bench and some walls bearing Mayan graffiti.

Judging from the jewelry, tools, semiprecious stones, and weaving materials found here, archaeologists believe this was once an important and well-ordered city. No one is sure why it was abandoned. Less than 2 miles south of Xunantunich are the ruins of an outlier called Actuncan, where pottery and trading items have been found.

Xunantunich was the first Mayan site in Belize to be opened to the public (in 1954), and it is now among the best maintained in the country.

If You Go: Heading west about 10 minutes from San Ignacio on the Western Highway, the tower of El Castillo is suddenly visible on the western horizon. Look for a sign and pedestrian shelter marking the turnoff on the right-hand side of the highway.

You will cross the Mopan River on a tiny, hand-cranked ferry secured to a steel cable (it can handle two cars at a time). There is no charge, as this is a public right-of-way. Follow the dirt road for about a mile up the hill to a small parking lot, then walk into the site. The road can be very slippery when wet. If you decide to go on foot, it takes about 40 minutes to walk up the hill from the ferry.

Besides passenger cars and package tours, trips to the Xunantunich ruins can be made via taxi from Benque Viejo or San Ignacio for about $4. An alternative is to take a bus from either town and ask the driver to drop you off at the river crossing. Xunantunich is an easy trip—usually occupying less than two hours—from the many resorts of the Cayo District or the hotels of Benque Viejo, San José Succotz, and San Ignacio.

About a mile from the site, on the Mopan River, is a stretch of surging rapids that some travelers enjoy traversing in canoes, kayaks, or rubber rafts. There are also several fine swimming holes in the area, and bird-watching is excellent.

Lamanai (Orange Walk District)

While the towering temples of Xunantunich and Caracol are impressive by any measure, a different kind of beauty awaits visitors making the scenic journey to Lamanai, the "submerged crocodile." The ruins are about 70 miles northwest of Belize City, on high ground that looms over the west bank of the beautiful New River Lagoon.

Lamanai is unusual in that it was occupied longer than almost any other known Mayan site, from about 1500 B.C. until at least A.D. 1650. Its history extends from the formative years of the civilization until well after Franciscan friars arrived from Spain to convert its "heathen" residents. The city enjoyed its greatest strength during the Pre-Classic era of A.D. 200 to 900, and Lamanai's major pyramid—variously referred to as the Southern Temple or N10-43—was completed around 100 B.C., then modified several times before A.D. 600.

Some of Lamanai's ruins are among the oldest surviving buildings from the Pre-Classic period, dating back to 700 B.C. Pollen samples show that corn was being cultivated here at least eight hundred years earlier. There are 700 buildings in the complex, which is believed to have supported at least 35,000 people when its population peaked. Only about 5 percent of the known structures have been excavated.

Thanks to records kept by early Catholic missionaries, we know that Lamanai is a Spanish corruption of Lamanain, the original Mayan name for this place (most other Mayan sites were named by their European discoverers). The term is fitting, since the lagoon nearby is perfect crocodile habitat. Many representations of the reptile have been found here, including ceramic decorations and plaster masks, some of which may be seen in the excellent on-site museum. A figure wearing a crocodile headdress, found in many forms throughout the area, is thought to represent one of Lamanai's rulers.

Although it is possible to drive here (about 2 hours from Belize City), many visitors prefer to come to Lamanai by boat up the New River, just as the ancient Maya did. After navigating through miles of constantly dividing tributaries and flat, closed-in landscape (teeming with water birds and their predators), the pyramid-shaped temple looming 112 feet above the New River Lagoon and main plaza is an awesome sight. When the crown of this temple was put in place in about 100 B.C., this may well have been the tallest building in the Mayan world.

Beyond the highest pyramid, N10-43, thick forest has taken over many of the unrestored limestone mounds where thousands of Indians once made their homes. At the apex of its considerable power, this well-situated city-state is said to have had a trading influence that extended over much of present-day Mexico, Guatemala, and Honduras as well as Belize.

The central core of the site covers about one square mile, with residential structures and smaller buildings spread over more than 1,000 acres. The overgrown vegetation makes it difficult to get a sense of perspective on the ground, so a hike to the summit of one of the temples is a good idea: three are over 100 feet tall.

In one section, accessible by a short path, are a few crumbling walls remaining from a couple of sixteenth-century Catholic missions, one of the only reminders of Spanish occupation extant in all Belize. Conversions of the Maya to Christianity began here in 1544. The Spanish remained until 1640, when the Indians rebelled and burned their church to the ground as part of a regional uprising that included Lamanai's sister city of Tipú, on the Macal River. A second chapel was later built at Lamanai using stones from one of the Maya's most sacred temples, which contributed to the friction between Europeans and Indians. In fact, a Mayan stela (still visible) was erected in front of this church after its destruction containing a written message firmly disavowing any allegiance to Christianity.

After the missionaries were eradicated, Lamanai was apparently devastated by successive epidemics of malaria, smallpox, and yellow fever. Virtually no one lived here when the British loggers arrived with their Jamaican slaves in the eighteenth century to extract mahogany and other trees. Chinese and East Indian laborers were imported about ninety years later to work in the local sugarcane fields, but they did not react well to the demanding climate or debilitating diseases, and most of the plantations were soon abandoned.

The ruin of a nineteenth-century sugar mill, complete with ficus-entangled flywheel and boiler, is still visible. It was built in 1866, then burned by the Maya (along with other European constructions) the following year. When the mill's manager succumbed to fever a short time later, the settlement was taken over by local Indians. A corroded molasses storage chamber, now home to bats, lies a short distance from the abandoned mill.

Many Guatemalan and a few Salvadoran refugees now live in the area as subsistence farmers. Some were relocated to the nearby village of Indian Church after they homesteaded within the park's boundaries.

Because of the ruin's protected status as an archaeological reserve, the number of black howler monkeys and other endangered mammals has been on the rise. In 1993, researcher Hal Markowitz of San Francisco State University began a long-term study of the behavioral ecology of howler monkeys here. Volunteers may work alongside the primate experts through tours offered by Oceanic Society Expeditions of San Francisco (see Inside Belize). Participants help in all aspects of noninvasive data collection and live in double-occupancy cabanas at the site.

Common trees here include the guanacaste, mahogany, rubber, poisonwood, cohune palm, and strangler fig. The lagoon, fed by a maze of underwater springs and aquifers, is teeming with fish and virtually unpolluted. On the western bank stretch miles of savannas that are an important habitat for jaguars and other cats.

Although most of Lamanai is still uncleared and unreconstructed, it has received much more serious archaeological attention than many Mayan sites in Belize. Minor excavation and mapping were carried out in 1917 and again during the 1930s and 1960s. An extensive and long-term project began in 1974 under the direction of Canada's Royal Ontario Museum and was largely completed in 1992. Among noteworthy findings by the Canadian research team were a tenth-century ball court marker and a cache of human remains that may have been sacrificed here during certain religious ceremonies. The bones of what appear to have been five small boys were exhumed in one temple, one of them found in the sitting position commonly used for sacred, ritualistic burials.

The wide array of artifacts found suggests that the people were enthusiastic and successful merchants. One ancient pottery vessel contained several small offerings floating in pools of liquid mercury, their purpose a complete mystery. Other oddities include an unusually small Mayan ball court and an extraordinarily preserved carved offering stone that lies prone under a protective palm thatch. It is believed that the latter object escaped destruction because it apparently fell face-forward to the ground during a Mayan fire ceremony and was therefore left unmolested for fear the event itself portended evil. An outstanding depiction of the Lamanai priest-king Lord Smoking Shell (whose reign began about A.D. 608) shows clearly his open-mouthed serpent headdress and other accoutrements. He holds a ceremonial bar in his arms, symbolizing his royal authority.

The small but impressive museum at Lamanai contains censers, burial urns, and chalices discovered here, along with eccentric flint carvings, tools, and many ceramic objects. If you are fortunate enough to stop by while the well-informed Mayan archaeologist Nasario Coo is in, you can obtain a very thorough account of Lamanai's fascinating history. Coo will provide a guided tour if his schedule allows.

If You Go: Lamanai is off the beaten track. Public transportation is limited to taxis (from Orange Walk Town), rental cars, supply trucks, and hired boats. A dirt road, occasionally impassable during the wet season, extends to the site from Orange Walk Town via the village of San Felipe. Watch for the signs directing you to Indian Church and/or Lamanai.

Most visitors arrange a boat trip through local hotels, travel agencies, or package tour operators. We recommend Mayaworld Safaris (2-32285) for a day trip via the New River to Lamanai. Wilfedo Novelo is a knowledgeable archaeological guide. Jungle River Tours (3-22293) and Carlos Godoy (3-22969) also offer fine New River/Lamanai tours. Another approach is to drive as far as Tower Bridge, Guinea Grass, or Shipyard (a Mennonite farming community), then head by locally hired boat up the New River. Boats can usually be rented on the spur of the moment in any of these riverside villages or can be arranged in advance through such hotels as the Victo-

Astronomical frieze at Mayan ruin of Xunantunich (Photo by Kevin Schafer)

ria in Orange Walk Town, the Adventure Inn in Consejo Shores, or the Maruba in Maskall.

The boat trip is very pleasant, affording opportunities for swimming and other water sports along the way. Many orchids and other flowering plants are visible in the trees overhead. Hollowed-out trunks along the riverbank provide a daytime home to a small, fish-eating bat. Many kinds of birds and animals live along the banks of the lagoon and are easily glimpsed during the crossing to Lamanai. Crooked Tree Lagoon (described in chap. 5) is only 8 miles to the east, and many species are present in both locations. Jabiru stork, snail kite, northern jacana, squirrel cuckoo, blue-crowned motmot, limpkin, cormorant, and night heron, along with huge flocks of parrots, are some of the birds recorded near Lamanai.

The accommodations closest to the ruins are a half mile away in Indian Church, at the highly recommended Lamanai Outpost Lodge. Rooms are also available in Orange Walk Town, about 20 miles to the northeast. A number of operators now schedule Lamanai as a day trip from Belize City or San Pedro.

Camping is not allowed at Lamanai, and no food or drink is sold here. The site has rest rooms, a picnic area, and several cut trails through the forest. Besides curator Nasario Coo, the resident caretakers can answer basic questions about the site. The structures are not well marked, however, and no literature is available. Bring your own guide or a map and guidebook as well as the usual insect repellent.

Cuello (Orange Walk District)

Cuello is located on private land, and permission is needed to visit this ancient site, a minor ceremonial center and settlement area about 4 miles southwest of Orange Walk Town. Arrangements can be made by calling the Cuello Rum Distillery, the site's owner, during business hours at 3-22141. Tours of the distillery, which bottles spirits under the Caribbean label, can also be scheduled. Permissions can usually be obtained by simply showing up; the facility is open Monday through Saturday.

Although not well developed for visitors, Cuello is one of the most exciting recent discoveries in the Mayan world. Before the exploration of this site in 1973 by Cambridge University, most experts believed the Mayan civilization had its start around 1500 B.C., which was the earliest date of any previously known settlement. Applying state-of-the-art carbon dating techniques to ancient maize fragments and wooden posts, it was determined that occupation by the Maya began here around 2600 B.C., possibly even earlier. Thus, the "start date" of the civilization was pushed back by a full millennium.

It was also once believed that the initial development of a distinct Mayan culture was spurred by contact with other ethnic groups, such as Mexico's early Olmec people. Trade artifacts found at Cuello suggest that the sophisticated social and religious institutions of Mayan life may have developed independently or through contact with still-unknown cultures. The jade and obsidian found here do not naturally occur in Belize and were probably traded for parrot feathers and animal skins collected from the nearby jungle.

Other findings at Cuello raise more unanswered questions. Why did a mass slaughter of at least thirty-two individuals take place here about 400 B.C.? Why were earthenware pots placed over the heads of the deceased in some of Cuello's burial chambers? Did the Maya originate their pyramid-plaza architectural style here, as many have suggested?

One certainty is Cuello's continuous occupation for thousands of years, until as recently as 1500. The site has yielded evidence that the Maya may have been able to build the strength of their city-state empire partly through the development of more productive strains of corn, their principal crop. The earliest known ceramics and masonry buildings in Belize have also been found here.

There is not a lot for the casual visitor to actually see at Cuello, which lies in a forested compound of the distillery and is surrounded by cattle pasture. Norman Hammond and his Cambridge research team continue to conduct research at the ruin, but they fill in excavated areas after their studies are completed. Still, this is an important historical site for any serious student of the Maya.

If You Go: Cuello can easily be reached by taxi ($6) or private car via Yo Creek Road, which begins in Orange Walk Town as Baker's Street.

No information or guides will be found at the site, although the Department of Archaeology can provide background materials in Belmopan.

About 25 miles down the same road are a number of traditional and modern Mennonite farms and settlements that fan out from Blue Creek Village (see chap. 7). By heading through August Pine Ridge and San Felipe, one will eventually reach the Mexican border crossing at La Unión. This is also the preferred route for those driving to Chan Chich Lodge, the Programme for Belize lands, and the Río Bravo Conservation Area.

Cerros (Corozal District)

About 20 miles northeast of Cuello, on an uninhabited stretch of Caribbean coastline overlooking Corozal Bay, are the ruins of Cerros (also known as Cerro Maya, or Mayan Hill). During the dry season the site can be reached by a dirt road, but it is more commonly visited by boat from either Corozal Town or Consejo. On a clear day, especially at sunset, the profile of the ruins is clearly visible from the opposite side of the bay.

Cerros is a late Pre-Classic era complex with virtually no construction after A.D. 100. Experts believe it was an important center of maritime commerce, probably handling much of the seagoing trade headed up the nearby New River to Lamanai. Its early demise may have been caused by a gradual early Classic period shift in Mayan trading patterns in favor of overland routes between the lowland and highland city-states. It was during this time that inland population centers such as Tikal and Caracol became established.

Although the archaeological reserve is small (53 acres), it includes three large acropolises that loom above several plazas and a few pyramid-like structures. The tallest temple is 72 feet and provides a sweeping view across the water. Cerros probably reached its peak between 400 B.C. and A.D. 100. During this period it appears to have shifted from an economy dependent on fishing, hunting, and farming to one reliant on the importation of pottery, salt, jade, and obsidian by dugout canoe. It was almost certainly linked by trade to the Yucatán interior via the Río Hondo about 10 miles to the north and to the many smaller trading sites on the Belizean cayes and atolls farther south.

Ancient ball courts, quasi-religious tombs, elegant residences, agricultural terraces, and boat canals have been found at Cerros, indicating that its social structure was at once highly developed. Surrounding the site is a man-made drainage canal that was nearly a mile long, 20 feet wide, and 6 feet deep. The immediate area has been uninhabited for some time, and part of the original complex is now underwater as a result of a rise in sea level.

Although long recognized as an archaeological site, almost no formal excavation or consolidation was carried out at Cerros until 1973, when a team from Southern Methodist University conducted preliminary field studies. The last SMU researcher departed in 1983, and no further archaeological work has been carried out since.

Some of the buildings at Cerros display large painted stucco masks that are up to 13 feet high. They depict images of human beings and animals. Unfortunately, because the sea air speeds erosion and no money is available for restoration, the masks have been plastered over to prevent further decay. The pyramid known as 5C, however, still has four masks: two identified as the sun and Venus, the others unknown. Some feel that the presence of these large friezes demonstrates that the divine Mayan elite were firmly in power by the end of the Pre-Classic era, or about A.D. 250.

If You Go: Largely unrestored and unexcavated, much of Cerros appears to the casual visitor as little more than a series of low mounds, with only the tallest ceremonial structures hinting at past grandeur. Several years ago a partnership was formed between a nonprofit Texas group and some American investors to create a tourist attraction here, complete with hotel, swimming pool, museum, and research center. The Cerro Maya Foundation collapsed without building anything, and Cerros remains without accommodations or services. Camping is not allowed. A resident caretaker will collect the requisite $1.50 entrance fee.

The roundabout road from Corozal Town passes by some idyllic lagoons and through the relaxed mestizo fishing villages of Chunox, Progresso, and Copper Bank. This route cannot be recommended during wet weather.

By easily secured boat at the Corozal Town public pier, Cerros is about 5 miles across Corozal Bay. It is roughly 10 miles from Consejo Shores, where boats can be hired at the Adventure Inn.

Because of the ruin's close proximity to the mouth of the New River and adjacent wetlands, insect repellent and long-sleeved clothing are necessary.

Santa Rita (Corozal District)

Amateur archaeologist Thomas Gann, a turn-of-the-century British physician living in Corozal, was perhaps the first European to recognize Santa Rita and Cerros as ancient Mayan sites. Located directly across the bay from the latter ruin and northeast of the Corozal Town center (encircled by private homes and businesses), Santa Rita flourished off and on from at least 2000 B.C. until the arrival of the Spanish in the 1500s. Some might convincingly argue that since part of the present-day town is built atop the Santa Rita ruins, human habitation has continued here without interruption since twenty centuries before the birth of Christ.

Gann theorized that Santa Rita was one of an important series of coastal towns strategically located so that signal fires could be used to send messages up and down the Yucatán peninsula. Although this theory has never been conclusively upheld, there is plenty of evidence that Santa Rita was in fact one of the region's most powerful Mayan communities and even regained some of its prominence after the disintegration of the civilization as a whole.

Santa Rita's location, on a limestone plateau overlooking the Chetumal and Corozal bays, immediately attracted the attention of Spanish conquistadors, who seized the city-state under the leadership of Alfonso Davila in 1531 from the Mayan warlord Nachacan. Although they were eventually routed by the Indians, the Spanish simply relocated farther north (at what is now the Mexican city of Chetumal) and managed to sever the remaining trade routes that fueled Santa Rita's prosperity. Within a few years the community was almost completely abandoned. The modern town of Corozal was subsequently established on the ruins' foundations in 1858 by survivors of the famous massacre at Bacalar, Mexico.

Despite its long and impressive history, only one visible structure remains at Santa Rita: a 50-foot-high and partially restored pyramid-shaped tomb, where two important burials were excavated. This site includes several chambers and an offertory niche. One of the rulers found buried here wore a kind of gold earring reserved only for the highest noblemen, another hint of Santa Rita's importance not only as a city but as a terminus for trade with other rich communities. Not incidentally, the discovery of gold objects here is believed to have prompted the first attack by the Spanish. Other artifacts have linked Santa Rita to the seacoast city of Tulum, some 200 miles to the north.

Like nearby Cerros, Santa Rita appears to have been an agricultural center long before the seagoing trade boom hit. Once its boats got under way, however, Santa Rita found eager markets for the prized commodities gathered or cultivated nearby, including cacao, vanilla, honey, and spices. Unlike Cerros, Santa Rita thrived through the Classic period and was still stockpiling turquoise and gold from the Aztecs long after more distant Mayan cities had collapsed. Relics from Santa Rita's tombs even include pottery made in the Andes mountains of far-off Peru.

Gann uncovered several burial sites, along with sculptured friezes and stuccoed murals. Much of this material has subsequently been lost—Indians deliberately destroyed six murals in 1900 before Gann could copy them—but some of the doctor's meticulous notes and drawings survive.

It was not until 1979 that a more thorough series of excavations was undertaken at Santa Rita, in a project led by Diane Chase and Arlen Chase, the same archaeologists responsible for the ongoing study of Caracol. Among important discoveries made here over a seven-year period was a skeleton adorned with jade and mica ornaments. Many of these findings are now held in the Archaeology Vault in Belmopan.

Sadly, since the founding of Corozal Town some 150 years ago, a good part of Santa Rita has been paved over or built on. Hundreds of ancient structures and artifacts have been lost forever as a result. To the horror of archaeologists, a good deal of this historical material was ground up into road-surfacing material years before it could be properly examined. (This was a common practice throughout Belize as late as the 1970s.)

If You Go: The last ancient building at Santa Rita, known as Structure 7, is an easy walk or car ride from the plaza of Corozal Town. Local residents will be happy to point you in the right direction: turn left at the Hilltop Bar and follow the road to the Coca-Cola bottling plant. No services are available at the site, although Pedro the caretaker (who once set up housekeeping in one of the tombs) is very helpful and knowledgeable. He collects a $1.50 fee during Santa Rita's hours of admission, 8:00 a.m. to 5:00 p.m. daily. Menzies Travel Agency, based on the south side of Corozal Town, is a recommended contact for excursions to Santa Rita and other Mayan ruins in the district.

Lubaantun (Toledo District)

Lubaantun is modern Mayan for "place of the fallen rocks," which aptly describes this Late Classic ceremonial center, noted for an unusual style of construction that is unique to southern Belize. The large pyramids and residences observed here are made of crystalline limestone blocks with no mortar binding them together, not unlike the Inca's constructions in the high Andes. This means that every hand-cut stone was carefully measured and shaped to fit together with the adjoining stone. The effect looks a bit like marble. The buildings that were then placed on top of these pyramids were made from perishable materials such as tree limbs and no longer remain.

The austerity of this site—Lubaantun is now essentially a single acropolis—is reminiscent of Quiriguá, about 100 miles away in southeast Guatemala, and there may have been close contact between the two city-states. Curiously, Lubaantun has impressive stone architecture but virtually no stone stelae. Nearby Nim Li Punit and Uxbenka have plenty of sculpted rock monuments but no large structures. This suggests to some authorities that a diverse social organization once prevailed in this area and that each site served a distinct purpose.

At Lubaantun, eleven large pyramid-platform structures are built around five main plazas and three ball courts. The tallest of these rises 45 feet above the jungle, and one can see the Caribbean (about 20 miles distant) from its top. There are thirteen smaller plazas and a number of other structures, but the entire complex is badly eroded.

It is believed that carvings and other types of building decorations commonly found in stonework at other Mayan sites were made out of wood at Lubaantun, which is located in one of the most rain-soaked corners of Belize. One theory persists that Lubaantun was an important religious, administrative, political, and commercial center—but only for a brief time (a couple of centuries at most, but perhaps as few as 20 years). No one knows what led to abandonment around A.D. 850, or why the hilltop site was not leveled before construction began, in the traditional manner. The Maya simply filled in gaps with stones and mortar instead.

Colonial officials began surveying Lubaantun with the help of Thomas Gann in 1903, and the British Museum started serious excavation work in 1926, joined the following year by the renowned Mayan authority J. E. S. Thompson. Some of the most impressive artifacts these teams unearthed were taken to museums in London and the United States. Archaeologists abandoned Lubaantun from

Mound and structure enclosing excavated stelae at Xunantunich (Photo by Richard Mahler)

1929 to 1970, when Norman Hammond returned with a team of Cambridge University researchers.

It is thought that the greatest wealth of Lubaantun came from the production and trading of cacao, which was so highly prized by the Maya that they used it as a form of currency. Even to this day the area is considered prime cacao-growing country, and the discovery of a ceramic musician wearing a cacao-pod pendant in 1970 lends credence to the notion that the prized beans were grown here in the eighth century. The cacao was probably exchanged for jade and obsidian.

The best-known discovery at Lubaantun is the remarkable Crystal Skull, supposedly unearthed in 1926 by Anna Mitchell-Hedges (daughter of archaeologist F. A. Mitchell-Hedges) on her seventeenth birthday. This artifact demonstrates superb artistry and workmanship; it is perfectly carved from an 8-inch-cube pure rock crystal and shows virtually no tool marks. The item appears to have been modeled after a specific human head, but the identity of that individual—and the Crystal Skull's significance—remains unknown. Some believe the skull was brought from somewhere else for a "staged" discovery at Lubaantun; others are convinced it is linked to the lost continent of Atlantis. As of mid-1993, the relic still remained in the hands of Ms. Mitchell-Hedges, a Canadian, although the Belize government has been negotiating for its eventual return. A similar crystal skull is on display at the Musée de l'Homme in Paris.

If You Go: Lubaantun, the largest archaeological site in southern Belize, is on a high limestone ridge just north of the Columbia River, one mile by unshaded dirt road past the village of San Pedro Columbia. Not directly accessible by public transit, the site is a 20-minute walk from the Southern Highway by a good trail. A steeper but shorter pathway leads to Lubaantun from the banks of the Columbia River.

Less than a half-mile walk behind the ruins is the Belize Agroforestry Research Center (BARC), a farm engaged in alternative forms of agriculture and permaculture, including pre-Columbian Mayan farming methods. It is operated by several expatriate Americans—all environmental activists—through the Tropical Conservation Foundation (14 N. Court St., Athens, OH 45701). BARC sponsors permaculture design courses catering to North Americans. Drop-in overnight guests are welcome at $5 a night; there is an additional fee for meals. There is considerable flora and fauna on the grounds, as well as many outlier ruins of Lubaantun.

Accommodations and services are also available in San Pedro as part of the "indigenous experience" offered by Dem Dats Doin in Punta Gorda (20 miles away). You can overnight in the latter town or San Antonio Village (5 miles).

Several hotels and travel agencies in the Toledo and Stann Creek districts arrange tours to Lubaantun and other nearby Mayan ruins. There are rest rooms and a picnic area here but no drinking water, food, literature, or guides. A resident Mayan caretaker, Santiago Coc, answers basic questions and collects a $1.50 fee.

Nim Li Punit (Toledo District)

Located north of Punta Gorda, this Late Classic ceremonial center remained hidden from outsiders until oil workers stumbled on it in 1976. Since then, excavations have revealed twenty-five stelae, including the tallest (31 feet) carved stone monument in Belize. The site's name is Mayan for "big hat" and refers to a headdress-adorned figure on the 31-foot stela mentioned above.

Archaeologists believe Nim Li Punit may have been affiliated with nearby Lubaantun, which flourished around the same time and is architecturally similar. Digging did not start here until 1983, after the site had been badly looted. Nevertheless, an impressive stela and royal tomb were uncovered in 1986. Archaeologist Richard Leventhal continues to oversee excavations.

There are several tall structures (up to 40 feet high) around two plazas and the remains of a fairly large settlement. More than two dozen monuments have been identified at Nim Li Punit, many of an unusually long and low design. One building, for example, is only 9 feet high but 215 feet long. It is believed that the site may have been a funerary cult center that served as a service community to the local elite, who were probably headquartered in Lubaantun. The true function of Nim Li Punit and its relation to other Mayan centers remains unclear.

If You Go: Nim Li Punit is one-half mile off the Southern Highway at Mile 75 near the Mayan village of Indian Creek. It is not directly accessible by public transportation, although, like Lubaantun, daily Z-Line buses pass by on their way to and from Punta Gorda and Dangriga.

A well-marked track leads visitors to the site from the highway in about 20 minutes. The trailhead is not far from Whitney's Grocery Store (if you pass Whitney's Lumber Mill, heading south, you have gone too far). The nearest accommodations are in Punta Gorda (25 miles south) or San Antonio Village (10 miles south). Several hotels and tour operators in the region make trips here, often in combination with Lubaantun.

The ruins overlook a mixture of second-growth jungle and milpa garden plots. Local Mayans use the nearby streams to bathe and do their laundry. Except for a small sun/rain shelter, there are no facilities at Nim Li Punit. Only the southernmost cluster of buildings is open to visitors.

Uxbenka (Toledo District)

Local Maya have known about Uxbenka—the "old place" in local dialect—for many years. But the outside world first learned of the site's existence in 1984, when reports of looting filtered back to Belmopan. On further investigation, officials learned that indeed this was a very ancient settlement. One of the seven carved stelae found here dates from the Early Classic period, the earliest archaeological date yet recorded in southern Belize, but most of the sculpted stones are too badly eroded to read. An additional thirteen noncarved stelae have been unearthed at Uxbenka, which also features a couple of unexcavated pyramids and a small plaza, plus some overgrown structural mounds.

The site, which is not extensive, perches on a ridge overlooking the foothills and valleys of the Maya Mountains. The nearby hillsides have been faced with cut terrace stones. This art form has not been found outside the Toledo District.

If You Go: Uxbenka is on the outskirts of Santa Cruz Village, about 4 miles west of San Antonio and 9 miles east of the Guatemala border. Besides private vehicle, the best transportation for visitors is through arranged tours from Punta Gorda or via the supply trucks that come through the area once or twice a week. You can also walk from San Antonio, where there is public transportation and a guest house.

Nohmul (Orange Walk District)

Nohmul is a major ceremonial center spread among privately owned sugarcane fields near the village of San Pablo, about 7 miles north of Orange Walk Town. Permission from the property owner is required before visiting. The site—located on a limestone ridge and dominated by a massive acropolis atop which a pyramid has been built—consists of two groups of buildings incorporating ten plazas and connected by a *sacbe*, or raised causeway.

Nohmul (Mayan for "great mound") was occupied first during the Pre-Classic era (350 B.C. to A.D. 250) and again during the Late Classic period (A.D. 600 to 900). At its height, the community was the seat of government for an area encompassing 8 square miles and including the nearby settlements now known as San Esteban and San Luis.

The dominant ceremonial structure at Nohmul, a large limestone-block rectangle, was built during the late Pre-Classic era with several modifications in subsequent years. Interestingly, this acropolis seems to have lost its religious significance over time and to have been converted into residential quarters by the end of Nohmul's Mayan occupation.

Thomas Gann first recorded the large mound as a Mayan site in 1897 and conducted digs here over the next thirty-nine years. He and his wife found jade, seashells, flint, obsidian, pottery, and human bones. Much of this material was removed from burial tombs and sent to the British Museum in London. Looting and the use of ancient buildings as road construction material took their toll on Nohmul before full-scale excavation could begin in 1982.

If You Go: Nohmul is about one mile west of the village of San Pablo, which straddles the Northern Highway midway between Orange Walk Town and Corozal Town. The site's owner, Esteban Itzab, should be contacted before proceeding to the ruin. He lives in the house directly across the street from the community water tower.

There are no facilities or services. Buses pass through the village hourly en route to Orange Walk Town or Corozal Town. Nohmul can also be easily reached by private car or taxi from either of these communities in about 20 minutes.

Cahal Pech (Cayo District)

The ridgetop ruin of Cahal Pech, practically within the town limits of San Ignacio, underwent extensive excavation and restoration during the early 1990s by San Diego State University, the University of Oregon, Canada's Trent University, and the Belize Department of Archaeology. Two adjacent sites on private land were still being excavated in 1993.

Cahal Pech derives its modern Mayan name, "place of the tick," from the large number of bovine parasites found here when the area was used as a cattle pasture. Local residents acknowledged the site's presence, but the ruins were not mapped until 1950 and were periodically looted until a complete survey was made in 1988.

This ceremonial complex of what was once a major Mayan settlement and political center consists of thirty-four structures spread across several acres. There are seven courtyards, plus a number of ball courts, stelae, and temple pyramids. The tallest building is 77 feet. The site functioned as a kind of castle, standing guard over the nearby confluence of the Mopan and Macal rivers. Cahal Pech is believed to have been closely associated with the nearby Buena Vista and Xunantunich cities dating from the same era.

Preliminary analysis indicates that Cahal Pech was occupied during the Late Classic period from 850 B.C. to about A.D. 1100, reaching its greatest strength around A.D. 600. Notable findings here include an altar, a mosaic mask, and what appears to be an ancient sweat lodge. Research supports the theory that the famous Classic Maya "collapse" of the ninth century came neither swiftly nor easily, at least at Cahal Pech. Based on new evidence of lingering squalor and decay, it appears that the breakdown of the civilization dragged on for as many as 100 years, until the early tenth century.

If You Go: Visitors are welcome at Cahal Pech, which is a pleasant 15-minute walk (or short drive) west of downtown San Ignacio along the Western Highway. Look for a sign where the road makes a sweeping turn. The site is on the south side of the road, out of view.

There is a worthwhile museum and visitors center. A very informative free pamphlet about Cahal Pech is distributed here, and an admission fee of $1.50 is collected.

La Milpa (Orange Walk District)

Also known as the Chan Chich site, these ruins are located on property that is simultaneously being developed and excavated under the direction of its owner, Barry Bowen (see above, Río Bravo Conservation and Management Area). Bowen has built a highly regarded jungle lodge on one ancient plaza, partly to deter the looters and marijuana growers who previously frequented the area and hauled off many artifacts.

Located near the village of Gallon Jug in the middle of the 250,000-acre Río Bravo tract, La Milpa comprises about forty structures scattered throughout thick forest. At least twenty courtyard groups have been counted, plus an elaborate system of reservoirs and causeways. Three pyramids rise to about 100 feet, and a "great plaza" here has been judged one of the ancient civilization's biggest. In fact, archaeologists now believe that La Milpa may be the third-largest Mayan complex in Belize, after Caracol and Lamanai.

Stelae and other artifacts indicate major occupation during the Early and Late Classic periods. Extensive mapping did not get under way here until 1990, and very few structures have been excavated or evaluated. With the establishment of a research center at Chan Chich in that same year, a better picture of La Milpa is emerging.

If You Go: The site is located in a very remote area that is inaccessible by road during wetter months. Most visitors arrive by private plane via the Gallon Jug airstrip and stay at Chan Chich, located a short distance from the main part of the ruins. Lodge bookings and archaeological tours are arranged through the Programme for Belize offices in Belize City and the United States (see Inside Belize). Arrangements should be made as far in advance as possible. Casual visitors who have obtained permission from Programme for Belize can drive to the site in about 4 hours from Belize City during dry weather, via Blue Creek Village in the Orange Walk District.

Other Ancient Mayan Sites

The following ruins have been documented by the Belize government and are in varying stages of study or excavation. In some cases, no work has been done beyond the most basic forms of mapping and cataloging. All are accessible to the public, although permission must be obtained in some instances from private landowners. There are, of course, many other Mayan sites in Belize, but in an attempt to discourage looting, the authorities prefer not to discuss locations that have not yet been evaluated.

The Colha site is located on the Rancho Creek Farm, about 7 miles north of Maskall on the (old) Northern Highway, roughly 40 miles northwest of Belize City in the Belize District. Permission of the landowner is required to see this small ceremonial site.

El Pilar is a Classic era ceremonial center being excavated by researchers from the University of California, Santa Barbara. At 50 acres, it is one of the largest unconsolidated Mayan ruins in the country, located in a cultivated part of the Cayo District near the

Belize River and about 16 miles directly north of Xunantunich. Archaeologists are especially intrigued by an unexplained causeway that extends from the site across the Guatemalan border into the dense Petén jungle. There are fifteen plaza groups built over many centuries. El Pilar can be reached by high-clearance private car or taxi. Drive to the village of Bullet Tree Falls and ask area residents for directions to the ruins. From San Ignacio, the trip takes about an hour. Guided tours by vehicle or horseback are also available from the highly recommended Parrot's Nest Riverside Treehouses in Bullet Tree Falls, which also runs trips to nearby chicle camps.

Buena Vista is located on a private cattle ranch, about 3 miles west of San Ignacio on the east bank of the Mopan River. The Cayo District site is fairly large but mostly unexcavated. Prior permission of the landowner is required to visit.

Floral Park and Baking Pot are two small but potentially significant sites on the south bank of the Belize River near Central Farm and Georgeville, respectively. The ruins are currently being excavated and evaluated. The vegetation-covered mounds of these sites can be seen from the Western Highway.

Maintzunun is a very small ceremonial site, unexcavated, about 10 miles north of the Cockscomb Basin Wildlife Sanctuary, just off the Hummingbird Highway. It is thought that the few remaining structures and artifacts are part of a larger complex that was occupied between A.D. 600 and 900.

Marco Gonzalez is a late Pre-Classic era residential and sea-trading center that was active for hundreds of years. It is in the thick mangrove swamp at the south end of Ambergris Caye. The ruins have been studied by the Royal Ontario Museum, which found no intact structures. Pottery, obsidian, and jade as well as basalt grinding tools, stelae, and temple mounds were unearthed here. Access to Marco Gonzalez, which has been heavily looted, is by foot trail from the town of San Pedro.

San Juan, excavated by a Texas archaeological team, is at the north end of Ambergris Caye and dates from the Pre-Classic period. It is one of about a dozen Mayan sites pinpointed on the island, all largely abandoned by A.D. 1000, as trading patterns shifted to overland routes. Many of the other cayes and atolls have similar sites and middens, the equivalent of Mayan trash heaps.

Pusilha is on the Moho River in the Toledo District, about one mile east of the Guatemala border. The ruins, built on top of a hill above the river, can only be reached by boat. The plaza contains about two dozen carved stelae.

Other lesser-known Mayan ruins include Shipstern, located south of Sarteneja Village in the Corozal District; El Posito, about 4 miles west of Guinea Grass in the Orange Walk District; Actun Balam, near Caracol in the Cayo District; Blackman Eddy, on the Macal River about 10 miles southwest of San Ignacio; Tzmin Kax, also in the Cayo wilderness; and Dolores Estate, an unexcavated Early Classic site near the Toledo District village of Dolores. An even smaller ruin in the Toledo District is Naheb, just west of the Southern Highway near Indian Creek Village.

Tikal

The famous Mayan ruin of Tikal is located about 50 miles (2½ hours) northwest of the Belize border in Guatemala. Because it is so close, many travelers make a side trip to the site, which is one of the most impressive in the entire Mayan world. (For a detailed discussion of Tikal and other nearby ruins, see Richard Mahler's *Guatemala: A Natural Destination*, published by John Muir Publications.)

In 1992, after nearly two centuries of discord, Belize and Guatemala normalized relations. There is now a Guatemalan embassy in Belize City and a consulate near the border in San José Succotz. Belize has an embassy in Guatemala City. If traveling to Tikal on your own, you can now obtain Guatemalan visas and/or tourist cards in Belize, and formalities at the border are straightforward. (If you travel from Belize to Tikal in a package tour, paperwork and fees are usually taken care of by the operator.) The border is open daily from 8:00 a.m. to noon and 2:00 p.m. to 6:00 p.m.; crossing during off-hours is sometimes possible for an extra fee.

Guatemalan tourist cards and, less reliably, visas are issued at the frontier, which runs along the east bank of Mopan River between the towns of Melchor de Mencos, Guatemala, and Benque Viejo, Belize.

Both documents require a $5 fee. If you are driving a vehicle, be sure to have your registration and insurance papers in order, and expect to pay a few dollars to have the car fumigated with insecticide on the Guatemalan side (this is required by law and is one reason Belizean companies will not allow their rental cars to enter Guatemala).

Bus passengers usually have to stop on the Belize side of the crossing and walk or take a taxi into Melchor de Mencos. The same thing happens going the opposite direction. Belizean taxi drivers often intercept passengers as they descend from buses on the Guatemala side and take them all the way to San Ignacio, for a fee of about $6 each. If you simply want a quick glimpse of Guatemalan life, Melchor de Mencos is the place to find it. There is a colorful market where handicrafts are sold and a bank where Belize dollars can be exchanged for quetzales (moneychangers at the border offer slightly lower rates). The hotels are inexpensive, and several offer reasonably priced tours to local Mayan ruins, including Tikal. Try the Hotel Melchor Palace on the Mopan River, which has a restaurant, a travel service, and a car rental agency. The operator, Marco Gross, also owns Arts & Crafts of Central America in San Ignacio (9-22823), where reservations for the Melchor Palace can be made.

The entrance to Tikal National Park is northwest of Melchor de Mencos via 2 hours of poor (but recently improved) road, then a half hour of paved surface to the ruins themselves. There is a $6 admission fee, good for the date of entry only. Because the site is so large, a good guidebook and/or map greatly enhances the experience. English-speaking, well-informed guides can be hired at the site. It takes several days to take in the majority of structures here, but the highlights can be seen in a few hours. Be sure to spend some time in Tikal's Silvanus G. Morley Archaeological Museum ($3 admission), where many artifacts recovered by researchers are on permanent display, including relics from a ruler's tomb.

En route to the park, you may be stopped by the Guatemalan military and asked to show your passport or other identification. These spot checks are ordinarily uneventful, but make sure you do not photograph any soldiers or military installations. If you do so, you may be detained for questioning and your film may be destroyed. The political situation in Guatemala is gradually improving, but parts of the Petén wilderness are still controlled by antigovernment guerrillas and outlaws.

As tourism has increased in Belize, the number of alternative ways for getting to Tikal has also increased. There are several scheduled flights each week between Belize City and Flores/Santa Elena (about 40 miles south of the ruins) offered by Tropic Air, Aerovías, and Aviateca. Charters can also be arranged. From the Flores airport there are frequent minibuses to Tikal, or a car can be rented for the 50-minute drive.

Both Novelo's and Batty's bus services carry passengers from Belize City to Melchor de Mencos, dropping passengers there for connections to Tikal and/or Flores. If you are heading directly to Tikal you will need to get off at El Cruce, an intersection about 15 miles south of the ruins. From there you can take a public bus or hitch the rest of the way, but there is a risk of getting stranded. Bus schedules being what they are, you will probably need to spend a night in Flores to catch the early morning public bus or a private minibus to the ruins.

The most popular, and in many respects the easiest, way to visit Tikal from Belize is as part of a package tour. Most of the Cayo lodges arrange such trips (by van or airplane) on a weekly or even daily basis, often including the services of a knowledgeable guide. Similar tours can be arranged from Belize City, San Pedro, and other towns. Prices for package tours of Tikal vary, depending on the number of persons traveling and the duration of the trip. Expect to pay at least $125 per person, however. Bear in mind that a one-day overland round-trip means being inside a vehicle for 5 hours or more.

Overnight visits require lodging and meals in Flores, Santa Elena, or Tikal National Park. Popular hotels in greater Flores include the Petén, Posada Tayasal, San Juan, and Itzá. Some of these places are very picturesque, situated beside the large lake that dominates this Spanish colonial town, built on the site of an ancient Mayan city.

There are three basic guest houses at Tikal National Park: the Jaguar Inn, the Jungle Lodge, and the Tikal Inn. The latter is highly recommended because of the conservation orientation of its owners, the Ortíz family. (Ask Mike Ortíz for directions to Tikal's various nature trails.) Rates are about $25 a night and up. There is also one campground, which charges about $6 a night for tent or hammock space. Water is scarce, so bring your own. Several restaurants and gift shops are also near the Tikal ruins, but there is no telephone. An overnight visit to the park is highly recommended because of the tremendous amount of wildlife, including monkeys, deer, and cats. Birders will be particularly rewarded. Because the area has been protected since the mid-1950s, many of the animals show little or no fear of humans.

7

Special Interests

For enthusiasts of diving, snorkeling, fishing, or simply taking it
easy, a trip to Belize presents almost unlimited opportunities.
Below is detailed information to help those with a special interest in
these pursuits. We have highlighted a few other activities that we can
recommend, such as bird-watching and nature trekking. For specific
details on individuals and services catering to these and other special
interests, please see Inside Belize following this chapter.

Diving and Underwater Sports

In 1989, *Skin Diver* magazine described Belize as "one of the western
Caribbean's premier dive destinations," praising its unspoiled waters
and easy access. Today, many of the publication's readers might
argue that Belize has since become the most highly regarded diving
spot in all the Caribbean, perhaps the entire Western Hemisphere.

With all those coastal waterways—along with literally thousands of
little-known reefs, sand bores, islands, and marine formations—to
choose from, there is something here for every specialty and level of
ability. The water of Belize is consistently calm, warm (averaging 80
degrees), and shallow enough to make long dives pleasurable. And
when you and your companion get tired of scuba, there is always
swimming, snorkeling, fishing, sailing, sea kayaking, windsurfing,

Sailboats in Belize City harbor (Photo by Kevin Schafer)

and sunbathing to choose from. Most of the major hotels, especially those on Ambergris Caye, offer one or more of these activities, plus whatever equipment may be required. The Ramada Royal Reef Hotel in Belize City is also a good place to inquire about diving trips and other water-related sports.

For the beginner, diving around San Pedro, Caye Caulker, Placencia, and Hol Chan Marine Reserve will provide more than enough variation in underwater scenery and marine life. But the more experienced diver or snorkeler will probably want to explore areas that have not suffered as much habitat damage at the hands of commercial fishermen and tourists. There are many small species of fish, sponge, and coral in the more well traveled areas, but such larger and more timid creatures as turtles and grouper are notably absent. (San Pedro and Caye Caulker are good places to find boats, escorts, and instructors, however.)

To experience the best of what Belize has to offer, such as the viewing of deep-water gorgonians, black coral forests, and the most exotic tropical fish, the underwater explorer has three basic options. First, one may elect to head for one of the more remote island hotels or resorts. Good choices include one of the several tourist operations on the Turneffe Islands, Glover's Reef, Lighthouse Reef, or South Water Caye. Second, one may sign on with one of the live-aboard dive boats shuttling among Belize's many uninhabited islands and isolated reef structures. And third, one may decide to charter a boat individually or as part of a larger group so as to have maximum flexibility in destination and schedule. Any of the three can be easily accomplished with the help of a local travel agent, dive shop, or major hotel.

Obviously, trade-offs are inherent in each selection. The more inaccessible lodges are relatively expensive and usually require a minimum stay of six days or more. Some of these also close during the hot, insect-plagued months of July, August, and September. Live-aboard dive boats are also somewhat costly, with fixed schedules and opportunities that generally exclude the Belize interior. The expenses of hiring a private boat can also add up quickly, and one may be circumscribed by the abilities of craft and crew.

Inside Belize contains a comprehensive roster of specialists involved in the three primary types of diving vacations we have described. For further details, we suggest you contact these sources directly for advice on what option may be most appropriate. Keep in mind that many dive resorts also cater to anglers, so it is feasible to combine both pleasures in a single Belizean vacation. Examples include the Belize River Lodge, Blue Marlin Lodge, Ramon's Village, Blackbird Caye, and Manta Reef Resort. Such operators usually have special rates for nondiving and nonfishing travelers or for off-season visitors.

Night diving and cave diving are increasing in popularity, and the major dive specialists can provide necessary guides, maps, lights, and other gear. You will see different species of animals at night, and the marine caverns here are some of the largest in the world. Belize Diving Services on Caye Caulker; Bottom Time Dive Shop and Reef Divers Limited on Ambergris Caye; Turneffe Lodge on Caye Bokel; Blue Planet Divers off Blackbird Caye; and Kitty's Placencia Dive Shop in Placencia are highly recommended. Favored dive spots include Socorrito Point and Mexico Rocks, both near Ambergris Caye, and The Elbow, off the southern tip of the Turneffe Islands. Glover's Reef and Lighthouse Reef also are excellent dive spots, especially in waters where the current stirs up plenty of oxygen and food sources for fish. There are a number of shipwrecks suited for diving as well.

A variation on the live-aboard approach to diving and snorkeling is an overnight cruise from San Pedro via the *Reef Roamer II*, a converted shrimp boat that is booked through local hotels. The 50-foot craft makes two- and three-night trips to dive the Blue Hole, Turneffe Islands, and Lighthouse Reef. From Caye Caulker, an outfit called Sea-Ing Is Belizing offers excursions that last up to eight days and include the outer atolls and reef structures. Your live-aboard vessel is a 28-foot sailboat. Other popular live-aboard boats include *La Strega*, *Greet Reef*, *Belize Aggressor*, and *Coral Bay*, all operating out of Belize City. These crafts are equipped with diving platforms, tank racks, freshwater rinses, and other services.

For underwater camera rental and overnight photo processing, try Island Photos in San Pedro, James Beveridge on Caye Caulker, or one of a couple of full-service photography stores in Belize City. For diving instruction, excellent courses are offered by Blue Planet Divers, based in Belize City and on Blackbird Caye in the Turneffe Islands.

Although most dive boats and diving resorts happily accommodate snorkelers and can easily supply any necessary equipment, it may be both easier and cheaper to arrange personalized day trips and hire your own boat operator. This is most easily done at hotels that have their own marinas, such as the Ft. George, Bellevue, Ramada, Sea Breeze, and Pyramid Island (Caye Chapel). Local fishermen and guides are often willing to drop off snorkelers and swimmers in good locations, then pick them up a few hours later. Small sandy cayes—notably, Congrejo, Goff's, Rosario, Montego, English, and Rendezvous—are especially recommended. Even on the more active islands of Ambergris, Caulker, Chapel, and St. George's, there is plenty of reef line away from populated areas and traffic lanes which offer an astonishing array of marine life.

Sailboards and Hobie Cats are available for rent at some of the hotels on Ambergris Caye and Caye Caulker. More sailing equipment is being added at outlying resorts, so be sure to inquire in advance if this is a pastime of interest. Some of the larger resorts now offer complimentary windsurfing, Sunfish sailing, and pier fishing in their vacation packages. Even small guest houses often have dories and canoes available for use by visitors.

Waterskiing and windsurfing are most popular off the waters of Ambergris Caye. Check with the San Pedro Tourist Center (tel. 26-2434) or Amigo Travel (tel. 26-2180) for suggestions. The Sunbreeze Hotel, Ramon's Village, and Journey's End Caribbean Club on Ambergris all rent waterskiing and windsurfing equipment.

Rental of a full compliment of scuba gear starts at about $40 a day, with an additional $70 and up for two tanks worth of diving. Full certification instruction costs $325 or more. Bring your certification card with you: reputable operators will not accommodate your scuba requests without it. Dive trips to Lighthouse Reef and other popular dive sites start at about $200 per day per person. Ambergris-based Out Island Divers has been recommended by experienced divers. Overnight trips on snorkel-only boats start at about $125 per person with charters about $20 higher, based on a two-person minimum. Day trips start at $40. The 45-foot catamaran *Stingray*, based at the Ramada Reef Hotel marina, has been recommended by experienced snorkelers. Contact owner/operators Michael and Donna Hill through the Ramada.

One cautionary note: some individuals have occasionally found rental equipment for water sports to be substandard in Belize. Whenever practical, it is always best to bring your own mask, snorkel, fins, and other paraphernalia to ensure reliability. The situation has improved greatly in recent years, but it is still a good idea to thoroughly examine any equipment offered for rent before heading offshore. You should also ask around before hiring a diving instructor, since the level of expertise varies considerably. And do not let anyone try to rent you a surfboard in Belize. Except during hurricanes, surf is nonexistent here.

If you do decide to bring your own underwater gear to Belize, ask your airline about special size and weight allowances. They are used to bulky baggage on the Belize City run and can usually accommodate all manner of equipment for little or no extra charge.

Before departure, we also recommend that the serious water sports enthusiast take a look at one of the specialty magazines or guidebooks that profile Belize on a regular basis. These are often available in large dive shops and sporting goods stores.

Once you have arrived in Belize, several factors may influence your choice of diving and snorkeling spots. Clarity of Inner Channel waters, for example, is reduced near the outlets of jungle rivers and urban areas like Dangriga and Belize City. Conditions improve on the Caribbean side of the barrier reef and the farther south one goes. The most crystalline water is found around the three atolls, where visibility is often in excess of 100 feet. Water temperatures range from about 74 degrees in winter to 84 degrees in summer. A bodysuit is adequate much of the year, and one never needs more than an eighth-inch wetsuit for thermal insulation.

Telephone service to the Belize mainland and the developed areas of Ambergris Caye and Caye Caulker is very good. Most of the outlying islands can only be reached by VHF marine-band radio. As in the

United States, channels 16 and 68 are the standard hailing frequencies. Live-aboard boats and charter craft also stand by on channel 78.

Once in Belize, divers and snorkelers should not enter the water before informing themselves of its possible hazards. Besides living coral polyps, which should not be touched or stepped on for reasons of ecology as well as health, there are the usual urchins, anemones, jellyfish, and stingrays to look out for. Fire worms (also called bristle worms) and certain types of sponges can cause a burning sensation if brushed against, and the aptly named scorpion fish will sting if stepped on. The sinister-looking barracuda and nurse shark cruise Belize's reefs by the hundreds but will not attack unless deliberately provoked or drawn by the scent of fresh food or blood. In general, it is best not to feed fish underwater. Every species is hungry, and some, such as the moray eel, have teeth sharp enough to remove a finger or two. A good pair of booties or Patagonia Reef Walkers will help reduce the risk of foot injuries.

Medical experts recommend that beginning or infrequent divers over age 35 get a physical exam before diving, preferably from a physician who is familiar with the sport. Among older divers, one out of every four fatalities involves cardiovascular problems. Other conditions that should preclude diving, at any age, are severe asthma, seizure disorders, insulin-dependent diabetes, and any disease that could result in a loss of consciousness.

Divers should always be aware of the risks of decompression sickness, or "the bends," caused by entrapment of nitrogen bubbles in the bloodstream. It is treatable by oxygen therapy or spending time in a decompression chamber. Treatments in a decompression chamber typically run $400 an hour, and only one unit is available in Belize. Because aircraft cabins are pressurized to the equivalent of about 8,000 feet, it is strongly recommended that scuba divers *not* fly sooner than 12 hours after a dive and preferably 24 hours.

Sportfishing

All the joys of the ocean are to be found in the waters of Belize. Great fishing—spin, fly, or troll—can be enjoyed year-round, and the abundance of fish guarantees excellent sport. Some anglers insist that it is impossible to go fishing in Belize and not catch something.

The estuaries and mouths of jungle rivers are known for their tarpon, black snapper, jack-revalle, cubera, and snook; lagoons and coral flats for their bonefish, permit, triggerfish, and barracuda; reef formations for their king mackeral, kingfish, jackfish, grouper, and snapper; and the deeper waters off the outer reefs and atolls for amberjack, sailfish, shark, wahoo, pompano, blackfin tuna, yellowfin tuna, bonito, and marlin.

There are many resorts, boat operators, lodges, and guides serving the needs of sportfishermen (see Inside Belize for a complete list of names and addresses). Almost any hotel near the water can easily provide you with a fishing guide, a boat, and tackle—for rent by the hour, day, or week. Flies, as well as extra tackle items, are available for sale to guests who need them. Many dive shops and diving boats also welcome fishing enthusiasts. You are advised that species vary considerably depending on the depth and clarity of water, or proximity to reefs and rivers.

Many saltwater fly-fishermen come to Belize to stalk the elusive bonefish, an almost transparent fish known for its feisty spirit and crafty ways. (As the name implies, the creature is too bony to make a decent meal.) Although the bonefish is relatively small—averaging 2 to 6 pounds—ounce for ounce it is considered perhaps the toughest fighter in the sea. The predator is often found in knee-deep, crystal-clear coral flats, particularly from November through April, where it attacks smaller fish with lightning speed.

The same waters also teem with the wily permit, especially on coral flats at incoming tides. Many fishing lodges claim Belize is the "permit capital of the world," with specimens weighing in at 30 or more pounds. Torpedo-shaped tarpon, sharp-eyed barracuda, and cubera snapper are equally plentiful near Belizean reefs. Forty-pound or larger tarpon are fairly common from June through August, and good-sized snook are reported all winter. The aggressive barracuda are notorious for breaking leader in the water or snapping at a fisherman's feet once they have been landed. Mutton snapper and jack also frequent the coral flats, along with the occasional grouper and red snapper.

Fisherman and his catch on Laughingbird Caye (Photo by Kevin Schafer)

The much deeper, ocean side of the barrier reef yields king and Spanish mackerel, grouper, snapper, bonito, blackfin tuna, and wahoo. Deep-water anglers can also land sailfish (March to May) and marlin (November to May). You will also encounter many shark, porpoise, and dolphin. The warmest months offer the best chance to hook grouper, mutton snapper, and mangrove snapper.

Lobster season is July 14 to March 15, but most of these spiny crustaceans (lacking the large claws of the cold-water species off the Maine coast) are taken by local fishermen, who also commercially harvest conch, shrimp, and other species.

Saltwater fly-fishing is best in the southern part of Belize, where the presence of divers, snorkelers, and Belizean fishermen has been felt the least. Anything south of Dangriga is likely to be especially promising. It is not unusual to go for days at a time without seeing another rod or line.

If fishing is the primary purpose of your trip, it is best to spend as little time as possible in Belize City. There is no beach here, and the waters are foul. Luckily, with some advance planning, one can easily transfer to a better base of operations on the day of arrival. Many fishing lodges have airport pickup service and often arrange overnight accommodations in Belize City, departing the next morning on chartered boats. Scheduled domestic airline service is also easily arranged from Belize City's municipal airport to Ambergris, Caulker, and Chapel cayes as well as the outlying coastal towns of Placencia (via Big Creek), Dangriga, Corozal, and Punta Gorda.

Many private fishing boat operators are also excellent guides. Some resorts hire locals whose only job is to help you find and catch the fish of your choice. With hundreds of varieties to choose from, simply making a selection may be a daunting task. Native Belizean "consultants" are sometimes included in the price of package tours, especially the week-long excursions to outer islands. The services of such native guides can also be engaged for about $200 a day, including boat, tackle, and fuel. Week-long fishing packages begin at around $1,100 for six days of actual fishing. These Belize-born experts are considered some of the best fly-fishermen in the world. Local guides such as Charles Leslie, of Placencia's Kingfisher Sports, Ltd., will take visitors to remote fishing camps as far away as Punta Negra (near the Guatemalan frontier). Other recommended guides include Richard Young, Jr., of Belize City and Whiprey Caye Guiding of Whiprey Caye (east of Placencia). During these visits to nearly virgin waters, anglers regularly complete a "grand slam"—by landing at least one tarpon, snook, bonefish, and permit within a 24-hour period.

On Ambergris Caye, the El Pescador lodge is recommended as a well-equipped base of operations for saltwater anglers. The resort, which has its own sportfishing boats, guides, and marina, was built by a German-American couple with the help of local Mennonite carpenters. The flats between here and the Belizean mainland are renowned for their tarpon (also called silver kings), recorded at up to about 100 pounds. Although they are not considered good eating, a large tarpon can easily take 90 minutes to subdue with a 10-weight fly rod. Prime time is considered April through August.

Although foreigners are allowed to take as much as 20 pounds of fish with them when they leave Belize, the more common practice is to measure the creature and throw it back for the next customer. An alternative is to share the game fish with one's guide, boatman, and fellow fishermen as a supper entrée. Some fishing lodges, such as Blackbird Caye Resort, require catch-and-release for ecological reasons.

Although some fishing equipment can be rented from local hotels and outfitters in Belize, the selection is limited (but it is improving over time). Live bait, for example, is sometimes hard to come by. Fortunately, one can usually make due with frozen shrimp or wriggling fingerlings plucked from the sea.

Indispensable for Inner Channel fishing (between the barrier reef and the mainland) is a good 9-foot fly rod, a sturdy reel, and an 8-weight floating saltwater tapered fly line. Experienced sportsmen often bring along one each of a light and medium spinning or fly rod, along with a heavier fly, spinning, or bait-casting rod and a deep-running lure.

Major resorts that specialize in sportfishing, such as the Paradise Hotel on Ambergris Caye or Pyramid Island on Caye Chapel, can make exact recommendations on tackle, line strength, lures, rods, and reels, depending on what the angler is after and the time of the year. The Golden Bonefish Lodge on Cockney Point Caye in the

Turneffe Islands is especially recommended for those eager to boat a bonefish or permit. In general, equipment will vary considerably for the following conditions: coral flats, mainland shoreline, mangrove lagoons, river-mouth casting, and deep-water jigging or trolling.

When fishing in tropical Belize, remember that reels in particular need daily cleaning in fresh water and regular lubrication. Other accessories that are often useful here include tennis shoes or Patagonia Reef Walkers for wading in coral flats and shoals, lightweight rip-stop nylon pants, and polarized sunglasses with side shields. The sun is so intense at these latitudes that a severe burn can occur after less than an hour of exposure. For that reason, we recommend that you bring long-sleeved shirts, cotton pants, wide-brimmed hats, bandannas, lip balm, and, of course, waterproof sunscreen (SPF no. 15 or higher).

One final note of caution. The sportfishing industry in Belize has been plagued in recent years by a number of "pirate" operators who illegally net large quantities of fish at the mouth of the country's biggest rivers, the feeding grounds for many important species. The netting is usually carried out at night, when the Department of Fisheries has difficulty keeping an eye out. Much of the catch, including even bonefish, is sold for local consumption in the public markets. Indiscriminate shark fishing has also been reported, with the catch destined for the Far East, where shark-fin soup is a prized delicacy. If, during the course of your visit, you should happen to come into contact with such outlaw fishermen, a discreet word to the local authorities would be appreciated by all who cherish Belize's fine recreational waters.

For a comprehensive list of reputable fishing guides, outfitters, and sportfishing resorts, see Inside Belize.

River Trips, Kayaking, and Sailing

Although Belize is a relatively small and low-lying country, it gets plenty of rainfall and boasts twenty major river systems, plus innumerable perennial streams. These sources supply the nation's domestic water needs and the demands of local agriculture.

For travelers looking for white water adventure, however, Belize may be a disappointment. Because of dramatic fluctuations in water levels and the long-term impact of dredging, there are few consistently reliable white water flows suitable for rafting, kayaking, or canoeing. Some rivers in the upland areas (especially of the Cayo District) have navigable white water during certain periods of the year, but it is best to check with tour operators specializing in such sport for their expert advice on where and when to go. The upper Macal and its tributaries is your best bet. See Inside Belize for local operators specializing in river trips.

Historically, rafts and canoes have always been common modes of transportation on Belizean waterways, and such vessels can easily be rented through most major hotels and travel agencies. The cottage resorts of the Cayo District, for example, often supply rafts, canoes, and occasional kayaks to their guests or even casual visitors. The area's Macal, Mopan, and Belize rivers are particularly well suited to these craft during the drier months, beginning in about January. Small boats can be rented for as little as one-half hour or as much as two weeks. Some operators arrange trips by raft or canoe all the way from the Guatemalan border to Belize City. This sort of journey is an excellent way to observe birds, plants, animals, and people along the riverbanks. Such travel is problematic during the rainy season, for obvious reasons.

Other popular destinations by boat include the offshore islands, the Crooked Tree Wildlife Sanctuary, the Community Baboon Sanctuary, and the Mayan ruins of Cerros, Lamanai, and Xunantunich. A trip up the New River from Orange Walk to Lamanai is a must for bird-watchers, and the New River Lagoon is arguably the loveliest body of fresh water in the country. Boat trips are also recommended to the Northern and Southern lagoons, Gale's Point, Placencia, Sittee River, Monkey River Town, and the Temash River.

Sea kayaking and windsurfing are rapidly increasing in popularity. The calm and relatively shallow waters of the Inner Channel (that portion of the Caribbean between the barrier reef and the mainland) are ideal locations for enjoying these activities, and the larger resorts of the islands can arrange equipment rental and instruction. Several of these hotels also rent small sailboats on a daily or weekly basis.

Areas favored by sea kayakers include the waters of Chetumal Bay, Ambergris Caye, Caye Caulker, and the Hol Chan Channel. Experienced kayakers can also follow the entire length of the barrier reef, camping along the way on such small islands as Bluefield Range, Colson Caye, and Northeast Caye. Windsurfers report the best conditions are on the leeward sides of the cayes, especially in the shallow waters west of Ambergris Caye.

Flora and Fauna

Belize has several of the world's richest habitats. No fewer than 4,000 different species of native flowering plants are found within its borders, along with about 700 species of trees and several hundred species of other plants. Scientists are only now beginning to carry out an exhaustive inventory of Belize's plants. The task is daunting: over 70 percent of the country is under some kind of forest cover, and almost half of Belize's primary forest is still standing.

In the animal kingdom, the numbers are even more staggering. Literally thousands of varieties of insects are native to the five major ecosystems of Belize, along with hundreds of mammals, reptiles, amphibians, and fish. Some of the rare or endangered species found here in relatively abundant numbers are the tapir, howler monkey, anteater, king vulture, Morelet's crocodile, sea turtle, mantee, and jaguar, the hemisphere's largest cat. The pamphlet entitled "Checklist of the Birds of Belize" (Carnegie Museum of Natural History) lists over 530 species that have been sighted here, including more than 200 migratory birds from North America who winter in the tropics. In many parts of the inland forest, it is not unusual to see as many as 120 different birds over a period of as little as four or five days. Of the world's more than 90,000 butterfly species, a large percentage are found here.

Part of this species diversity is a result of Belize's relatively small population and the pristine quality of its wilderness. El Salvador, which has more than twenty-five times as many people in only a slightly smaller area, has many fewer plants and animals. Another rea-

Cashew fruit with nut in Crooked Tree Village (International Expeditions Photo)

son for the incredible assemblages of flora and fauna found here is the variation in habitat zones. There are five basic ecological regions: northern hardwood, southern hardwood, mountain pine ridge, coastal savannas and pine ridges, and mangroves and beaches. Within these categories, distinctions can be drawn based on rainfall amounts (varying widely from north to south), altitude (from sea level to nearly 4,000 feet), and soil types (from very poor to very fertile).

It is beyond the scope of this book to discuss each of these habitats in detail. For the reader with a serious interest in the natural history of Belize, or specific aspects of its flora and fauna, we suggest looking at some of the specialized publications listed in the Appendix.

Scientists are still finding plants and animals in Belize which are completely new to science or previously unrecorded in Belize. One expedition into the Maya Mountains, for example, turned up a bird in the latter category dubbed the scaly-throated foliage gleaner. Several new species of amphibians and flowering plants have been found during the 1990s.

Rather than attempt an exhaustive discussion of Belizean ecosystems and their native inhabitants in this limited space, we will simply provide a few thumbnail sketches of some of Belize's most intriguing flora and fauna. Keep in mind that this represents only a tiny fraction of what Belize has to offer.

Jabiru Stork

The jabiru is the largest flying bird in the Western Hemisphere, standing up to 5 feet tall and with a wingspan of up to 10 feet. It is also one of the rarest birds in Central America. Besides its size, the jabiru can be identified by its massive black bill that turns slightly up and its bare black head, which has a wide, inflatable crimson band at the base of the neck.

In Belize, where the jabiru is fully protected, a population of about 30 storks nest during winter months along swamp edges and roadside pools as well as wet savannas and lowland pine ridges. Belize's jabirus return from Mexico around November to make their nests, usually at the top of a tall, secluded tree. Breeding continues until early April, when the birds begin migrating back to Mexico for the summer. The Crooked Tree Wildlife Sanctuary is a favorite breeding ground of this enormous bird.

Parrots

Seven species of parrots, one species of parakeet, and one species of macaw make Belize their home. Parrots have few enemies in the jungle except for larger predators, who tend to eliminate the weakest or most vulnerable birds. A far bigger threat is posed by humans, who continue to destroy the parrot's forest habitat, capture the animal for commercial purposes, or even kill it for food.

The capture of young parrots usually does considerable damage to the environment, since nesting trees are often cut down in the hope that chicks will somehow survive the fall. In an effort to discourage collection of these birds, the Belize Zoo and U.S. Fish and Wildlife Service have produced a conservation poster urging people, "Keep a Poster, Not a Parrot." The species captured in greatest numbers here is the yellow-headed parrot, prized in North America as a fluent and easily trained "talker." Other vocal members of the same family are

Red-lored Amazon parrot (Photo by Kevin Schafer)

the Aztec (or olive-throated) parakeet and mealy (or blue-crowned) parrot. The latter mates for life and almost always flies in a two-by-two formation with its partner. These species are quite social and like to live near others of their kind.

The common names of parrots are inspired by easily identifiable head markings ("lore" refers to the area between eyes and beak, "crown" is the top of the head, and "front" is the forehead, while "hood" and "head" are self-explanatory). The less gregarious parrots found in Belize are the brown-hooded, red-lored, yellow-lored, yellow-headed, white-fronted, and white-crowned. Only sharp-eyed birders are usually able to tell the latter two sets of species apart.

Like many tropical animals (and people), parrots usually take a nap during the heat of the day and are most often seen during later afternoon and early morning feeding periods. The birds roost overnight.

Scarlet Macaw

One of the rarest birds in Belize is the scarlet macaw, the third-largest of the world's sixteen surviving macaw species. It is one of eight such species in danger of extinction throughout much of its range, which extends from subtropical Mexico south to Bolivia.

A macaw sighting is an unforgettable experience. Mature birds, locally referred to as parrots, are over 2 feet tall and adorned with brilliant plumage, particularly bright red wing feathers adorned with dabs of yellow, orange, and blue.

The greatest threat to this magnificent bird is the destruction of its forest habitat, nest-robbing for the wild bird trade, and killing for meat and feathers. The first (and only) systematic study of scarlet macaws in Belize was carried out by the Center for the Study of Tropical Birds. It concluded that the bird has a relatively confined range in the dense central forests of the country, extending from the Maya Mountain divide north to the Mountain Pine Ridge. A few individuals and small flocks have been seen in other areas from time to time. In recent years, however, no more than 30 birds have ever been seen at any given time or location. Researchers noted about 40 separate sightings of scarlet macaws in central Belize from mid-1985 through mid-1989, typically involving two to four birds each.

"It is certain that the status of the scarlet macaw in Belize is precarious," concluded the final report of the Center for the Study of Tropical Birds. "Not only are there the persistent threats of habitat destruction and disturbance by British Armed Forces, logging operations, plant collectors, etc., but the threat of wild birds being caught for the pet trade continues," despite the latter's illegality. Fortunately, a 1991 expedition to the Raspaculo wilderness found a healthy population of macaws in Belize's most remote interior jungles.

Blue-crowned motmot (Photo by Kevin Schafer)

Blue-Crowned Motmot

This beautiful and relatively large bird is sometimes called Good Cook, because its deep-throated call (usually heard at dawn or dusk) resembles those two words. It is also distinguished by its indigo head feathers and long tail. The latter acquires an oddly pointed shape through removal of central feathers by preening and wear. While the blue-crowned motmot is fairly common, its cousin, the keel-billed motmot, is one of the rarest birds in Central America. Only a few sightings have been documented, notably, near Mountain Equestrian Trails and Caracol in the Cayo District. The bird is believed to be locally extinct in all the countries surrounding Belize.

Roseate Spoonbill

One of the rarest birds in Belize, this large, pinkish creature with a distinctive spoon-shaped bill once nested in marshy areas around Ambergris Caye until those habitats were destroyed by local fishermen. This species breeds in the Shipstern area, and as many as 30 spoonbills (possibly migrants) can sometimes be seen around Big Falls, Crooked Tree Lagoon, Ambergris Caye, Mussel Creek, and the northern wetlands.

Jaguar

The jaguar was among the most revered animals of the ancient Maya, and even today this jungle cat commands great respect among Belizeans, who often refer to it as a tiger or *el tigre*. Up to 6 feet long and weighing as much as 250 pounds, its likeness turns up on modern T-shirts as well as eroded Mayan ornaments. Originally found from the southwestern United States to Argentina, the jaguar (largest cat in the Western Hemisphere) has become extinct or endangered throughout its range. In Belize, however, the animal is common in many areas, even within a half-hour drive of Belize City. This nocturnal predator feeds primarily on peccary, paca, tapir, or deer, along with an occasional bird, lizard, turtle, or fish.

Contrary to local belief, jaguars will not attack humans unless provoked and usually do not steal livestock unless they are sick, injured, or very old. In fact, they are the least known of large cats to attack people. Human encroachment continues to limit their territory, and hunters, operating illegally, occasionally kill perfectly healthy animals in Belize for their hides. Alan Rabinowitz, during an intensive field study, brought the jaguar into the international spotlight as a means to protect the Cockscomb Basin Wildlife Sanctuary, the only designated jaguar preserve in the world.

Jaguars are very territorial, ranging over as much as 60 square miles of forest and savanna. The male, a solitary creature who partners with one female at a time, marks the boundaries of his kingdom with tree scratches and ground scrapings. The other four native cats of Belize are the puma, ocelot, margay, and jaguarundi.

Baird's Tapir

Called a "mountain cow" by locals, this nocturnal species is the national animal of Belize. Still fairly plentiful here, the Baird's tapir has almost disappeared from the rest of its native Central America and Mexico, earning it a place on the endangered species list. It feeds on fruits, aquatic plants, grasses, and shrubs. Despite the fact that tapirs have thick hides and a disagreeable flavor, their ranks have been thinned by native hunters, many of whom mistakenly believe these docile vegetarians will attack and kill their domestic animals. The tapir is adaptable to almost any Belizean environment, but today it is most plentiful in mountain forests where there is water nearby. Although it can weigh up to 650 pounds, the Baird's tapir is surprisingly agile and has splayed feet for navigating mudholes. The herbivore's long, flexible upper lip and strong molars are well suited for foraging and swallowing twigs, nuts, and other tough plant tissues. The tapir has an excellent sense of smell and hearing, although its eyesight is weak. The docile beasts are usually solitary and tend to avoid confrontation by steering clear of other large animals. Perhaps the best-known Baird's tapir is named April and lives in the Belize Zoo, where she has become both a favorite of visiting schoolchildren and a national mascot of sorts.

Hickatee

The Central American river turtle is making one of its last stands along the waterways of Belize. Locally referred to as the hickatee, it can only be found here and in the most isolated parts of southern Mexico and northern Guatemala. Prized as a food source (slowly dying specimens can be seen for sale in Belizean markets), this turtle spends almost its entire life in the water, except when it lays its eggs in rotting vegetation along the riverbanks, where they incubate themselves. The hickatee is brown or olive drab on its back, with a cream-colored underbelly. Large males weigh as much as 50 pounds. Unfortunately, the animal seeks out fish and aquatic plants by night, then sleeps or floats much of the day, making it an easy target for man.

Sea Turtles

Three of the world's eight species of sea turtles are known to nest in Belize: the green, loggerhead, and hawksbill. Although the situation is changing, many are still taken for their flesh, eggs, and shells. Increasingly, turtles are being kept from their traditional nesting areas by fences, buildings, people, pets, bright lights, and loud noises. For these reasons, all three species found in Belize have been declared endangered. Visitors are urged to respect the nesting season (June 1 to August 31), refrain from buying turtle meat or products, and avoid throwing into the sea plastic bags in which turtles can become entangled.

No one knows how the female loggerhead turtle, called *lagra* in Belize, can find her way back to nesting beaches as many as fifty years after the same animal left that same stretch of sand to spend her life in the sea. Yet that is exactly what happens when this large turtle (up to 300 pounds) returns to Belize to lay up to 100 leathery eggs at a time. After a two-month incubation, tiny babies emerge from the shells and make a mad dash for the water. Most are caught en route by birds, crabs, lizards, and humans. Less than 5 percent typically survive to reproduce.

The green turtle is an even larger species, measuring up to 4 feet in length and weighing up to 600 pounds. Because its greenish meat and tender eggs are considered delicacies, this turtle has been hunted extensively. It also sometimes gets caught in shrimp nets while surfacing from the sea grass beds where it feeds. Although it cannot legally be exported, the green turtle may still be purchased in the Belize city market and found on the menu of local restaurants.

One of the smaller sea turtles is the hawksbill, which gets its name from its sharp, hooked beak. The animal's top shell is covered with multicolored scales that have long been popular for use in combs, eyeglass frames, hair clips, and jewelry. The hawksbill is often killed before it reaches maturity, which has had a devastating effect on the species' ability to reproduce.

Dolphins

Bottlenose dolphins are common off the coast of Belize, and research is now being done on these marine mammals at Blackbird Caye on the Turneffe atoll. Thanks to the media exploits of Flipper, the bottlenose is the most well-known dolphin species in the world. Individuals may be gray or whitish in color and can grow up to 10 feet long. These very social animals can often be seen riding the bow wake of powerboats. They breathe air and give birth to live young, which they subsequently nurse. The complexity of the social interactions among dolphins, scientists believe, may help explain the evolution of their large brains. The creatures emit a variety of complex buzzing, whistling, and clicking sounds that bounce off objects like sonar echoes and enable dolphins to "see" those objects. This process is called echolocation. The sound beams can apparently even penetrate living tissue, which seems to allow male dolphins to "see" when a female is approaching fertility and force her to follow them for mating purposes.

Basilisks and Iguanas

Once you've seen a basilisk in action, you'll know why Belizeans have labeled it "the Jesus Christ lizard." The prehistoric-looking animal moves with such great speed, often on its hind legs, through its riverside habitat that it seems to be able to skim right across the surface of a creek or river without sinking, disappearing into foliage on the opposite bank. The basilisk is virtually impossible to catch: extra flaps of skin across the toes of enlarged rear feet make this water-walking trick possible. While these omnivorous reptiles appear fierce—like miniature *Tyrannosaurus rex*—they prefer to munch on leaves, flowers, and fruit in their favorite trees (often a giant ficus), in addition to the occasional insect and bird. They can be distinguished by their ridged backs, ranging in color from yellow-brown to muted gray, and (among males) reddish throat sacs. Local people love to eat the raw eggs of the female basilisk, and the creatures are becoming scarce in areas where pesticides are used. Predatory birds are another enemy. The dominant males are quite territorial and can be seen perched on high tree limbs from which they can survey their domains along inland waterways.

Two iguanid species also live in Belize: the green iguana or "bush-chicken" and the black or land iguana, locally called a "wish-willy." These creatures spend most of the day sunbathing and are very territorial, responding to trespassers with repeated patterns of head-bobbing. These animals (and their eggs) are easy prey for hungry villagers as well as birds, snakes, and coati. Wish-willies are commonly encountered on the offshore cayes of Belize, where they frequent vegetation near beaches and mangrove forests.

Fer-de-lance
Variously known as the yellow-jaw tommygoff, barba amarilla, and tres minutos, the fer-de-lance is a nocturnal pit viper related to the water moccasin and tropical rattlesnake. Because of its fast-acting venom, the fer-de-lance is considered to be among the world's deadliest snakes. There are many reliable reports in Belize of individuals who have died soon after stumbling on the animal in the bush. However, unless provoked, or you are very unlucky, the vipers will avoid you and stick to smaller game, such as birds, rats, and other small mammals. The fer-de-lance is at home in any part of Belize, including cities, and can be vicious if it does decide to attack. Adults can reach 8 feet in length, enabling them to strike from a coiled position. Their two retractable fangs are the largest of any snake, in proportion to size. Keen awareness of smell and temperature enables the fer-de-lance to accurately pinpoint warm bodies in the dark, when it is most likely to be active. It is easily identified by its arrow-shaped head, diamond-patterned back, and thick-set body. If you are bitten, medical help should be sought at once. The best prevention is wearing boots, however, since most fer-de-lance bites are in the feet and ankles.

Palm Trees

The cohune palm, widespread throughout Belize, is one of the forest community's most useful members. Its fronds are used as thatch in roofs, and a valuable oil can be extracted from its fruit. Husks from the tree's palm nuts make excellent fuel, and the nut meat can be pounded into a flour that will store many weeks without spoiling. The cohune was highly regarded by the ancient Maya, who considered it a symbol of fertility. Because of the many practical uses of the palm, this plant is almost always spared when forests are cut down for subsistence agriculture.

Dominant in low-lying marshes and along riverbanks are palmetto palms, which can grow to great heights and provide fronds used in traditional house construction.

Mangroves

Almost the entire coastline of Belize, including the fringes of its many cayes, are covered by dense stands of black, white, and red mangrove, with the latter species dominating. Different types of mangroves are adapted to varying degrees of salinity, and you will notice them changing as you go away from sources of salt water. While 90 percent of the world's original mangrove forests have been destroyed, Belize can boast that 90 percent of its mangrove habitat remains intact. The ancient Maya made extensive use of the mangrove wetlands, as evidenced by the use of crocodile and manatee images in their artwork. Mangroves as tall as 100 feet or more can be seen along some waterways, such as the Toledo District's Temash River. Although these tangled saltwater thickets have traditionally been despised by settlers, who often cleared them as quickly as possible, they protect shorelines from erosion during storms and provide an irreplaceable nursery for small fish and crustaceans. Snorkeling near mangrove roots often is more rewarding, in terms of marine life, than swimming in open water or near coral reefs. Above the waterline, visitors can see egrets, herons, ibises, spoonbills, pelicans, frigatebirds, raptors, and boobies amid the tangled roots and branches. Coatimundis, crocodiles, anteaters, tapirs, jaguars, raccoons, and boa constrictors are also found in these wetland areas.

Bicycling

Bicycling opportunities in Belize are limited, and until recently the sport of mountain biking was virtually unknown. Nevertheless, a growing number of tour operators, resorts, and lodges are now catering to the needs of bicycle enthusiasts, and an infrastructure is gradually developing. Check the list of tour operators in Inside Belize for specialists in this sport. Three of the best are Bike Belize in Belize City, Red Rooster Bicycle Tours in San Ignacio, and Paradise Bicycle Tours in Evergreen, Colorado.

The biggest problem bikers will encounter in Belize is the limited network of roads in the country and an even smaller number of trails suitable for bicycle transportation. Belizean roads are notoriously bad, characterized by an unusual number of potholes, mud bogs, sharp rocks, and sand traps. Even the best thoroughfares, such as the Western Highway from Belize City to Benque Viejo, typically have narrow traffic lanes, few service stations, and virtually no shoulders.

Due to the rainy climate and lush vegetation, trails are often difficult to negotiate, even for those on foot. Bicyclists should be aware that unstable, slick, and mucky surfaces and narrow passageways are the *norm* off-road, not the exception. Trails are frequently blocked by fallen trees and branches, including those of many plants whose burrs, thorns, and nettles can lead to painful rashes and puncture wounds. Some very common varieties, such as the aptly named "give-and-take" palm and "sticky" bamboo, cause cuts that can become easily infected.

A different set of obstacles confronts bikers setting out on the crowded streets of Belize City and other big towns. Roads are sometimes very narrow and congested, crammed with jostling people, cars, trucks, and other bicycles. In addition, your bike may be much coveted by an impoverished Belizean, so make sure it is secured when unattended. Better yet, bring it indoors whenever possible.

On the cayes, sandy lanes that pass for modest thoroughfares may jam gears and swallow up narrow-tired bicycles. Ambergris Caye has the most navigable trails, and Amigo Travel in San Pedro (among others) rents bikes for a reasonable fee. The proprietors can direct visitors to some scenic areas north and south of the town.

Currently the most accessible and rewarding area of Belize for bicyclists is the Cayo District, especially the Mountain Pine Ridge forest reserve. Mountain biking is increasingly popular, and many lodges now have bikes to rent. Try the Maya Mountain Lodge near Santa Elena or Red Rooster in San Ignacio. Most of the region's many attractions are easily reached from any of the Cayo's lodges or campgrounds, and there are many destinations worth visiting (see chap. 6). The main routes are well-maintained dirt roads, and they are relatively uncrowded. This area's primary advantages are slightly cooler temperatures and lower humidity than the coast, with relatively few biting insects. Watch for rain, however, as these mostly dirt roads turn into mud in a hurry.

Side trips from either the Cayo or Belize District include the Belize Zoo, Guanacaste National Park, Community Baboon Sanctuary, Blue Hole National Park, St. Herman's Cave, Five Blues National Park, Crooked Tree Nature Sanctuary, Gale's Point Manatee Sanctuary, and the Mayan ruins of Altun Ha. Because Belize is a narrow country (about 70 miles), an ambitious bicyclist can make it all the way from Belize City to Guatemala in a single day. Another popular one-day excursion is from Dangriga to the Cockscomb Basin Wildlife Sanctuary, with interesting rest stops en route at Hopkins and Maya Center.

Customs officials at the international airport and land border crossings are now accustomed to seeing tourists bring bicycles into Belize, but it is a good idea to carry proof of ownership or have your passport stamped with the bike specifically listed. This is a precaution against having to pay import duty on the item, since authorities may assume the bicycle will be sold in Belize, where they are quite expensive. In traveling to the cayes, remember that domestic airplanes are small, propeller-driven craft that may be unable to accommodate large bicycles unless they are disassembled. Most passenger boats, however, can easily store such cargo. High-quality mountain bicycles are now being manufactured in Belize as well, and you may wish to inquire about their purchase before starting your trip.

Mennonite Country

The lush subtropical landscape of Belize has been radically trans-
formed into something out of the American Midwest in the various
Mennonite farming communities established during the more than
thirty-five years since these denim-clad newcomers began settling
here. Most of the Mennonite migration took place from 1958 to
1962, when thousands left their rural homesteads in Canada and
Mexico and headed south for steamy Central America. These hard-
working and deeply spiritual immigrants have taken raw, nutrient-
deficient land and made it amazingly productive. Today Belize's estimated 6,000 Mennonites feed not only their own families but much
of the rest of the country. Besides most grains and fresh vegetables,
they also contribute much of the nation's poultry and dairy products.
Mennonite furniture is also highly prized.

Visitors may not think of the Mennonite colonies as an appropriate item for a tourist's agenda. After all, the Mennonites of Belize
tend to stick to themselves, only venturing into town to visit the doctor, deal with bureaucracies, or buy the few supplies that they cannot
provide for themselves. A large percentage prefer to be left alone and
should not be approached even by well-meaning outsiders. The most
traditional Mennonites do not wish to be photographed. Yet a small
segment of the Mennonite population welcomes limited contact with
the secular community, and many of these individuals will be happy
to show off their accomplishments. If you are lucky, you may even be
invited into a Mennonite home for conversation and a meal.

Contrary to popular belief, not all Mennonites are alike. Take a
drive west of Orange Walk Town, for example, and you will pass
many smiling Mennonites driving pickup trucks or tractors with their
radios blaring, heading for farmhouses equipped with electricity, telephones, and even satellite dishes. Wander around the backroads of
Upper Barton Creek, however, and you will just as likely come across
somber Mennonites squinting into the sun atop horse-drawn wagons.
They are easily identified by their plain clothing and shy manner.

Adherence to ancestral traditions and religious values varies considerably among the Mennonites of Belize, and the majority now
accept some degree of modernization. The softening can most readi-

ly be seen in their mode of dress. Conservative Mennonite men still favor suspenders, long-sleeved shirts buttoned to the neck, straw hats, and dark trousers, while their wives and daughters prefer dark long dresses and wide-brimmed bonnets. But an increasing number of individuals are adorning themselves with brightly colored fabrics and wrapping jaunty ribbons around their hats. Some wear casual western clothing.

Despite these differences, all Mennonites can trace their heritage back to 1531, when the Dutch priest Menno Simons founded their faith during the Radical Reformation, a backlash against the Roman Catholic hierarchy. Members of the pacifist Anabaptist sect were frequently persecuted over the years by both religious leaders and political officials, angry over their militant refusal to pay land taxes or support the military. As a result, the Mennonites migrated as a tight-knit group from Holland to the Friesen Islands of Germany, then to Switzerland and finally to Prussia. During the seventeenth and eighteenth centuries, many headed for the hinterlands of Canada and the United States, particularly Manitoba and Pennsylvania, where they could continue their simple, agricultural life-style in peace. The Canadian colony split after World War I, with a large group heading for Chihuahua and Durango in Mexico. Then, in the late 1950s, crowding and political changes in their host countries prompted about 3,000 Mennonites to set out once again for a life free of religious persecution and the pressures of modern society. Their destination was the Río Hondo valley of British Honduras, now called Belize.

The Mennonites have settled mostly in the empty western quadrants of the Corozal, Orange Walk, and Cayo districts, where unoccupied land was available free of charge from a government anxious to see it developed. Huge tracts of up to 148,000 acres were acquired by the new colonists, who pooled their resources to quickly become the most productive farmers in their adopted homeland. The more traditional Mennonites have managed this without using electricity and most forms of mechanization, relying instead on human and animal labor. Over the years, some progressive Mennonites have started using power tools, motorized vehicles, and electricity. A few are now praised as the best mechanics in Belize.

Among themselves, Mennonites still speak in the same form of archaic German-Dutch dialect they have relied on throughout 400 years of dislocation. Many children and women speak no other language. They operate their own churches, schools, banks, and businesses and by government decree are exempt from military service and certain forms of taxation. They prefer not to vote or participate in electoral politics, but Belizean officials have welcomed their many contributions, which include the establishment of new roads, lumber mills, small-scale factories, and power plants. Mennonites established the first successful dairies in Belize and were the first to raise chickens on a large scale.

As the Mennonite subculture has evolved, some of their churches have started to absorb many native Belizeans, of all colors and creeds. There are now Mennonite congregations made up of Spanish-speaking mestizos, Mayan Indians, Garifuna fishermen, and Creole farmers. Intermarriage is increasingly common.

At least twenty-eight different branches of the Mennonite faith now coexist in Belize, although the colonies are divided into two basic camps: the modern Progressives (also called the Evangelical Mennonite Mission Church) and the conservative Old Colony (or Kleine Gemeinde Church). Strongholds of traditional Kleine Gemeinde values include the "camps" (as colonies are known) of Shipyard, Little Belize, and Barton's Creek. Progressives have congregated in Linda Vista and Rosita, among other villages. Mixed enclaves are found around Blue Creek, Georgeville, Orange Walk Town, Hattieville, and Spanish Lookout.

The Mennonite communities have no tourism infrastructure, so it is necessary to inquire among hotel and tour operators and local residents if you wish to visit their homesteads and churches. Belize Services, Mountain Equestrian Trails, Lamanai Outpost Lodge, and Chaa Creek Cottages have expertise in this area. Mennonite markets and businesses are of course open to the public, although these are not well marked in traditional communities, which shun any form of ostentatiousness. The Cayo village of Upper Barton Creek, south of Georgeville, is a good place to buy fresh fruits and vegetables from Mennonites, and you can sample delicious ice creams and cheese in their Georgeville stores. Maya Ranch (92-2188) arranges buggy rides with Mennonites in the Upper Barton Creek area.

The Spanish Lookout community about 20 miles east of San Ignacio in the Cayo District is open to casual visitors who wish to tour the Mennonite countryside by private car, bicycle, or even boat. Sundays are good days to visit: after attending church, Mennonites visit their neighbors to talk and share meals. When the weather is good, some families go to the nearby Aguacate Lagoon on Cadena Creek to swim, fish, and picnic.

There are a handful of Mennonite guides catering to tourists, notably to the Lamanai Mayan site on New Lagoon. David and Jacob Klassen are two riverside farmers at Shipyard's Camp One who provide boat trips to the ruins. One of the leaders of the 2,000-member Shipyard community, Jacob Wall, runs the Belize Mills sawmill where visitors are welcome to buy high-quality Mennonite bowls, chairs, doors, and other furniture. His is one of five sawmills in the area processing mahogany, santa maría, cedar, and other tropical woods used domestically and in the United States. Wall can be reached via local two-meter VHF radio (there are no telephones in this part of Belize).

Farther to the northwest in the Orange Walk District is the Blue Creek hydroelectric power generator, near the confluence of the Río Bravo (Blue Creek) and the Río Hondo. Built to serve a large group of Mennonite families, this is the only water-powered electricity station in Belize and visitors are welcome. Not far away, in Blue Creek Village, outsiders may shop or refuel at the Mennonite-owned Linda Vista Shopping Center and eat a taco or hamburger at Jacob Neufeld's Store, a genuine Mennonite fast-food emporium.

Inside Belize

Where to Stay

Note: Many hotels, lodges, and guest houses in Belize automatically add a 10% service charge and/or a 5% mandatory government room tax to all bills. A surtax of 3% on all credit card charges is also commonplace.

Rate schedule (double occupancy, all prices in U.S. dollars, accurate as of mid-1993):
HIGH: $60 and up
MODERATE: $30 to $59
LOW: $29 or less

Belize District

HIGH

Belize Biltmore Plaza
Mile 3, Northern Highway
Belize City
Tel. 2-32302, fax 2-30132,
U.S.A. (800) 327-3573
(shops, swimming pool, restarant, bar, karaoke, tours)

Bellevue Hotel
5 Southern Foreshore
Belize City
Tel. 2-77051, fax 2-73253
U.S.A. (800) 223-9815
(also rents cottages on St. George's Caye)

Château Caribbean
6 Marine Parade
Belize City
Tel. 2-30800, fax 2-30900
(restaurant and bar overlooking Caribbean)

Radisson Ft. George Hotel
Box 321, 2 Marine Parade
Belize City
Tel. 2-77400, fax 2-73820
U.S.A. (800) 633-4734, Canada (402) 967-3442
(swimming pool, travel agency, gift shop)

Maruba Resort and Jungle Spa
Maskall Village
Tel. 3-22199
U.S.A. (800) 627-8227 or (713) 799-2031, fax (713) 795-8573
(10 miles north of Altun Ha ruins; offers boating, bird-watching, swimming, and complete spa)

Ramada Royal Reef Hotel
Newton Barracks Road
Belize City
Tel. 2-32672, fax 2-31649
U.S.A. (800) 228-9898
(restaurant, gift shop, convention center, swimming pool, marina)

Villa Hotel
13 Cork Street
Belize City
Tel. 2-32800, fax 2-30276
U.S.A. (800) 421-0000, fax (213) 487-5467

MODERATE

Belize Guest House
(Charles Hope)
2 Hutson Street
Belize City
Tel. 2-77569

Bird's Eye View Lodge
Crooked Tree Village
Tel. 2-72304
(bird-watching, boating, nature treks)

Chaa Hiix Lodge
(Robert Brooks)
Spanish River
(bird-watching specialist near Crooked Tree; access by boat)

Dibasei Guest House
26 Hydes Lane
Belize City
Tel. 2-33981, fax 2-32136
(Garifuna owned and operated with gift shop and restaurant on premises; cultural tours to Dangriga and surrounding Garifuna villages)

Fort Street Guest House
(Rachel Emmer)
Box 3, 4 Fort Street
Belize City
Tel. 2-30116, fax 2-78808
U.S.A. (800) 538-6802
(assist in trips to interior, cayes, atolls; popular among adventure outfitters and conservation groups; room rates include breakfast)

Glenthorne Manor
(Winil Grant Borg)
27 Barracks Road
Belize City
Tel. 2-44212
(Belizean-style bed and breakfast)

Hotel El Centro
Box 122, 4 Bishop Street
Belize City
Tel. 2-72413, fax 2-74553

Kahlua Guest House & Bar
(James and Delia Wang)
120 Eve Street
Belize City
Tel. 2-31130, fax 2-31185
(air-conditioning; cable TV; oceanfront; occasional entertainment at night)

Hotel Mopan
(Tom and Jean Shaw)
55 Regent Street
Tel. 2-77351 or 2-77356
(bar and travel agency on premises, assists in conservation-oriented trips)

Mom's Triangle Inn
(Sue Williams)
11 Handyside Street
Tel. 2-45523 or 2-45073, fax 2-31975
(restaurant; tours arranged to zoo, cayes, and fishing areas; agent for Maya Mountain Lodge, Mountain Equestrian Trails)

Paradise Inn
(Rudy Crawford)
Crooked Tree Village
Tel. 25-2535, fax 2-52534,
U.S.A. (718) 498-2221
(bungalows on Crooked Tree Lagoon, restaurant, horseback riding, canoeing, boating, guided tours, fishing, Mayan ruins, bird-watching a specialty)

Royal Orchid Hotel
New Road & Douglas Jones Streets
Belize City
Tel. 2-32112, fax 2-32789

LOW

Community Baboon Sanctuary Bed and Breakfasts
Contact: Belize Audubon Society
Tel. 2-77369 or 2-78562
(stay with a Creole family, reservations preferred)

Eyre Street Guest House
7 Eyre Street
Tel. 2-77724
(basic rooms with communal shower and bath area)

Freddie's Guest House
86 Eve Street
Tel. 2-44396

Golden Dragon Hotel
29 Queen Street
Tel. 2-45271
(also operates Chinese restaurant)

Little Eden Bed and Breakfast
(Fred and Sally Cuckow)
Burrel Boom Cutoff, Northern Highway
Box 1317, Belize City
Tel. 2-8219
(budget accommodations near howler monkey sanctuary)

Monkey Bay Wildlife Sanctuary
(Matthew Miller)
Mile 32, Western Highway
Tel. 8-23180
(camping under thatch shelters at private nature reserve)

North Front Street Guest House
124 N. Front Street
Tel. 2-77595
(basic rooms with communal bath and shower, breakfast available)

Seaside Guest House
(Philip Remare)
3 Prince Street
Tel. 2-78339
(breakfast available; popular among conservationists; makes arrangements for Gales Point homestays and Parrot's Perch Lodge in Cayo District)

Ambergris Caye and Caye Caulker

HIGH

Journey's End Caribbean Club
(John and Jennie Rietz)
Box 13
San Pedro
Tel. 26-2173, fax 26-2028
U.S.A. (800) 447-0474
(waterfront cabanas, poolside villas; 4.5 miles north of San Pedro; windsurfing, snorkeling, sailing)

Mata Rocks Resort (formerly House of the Rising Sun)
Ambergris Caye
Tel. 2-62336
U.S.A. (503) 645-7323, fax (503) 690-9308
(rooms with kitchens, 1.2 miles south of San Pedro)

Paradise Resort Hotel and Villas
Box 25
Belize City (located near San Pedro)
Tel. 2-62083
(fishing, boating, restaurant and bar)

Ramon's Village Resort
(Ramon Nuñez)
San Pedro
Tel. 2-62071, fax 2-62214,
U.S.A. 800-MAGIC or (601) 649-1990
(diving instruction and services, sailing, fishing, snorkeling, boat charters)

Rock's Inn
San Pedro
Tel. 2-62326, fax 2-62358
(air-conditioned suites with kitchens, on beach north of San Pedro)

Spindrift Hotel
San Pedro
Tel. 26-2018, fax 2-62251
(Italian restaurant on premises)

Sun Breeze Beach Resort
San Pedro
Tel. 2-62191, fax 2-2346
(sailing, snorkeling, windsurfing, diving, scuba, volleyball)

Victoria House
Box 22
San Pedro (2 miles south)
Tel. 2-62067, fax 2-62429
U.S.A. (800) 247-5159
(popular among adventure outfitters)

MODERATE

Barrier Reef Hotel
(Old Blake House)
San Pedro
Tel. 2-62075, fax 2-62719

Conch Shell Inn
San Pedro
Tel. 2-62062

Coral Beach Hotel and Dive Club
San Pedro
Tel. 2-62013, fax 2-62864
(diving, snorkeling, fishing)

El Pescador
Punta Arena Beach
San Pedro
Tel. and fax 2-62398
(3 miles north of San Pedro, fishing specialists)

Lena's Hotel
Caye Caulker
Tel. 22-2106

Lily's Caribbean Lodge
San Pedro
Tel. 2-62059

Royal Palm Inn
Box 18
San Pedro
Tel. 2-62148, fax 2-62329

San Pedro Holiday Hotel
(Celi McCorkle)
San Pedro
Tel. 26-2014, fax 2-62295
(rooms, bungalows, or apartments; complete dive shop; arranges snorkeling, fishing, and glass-bottom boat trips)

Thomas Hotel
San Pedro
Tel. 2-62061
(scuba services)

LOW

Ignacio Beach Cabin's
Caye Caulker
Tel. 2-22212
(beach bungalows and camping, reef trips)

Marin's
(John Marin)
Caye Caulker
Tel. 2-22110
(reef trips)

Mira Mar
(Melvin Badillo)
Caye Caulker
Tel. 2-22110

Martha's Hotel
San Pedro
Tel. 2-62053, fax 2-62589

Rivas Guest House
Caye Caulker
Tel. 2-22127

Rubie's Hotel
San Pedro
Tel. 2-62063
(ask for Richie Woods, resident naturalist and reef expert)

San Pedrano Hotel
San Pedro
Tel. 2-62054

Shirley's Guest House
Caye Caulker
Tel. 2-22145

Tom's Hotel
(Tom Young)
Caye Caulker
Tel. 2-22102
(snorkeling, reef trips)

Vega's Far Inn
Caye Caulker
Tel. 2-22142, fax 2-31580
(camping and rooms)

Other Cayes

HIGH

Blackbird Caye Resort
(Al Dugan, Betty Taylor, Ray Lightburn)
On Blackbird Caye, Turneffe Islands
Box 1315, Belize City
Tel. 2-30882
1415 Louisiana, Suite 3100
Houston, TX 77002
(800) 537-1431 or (713) 658-1142
(conservation-oriented resort, diving, fishing)

Blue Marlin Lodge
(Mike and Rosella Zabaneh)
Box 21
Dangriga on South Water Caye, 27 miles east of Dangriga)
Tel. 5-22243, fax 5-22296
U.S.A. (800) 798-1558
(diving and fishing lodge; offers dive boats, tanks, snorkeling, trips to Glover's Reef; complete dive shop)

Castaways Lodge
Long Caye
Tel. 2-75785
(snorkeling, fishing, swimming)

Lighthouse Reef Resort
Northern Two Caye, Lighthouse Reef Atoll
Box 26, Belize City
Tel. 2-31205, U.S.A. (800) 423-3114
(fishing, diving, snorkeling, swimming; private airstrip)

Little Water Caye Resort
(off Placencia)
Box 1666, Belize City
Tel./fax 6-22267
(fishing, boating, snorkeling)

Manta Reef Resort
Glover's Reef Atoll
Box 215, Belize City
Tel. 2-31895, VHF channel 70
U.S.A. (800) 342-0053
(diving, fishing, snorkeling, swimming)

Pyramid Island Resort
(on Caye Chapel)
Box 192
Belize City
Tel. 2-44409, fax 2-32405
(full-service diving and fishing lodge, airport)

St. George's Caye Lodge & Cottages
(Fred Good)
Box 625
Belize City
Tel. 2-44190, fax 2-30461
U.S.A. (800) 678-6871
(full-service diving and fishing lodge)

Spanish Bay Resort
(on Spanish Lookout Caye)
Box 35, 71 N. Front Street
Belize City
Tel. 2-77288, fax 2-72797,
U.S.A. (800) 359-0747
(diving, snorkeling, fishing, nature trips, restaurant; dive shop and dive instruction)

Turneffe Flats
Blackbird Caye, Turneffe Islands
Box 1676, Belize City
Tel. 2-30116, fax 2-78808
(flyfishing specialists; also snorkeling, beach camping, diving)

Turneffe Islands Lodge
Caye Bokel, Turneffe Islands
Tel. 2-2331
U.S.A. (800) 338-8149, fax (904) 641-5285
(diving specialists)

Wippari Caye Lodge
near Point Placencia
Tel. 6-23130
(fishing specialists)

MODERATE

Fairweather and Friends
(Elwood Fairweather)
(on Tobacco Caye)
Box 240
Belize City
Tel. 5-22201
(cabins; fishing, boating, reef tours)

Gaviota's Coral Reef Resort
Tobacco Caye
Tel. 5-22244
(cottages with restaurant and bar; fishing, boating, snorkeling)

Golden Bonefish Lodge
Cockney Point Caye, Turneffe Islands
Box 294
Rockford, MI 49341-0294
(diving, snorkeling, fishing, swimming)

Island Camps
(campground on Tobacco Caye)
51 Regent Street
Belize City
Tel. 2-72109 or 5-22201
(tents only)

Leslie Cottages
South Water Caye
Tel. 5-22004, fax 5-23152
U.S.A. (800) 548-5843
(cottages and dorm-style accommodations, snorkeling, boating)

Ocean's Edge Lodge
Tobacco Caye
Tel. 5-22171

Ranguana Reef Resort
(Eddie Leslie)
Ranguana Caye
Tel. 6-23112
(four rustic cabanas with kitchens; fly-fishing, snorkeling, boating, swimming)

Ricardo's Beach Huts & Lobster Camp
Bluefield Range
Box 55 or 59 N. Front Street (Mira Río Hotel)
Belize City
Tel. 2-44970 or marine VHF channel 68
(snorkeling, diving, fishing, camping, tours)

The Wave
Gallows Point Caye
9 Regent Street, Belize City
Tel. 2-73054
(boating, scuba, fishing, reef tours)

LOW

Camp Mt. Zion
Punta Rocker's Island
Box 10, Dangriga
Tel. 5-22142
(cottages; fishing, boating, snorkeling)

Glover's Atoll Resort
(The Lomont Family)
Long Caye, Glover's Reef
Box 563, Belize City
Tel. 8-22149 or 92-3310
(beach bungalows; fishing, camping, snorkeling, diving, kayaking, swimming; facilities on North East Caye)

Moonlight Shadows Lodge
(Rudolfo Avila)
Southern Long Caye
Tel. 8-22587
(snorkeling, diving, fishing; restaurant)

Reef End Lodge
(Roland Jackson)
Tobacco Caye
Box 10
Dangriga
(cabins and camping; boating, snorkeling, fishing, reef trips)

Cayo District

HIGH

Belmopan Convention Hotel
Box 237, Bliss Parade and Constitution Drive
Belmopan
Tel. 8-22340, fax 8-23066

Blaqueano Lodge
(Nancy Woodruff)
Mountain Pine Ridge
(cabana-style accommodations, catering especially to writers and artists)

Chaa Creek Cottages
(Mick and Lucy Fleming)
P.O. Box 53
San Ignacio
Tel. 9-22037, fax 9-22501
(meals available, also tours throughout Belize and to Tikal; swimming, horseback riding, canoeing, caving, overland expeditions; arranges joint vacations with Placencia's Rum Point Inn)

DuPlooy's Riverside Cottages & Hotel
(Ken and Judy duPlooy)
Big Eddy, Chaa Creek Road
San Ignacio
Tel./fax 9-23301
U.S.A. (800) 359-0747
(on 20 acres, 9 miles southwest of San Ignacio next to Macal River; offers swimming, canoeing, fishing, horseback riding, caving, pack trips, nature treks, orchid garden, and tours)

Ek' Tun
(Ken and Phyllis Dart)
701 George Price Boulevard
Benque Viejo
Tel. 9-32536, fax 93-2446
U.S.A. (303) 442-6150
(remote cottage on Macal River; nature and cave tours; bird-watching; hiking; canoe and boat trips)

Hidden Valley Inn
(Bull or J. Christian Headley II)
Mountain Pine Ridge Forest Reserve
Box 170, Belmopan
Tel. 8-23320, fax 8-23334
U.S.A. (800) 334-7942
(meals included; tours available, advance reservations required; 18,000 acres includes Thousand -Foot Falls; 90 miles of trails for bird-watching, hiking, and camping)

Mountain Equestrian Trails
(Jim and Marguerite Bevis)
Mile 8, Mountain Pine Ridge Road
Central Farm Post Office, Cayo
Tel. 2-44253/9-23310, fax 8-23235
(horseback trips throughout Mountain Pine Ridge, Maya Mountains, Vaca Plateau, Chiquibul Forest; swimming, horse-drawn wagons, nature treks, river rafting, guided wilderness camping trips)

Windy Hill Cottages
(Bob and Lourdes Hales)
Graceland Ranch
San Ignacio
Tel. 9-22017, fax 92-3080
(ranch on outskirts of San Ignacio at confluence of Belize and Mopan rivers offering horseback riding, canoeing, swimming, hiking, tours of interior; outdoor pool)

MODERATE

Banana Bank Ranch
(John and Carolyn Carr)
Box 48, Mile 47, Western Highway
Belmopan
Tel. 8-23180, fax 8-22366
(popular among adventure outfitters; horseback riding, canoeing, hiking, tours)

Black Rock Enterprises/Caesar's Place
Box 48
San Ignacio
Tel. 92-2341, fax 92-3449
(guest house at Mile 62, Western Highway; camping and cottages on Macal River, 8 miles southwest of San Ignacio)

Bullfrog Inn
25 Half Moon Avenue
Belmopan
Tel. 8-22111, fax 8-23155

Circle A Lodge
35-37 Half Moon Avenue
Belmopan
Tel. 8-22296

Crystal Paradise Resort
(Victor Tut)
Cristo Rey Village
Tel. 92-2823
(horseback riding, boating, birding, nature treks, and tours; restaurant; operated by Mayan-Creole family)

Las Casitas
22 Surrey Street
San Ignacio
Tel./fax 9-22475
(horeseback riding, fishing, boating; restaurant and bar)

Maya Mountain Lodge and Educational Field Station
(Bart and Suzi Mickler)
Box 46
San Ignacio
Tel. 9-22164, fax 9-22029
U.S.A. (800) 344-MAYA
(1 mile from San Ignacio in foothills of Mountain Pine Ridge; offers horseback riding, mountain biking, canoeing, hiking, and tours; field station accommodates study groups with classroom and reference library)

Mida's Eco-Resort and Eco-Tours
(Mike and Maria Preston)
Branch Mouth Road
San Ignacio
Tel. 9-23172/2101, fax 9-23172
(bungalows on river, nature-oriented tours)

Pine Ridge Lodge
17 Mile Mountain Pine Ridge Forest Reserve,
Box 2079, Belize City
Tel. 9-23310
U.S.A. (216) 781-6888
(American-owned cabin complex in pine forest; swimming, hiking; equestrian, river, archaeological, naturalist, bird, cave, and jungle tours)

Plaza Hotel
4a Burns Avenue
San Ignacio
Tel. 92-3332

Rancho Los Amigos
(Ed and Virginia Jenkins)
San José de Succotz
Tel. 93-2261
(built beneath Mayan pyramid, swimming, hiking)

San Ignacio Hotel
(Escandar Bedran)
8 Buena Vista Street
San Ignacio
Tel. 9-22034 or 9-22125, fax 9-22134
(on a hill overlooking Macal River within town of San Ignacio, restaurant and bar)

Snooty Fox Guest House
(Michael Waight)
64 George Price Avenue
Santa Elena
Tel. 92-3556 or 92-3193
(cottages and private rooms with a shared kitchen)

Warrie Head Ranch & Lodge
(located in Teakettle Village)
P.O. Box 244
Belize City
Tel. 2-77185, fax 2-75213
(old logging camp now a working ranch, located 6 miles from Belmopan; swimming, canoeing, hiking, tours, art sales)

LOW

Central Hotel
24 Burns Avenue
San Ignacio
Tel. 9-22253

Clarissa Falls Cabins
5.5 Mile, Benque Viejo Road
Tel. 93-2424
(boating, horseback riding, nature treks; cottages located on riverbank)

Cosmos Camping
(Chris Lowe)
Branch Mouth Road
San Ignacio
Tel. 92-2755
(riverside camping)

Guacamallo Ruins Campground
(Dave and Eddie)
Macal River (8 miles southwest of San Ignacio)
Tel. 92-2028
(camping, boating, nature treks, Mayan ruins)

Hi-Et Hotel
12 West Street
San Ignacio
Tel. 92-2828
(breakfast available)

Maya Hotel and Restaurant
11 George Street
Benque Viejo
Tel. 9-32116

Nabintunich
(Rudy Juan)
San Lorenzo Farm
Tel. 9-32309, fax 9-32096
(swimming, canoeing, horseback riding near Mopan River)

Okis Hotel
47 George Street
Benque Viejo
Tel. 9-32006

Parrot's Nest
(Fred Prost)
Bullet Tree Falls
Tel. 2-78339 or through Eva's Hotel, San Ignacio
(horseback riding, Mayan ruins, nature treks, boat trips; stay in treehouses above the Belize River next to bromeliad farm; German spoken)

Piache Hotel
18 Buena Vista Road
San Ignacio
Tel. 9-22032
(thatched cottages, tours available)

Corozal District

HIGH

Adventure Inn
(located in Consejo Shores)
Box 35
Corozal Town
Tel. 4-22187, fax 4-22243
(palapa cottages overlooking Caribbean; swimming, sailing, windsurfing, kayaking, bicycling, tennis, tours to cayes, interior and Mayan ruins; bar and restaurant on premises)

Tony's Inn
Box 12, South End
Corozal Town
Tel. 4-22055, fax 4-22829
(arranges tours throughout Corozal District)

MODERATE

Caribbean Motel & Trailer Park
Barracks Road, South End
Corozal Town
Tel. 4-22045
(rooms and camping; RVs and campers okay; restaurant, travel information)

Hotel Maya
Box 112, South End
Corozal Town
Tel. 4-22082, fax 4-22827
(oceanfront view, good restaurant)

LOW

Blue Heron Cove
Lowrey's Bight
Box 115, Corozal Town
Tel. 4-22950
(fishing, boating, meals)

Diani's Hotel
Sarteneja Village
Tel. 4-32084
(fishing, boating; restaurant and bar)

Nestor's Hotel
123 Fifth Ave. So.
Corozal Town
Tel. 4-22354
(Mexican restaurant on premises)

Orange Walk District

HIGH

Chan Chich Lodge
(near Gallon Jug, Río Bravo Conservation Area)
Box 37, 1 King Street
Belize City
Tel. 2-75634, fax 2-75635
U.S.A. (800) 343-8009
(located in the plaza of an anicient Mayan ruin within 250,000 acres of mostly pristine tropical forest wilderness; hiking and horseback riding, nature tours, canoeing, birdwatching)

Lamanai Outpost Lodge
(Colin and Ellen Howells)
Indian Church
Box 63, Orange Walk Town
Tel./fax 2-33578
(canoeing, windsurfing, tours of Mayan ruins, swimming, horseback riding, nature treks, boat trips, fishing)

MODERATE

D-Star Victoria Hotel (formerly Baron's)
40 Belize/Corozal Road
Orange Walk Town
Tel. 3-22518, fax 3-22847
(arranges jungle tours to Lamanai)

LOW

Chula Vista Hotel
Trial Farm
Tel. 3-22227

Jane's Hotels
2 Baker's Street and Market Lane
Orange Walk Town
Tel. 3-22473 or 3-22526
(Chinese restaurant on Baker's Street premises)

La Nueva Ola
73 Otro Benque Road
Orange Walk Town
Tel. 3-22104

Mi Amor Hotel
19 Belize/Corozal Road
Tel. 3-22031

Stann Creek District

HIGH

The Cove Resort/Mother Ocean's Tropic Hotel & Environmental Research Station
(Clint and Kelly Whitehead)
Box 007
Placencia
Tel. 6-22024, fax 6-22305
U.S.A. (800) 662-3091
(fishing and reef trips arranged; bungalows, restaurant)

Manatee Lodge
(Bull and Christian Healey)
Box 170
Belmopan (located in Gales Point)
Tel. 8-23321, fax 8-23334
(sportfishing, diving, manatee watching, birding, nature tours)

Rum Point Inn
(George and Corol Bevier)
Placencia
Tel./fax 6-22017
U.S.A. (800) 747-1381, fax (504) 464-0325
(Mayan-style lodge 3 miles north of Placencia Village; expedition outfitter, camping, fishing, diving, river, nature tours; arranges joint vacations with Cayo's Chaa Creek Cottages)

MODERATE

Kitty's Place
Placencia
Tel. 6-22027
(camping, rooms, dive shop, sportfishing and jungle trips; restaurant)

Paradise Vacation Resorts
(Dalton Eiley)
Placencia
Tel. 6-23118 or 6-23179
(diving and fishing trips, nature tours, windsurfing)

Pelican Beach Resort
(Therese and Tony Rath)
Box 14
Dangriga
Tel. 5-22044 or 5-22541, fax 5-22570
(tours arranged to reef, Cockscomb Basin Wildlife Sanctuary, Hopkins Village, Mayan ruins, Manatee Lagoon; also rents bungalows on South Water Caye)

Possum Point Biological Station/Bocatura Bank Campground
(Paul and Mary Shave)
Sittee River
Tel. 5-22006
(nature tours, reef trips, swimming, fishing, camping, snorkeling; also operate Wee Wee Caye accommodations)

Serenity Resort
between Placencia and Seine Bight
Tel. 6-22305, U.S.A. (800) 331-3797
(cabanas on the beach; reef and inland tours)

Singing Sands Inn
Maya Beach
Box 662, Belize City
Tel. 2-30014 or 6-22243
(cabanas and restaurant on remote beach; fishing, snorkeling, canoe trips)

Sonny's Resort
Placencia
Tel. 6-23103
(on the beach in the village; restaurant and bar; tours arranged)

Toucan Inn
(Craig and Maureen Griffith)
(located in Big Creek)
Box 1137
Belize City
Tel. 6-22092
(also pub-style bar, the Tipsy Toucan)

Turtle Inn
(Skip and Chris White)
Placencia
Tel. 6-22069, fax 6-23203
U.S.A. (303) 444-2555
(fishing and nature tours, dive shop with full certification)

LOW

Cameleon Central
119 Commerce
Dangriga
Tel. 5-22008

Caribbean View Hotel
Hopkins Village
Tel. 5-22033

Catalina's Hotel
37 Cedar Street
Dangriga
Tel. 5-22390

Gales Point Bed & Breakfast
Gales Point
Tel. 2-78339
(community-operated guest house system; stay with a Creole family)

Hello Hotel
(Antonio Zabaneh)
Mango Creek
Tel. 6-22011

Hotel Arrow
Hopkins Village
Tel. 5-22033

Lomont's Guest House & Camping
(Gil Lomont)
Sittee River
Tel. 8-22149
(guest house and campground on river, co-owned with Glover's Atoll Resort)

Prospect Guest House
(Isaac Kelly)
Sittee River
(rooms and meals in Creole village, local tours arranged; same owner as the Hub Hotel & Restaurant in Dangriga)

Ran's Travelodge Villas
Placencia
Tel. 6-22027
(furnished apartments, available long-term)

Riverside Hotel
135 Commerce Street
Dangriga
Tel. 5-22168, fax 5-22296
U.S.A. (800) 256-REEF

Sandy Beach Lodge
Hopkins
Tel. 5-22033
(community-operated bungalow lodge and restaurant)

Seaspray Hotel
Placencia
Tel. 6-23148
(beachfront rooms with ceiling fans)

Sophie's Hotel
970 Chatuye Street
Dangriga
Tel. 5-22789

Toledo District

HIGH

Mira Mar Hotel
Box 2, 95 Front Street
Punta Gorda
Tel. 7-22033
(arranges tours)

Traveller's Inn
Punta Gorda
Tel. 7-22568
(restaurant and bar; tours arranged)

MODERATE

G & G's Inn
49 Main Middle Street
Punta Gorda
Tel. 7-22086, fax 7-22469
(restaurant and bar, tours arranged)

Safe Haven Lodge
2 Prince Street
Punta Gorda
Tel./fax 7-22113
U.S.A. (800) 367-6823
(fishing, tours)

St. Charles Inn
23 King Street
Punta Gorda
Tel. 7-22149

LOW

Bol's Hilltop Hotel
(Dominicio Bol)
San Antonio Village
(no electricity; tours of Mayan villages and ruins)

Dems Dats Doin/Toledo Visitors Information Center
(Alfredo and Yvonne Villoria)
Box 73
Punta Gorda
Tel. 7-22470
(arranges overnight trips to stay with Kekchi and Mopan Maya families; also, trips to caves and Mayan ruins)

Laguna Village Guest House
Box 75
Punta Gorda (located in Laguna Village)
Tel. 7-22119
(accommodations in a Kekchi Maya village)

Nature's Way Guest House/Belize Adventure Travel
(William Schmidt)
Box 75, 65 Front Street
Punta Gorda
Tel. 7-22119
(tours arranged, trips by boat available; contact point for Mayan villages' guest house system and Garifuna model village)

281

Where to Eat

Belize City

Dit's
50 King Street
Tel. 2-73330

Fort Street Restaurant
4 Fort Street
Tel. 2-45638
(Belizean and continental cuisine, famous desserts; reservations for dinner recommended)

G.G.'s Cafe and Patio
2-B King Street
Tel. 2-74378
(lunch and dinner in patio atmosphere)

Golden Dragon
Queen Street
Tel. 2-72817
(Chinese food)

Goofy's
6 Douglas Jones Street
Tel. 2-32480
(excellent Jamaican cuisine)

The Grill
164 Newtown-Barrack Road
Tel. 2-45020
(lunch and dinner, specializes in seafood)

King Street Pizza House
11 King Street
Tel. 2-73966
(also featuring fruit shakes)

Lumba Yaad Bar and Grill
Mile One, Northern Highway
Tel. 2-44068
(Belizean barbecue, live music weekends)

Macy's Cafe
18 Bishop Street
Tel. 2-73419
(native Belizean and Creole cooking)

New Chon Saan
55 Euphrates Avenue or
184 N. Front Street
Tel. 2-72709 or 2-30709
(Chinese food)

New Chon Saan Palace
1 Kelly Street
Tel. 2-33008 or 2-33009
(air-conditioned, more elegant atmosphere)

Mom's Triangle Inn (see above)

Pearl's Pizza
13 Handyside Street
Tel. 2-31120
(best pizza in Belize City; take-out available)

Belmopan

Bullfrog Inn
25 Halfmoon Avenue
Tel. 8-2111
(a favorite meeting place; restaurant and hotel)

Little Dragon
Tel. 8-22466
(Chinese food)

Cayes

Elvi's Kitchen and Bar
Pescador Drive (Middle Street)
San Pedro, Ambergris Caye

The Hut
San Pedro, Ambergris Caye
Tel. 2-62070

Lily's Restaurant
San Pedro, Ambergris Caye
Tel. 2-62059
(seafood)

Little Italy Restaurant
San Pedro, Ambergris Caye
(Italian and Belizean cuisine, located in Spindrift Hotel)

Marin's Bar and Restaurant
Caye Caulker
Tel. 2-45937, ext. 104
(seafood)

Melvin's
Caye Caulker
(lobster)

Mrs. Rodriques'
Caye Caulker
(lobster)

The Pier
San Pedro, Ambergris Caye
Tel. 26-2249
(in Spindrift Hotel, known for chicken racing)

The Pizza Place
San Pedro, Ambergris Caye
Tel. 25-244
(pizza, sandwiches; eat in, take out, or have delivered)

Royal Palm
San Pedro, Ambergris Caye
Tel. 2-62148
(East Indian food)

San Pedro Grill
Fido's Courtyard
San Pedro, Ambergris Caye

Tropical Paradise
Caye Caulker
(seafood)

Cayo District

Belbrit Restaurant and Bar
30-A Burns Avenue
San Ignacio
(Belizean and British food and drink)

Caesar's Plaze
Mile 62, Western Highway
Tel. 9-22188
(also rents rooms and sells black coral, silver jewelry, and wood carvings)

Eva's Restaurant
(Bob and Nestora Jones)
22 Burns Avenue
San Ignacio
Tel. 92-2267
(also gift shop and tourist information, radio contact with many lodges and tour operators)

J.B.'s Place
Mile 33
Western Highway (near Belize Zoo)
(food, gift shop, gas station)

Serendib
27 Burns Avenue
San Ignacio
Tel. 92-2302
(Sri Lankan and Belizean food)

Corozal District

Adventure Inn
Consejo Shores
(bar and restaurant; American and continental food)

Crises Restaurant
Corozal Town
(Belizean cuisine, evening dancing)

Dubie's
44 Fifth Avenue
Corozal Town
Tel. 4-22335
(Belizean food)

Hotel Maya Restaurant & Bar
Corozal Town

King of King's Chinese Restaurant
4th Avenue
Corozal Town
Tel. 4-22438

Rexo's Chinese Restaurant
N. 5th Street
Corozal Town

Tony's Inn & Beach Resort
Corozal Town
(outdoor bar facing Corozal Bay; full-service restaurant inside)

Orange Walk District

ALL IN ORANGE WALK TOWN

Eddie's Cabin
46 San Antonio Road
Tel. 3-22095
(Belizean cuisine; national and international drinks)

Jane's Chinese Food
21 Main Street
Tel. 3-22389

Lamanai Outpost Lodge
Indian Church
(fresh fruit and fish a speciality)

New Paradise
6 San Antonio Road

Stann Creek District

BJ's Restaurant
Placencia
Tel. 6-23106
(specializing in seafood and juices)

Burger King
St. Vincent's Street
Dangriga
(hamburgers and American-style food, not connected with the franchise of the same name)

Flamboyant Restaurant and Bar
Placencia
Tel. 6-23174

The Galley
Placencia
Tel. 6-23133
(seafood and hamburgers, full bar)

Hummingbird Cafe
Mile 25.5 Hummingbird Highway

Jene's Restaurant and Bar
Placencia
(fresh seafood on the beach)

Stone Crab Restaurant
Placencia
(seafood; bar and hotel on premises)

Tentacles Restaurant and Bar
Placencia
Tel. 6-23156
(Italian food, seafood, chops, Sunday buffet)

Starlight Cafe
121 Commerce Street
Dangriga
Tel. 5-2072
(Chinese food)

Toledo District

Kool Spot
Big Falls
Tel. 7-2126

Kowloon Restaurant
35 Middle Main Street
Punta Gorda
(Chinese food)

Man Man Restaurant
81 St. Vincent Street
Punta Gorda
(Belizean food)

Tourist Information

Belize Tourism Industry Association
Box 62, 99 Albert Street
Belize City
Tel. 2-75717, fax 2-78007

Belize Tourist Board
Box 325, 83 N. Front Street
Belize City
Tel. 2-77213 or 2-73255,
fax 2-77490

New York Office:
(Jeremy Pask, Suzanne Stephan)
15 Penn Plaza, 415 Seventh Ave., 18th
Floor
New York, NY 10001
Tel. (800) 624-0686 or (212) 268-8798
fax (212) 695-3018

Belize Embassy
2535 Massachusetts Ave. NW
Washington, D.C. 20008
Tel. (202) 332-9636, fax (202) 332-6741

Transportation

Air Travel

The Phillip Goldson International Airport is 9 miles west of Belize City on the Northern Highway. The municipal airport is in the northeast part of the city on Barracks Road.

INTERNATIONAL AIRLINES

Aerovías
Tel. 2-75445
U.S.A. (305) 885-1775
(semiweekly flights to and from Flores)

Air France
Marine Service Bldg.
34 Regent Street
Belize City
Tel. 27-3448
(special rates from Paris, London, and Madrid via Sahsa Airlines)

American Airlines
U.S.A. (800) 624-6262,
Canada (800) 433-7300, Belize 2-32522
(daily flights from Miami)

Aviateca
International Airport
Belize City
U.S.A. (800) 327-9832
(semi-weekly flights to and from Flores, Guatemala City, and Cancún)

Continental
32 Albert Street
Belize City
U.S.A. (800) 231-0856, Canada
(800) 525-0280, Belize 2-78309
(daily flights from Houston with connections to the rest of Central America; supports conservation work)

Sahsa (formerly Tan Sahsa)
Queen Street at New Road
Belize City 2-77080,
U.S.A. (800) 327-1225 or (305) 526-4300
(daily flights from New Orleans, Houston, and Miami with special baggage allowance for diving gear; connections to the rest of Central America)

TACA
Belize Global Travel
44 Albert Street
Belize City 2-77185 or 2-77363,
U.S.A. (800) 535-8780,
Canada (800) 387-6209 (except Quebec, 800 263-4063, and Ontario, 800 263-4039)
(daily flights from Houston, Miami, New Orleans, New York, Washington, San Francisco, and Los Angeles; connections to the rest of Central America)

DOMESTIC AIRLINES

Island Air
General Delivery
San Pedro, Ambergris Caye
Tel. 2-62180 or 2-31140, fax 2-62192
(daily flights to and from San Pedro, Caye Caulker, Caye Chapel, Municipal airport, International airport, plus charters)

Maya Airways
Box 458, 6 Fort Street
Belize City
Tel. 2-7215 or 2-62611
U.S.A. (800) 552-3419
(daily flights to and from 7 airports in Belize; charters available to other destinations)

Sky Bird
Belize City
Tel. 2-32596 or 2-52045, ext. 515
(daily flights between Belize City and Caye Caulker)

Tropic Air
P.O. Box 20
San Pedro, Ambergris Caye
Tel. 2-62012, fax 2-630807; in Belize City 2-45671; in U.S.A. (800) 422-3435, except Texas (713) 449-5230
(daily flights to and from 7 airports in Belize, plus twice weekly to Flores/Santa Elena in Guatemala; charters available to Cancún, Mérida, Cozumel, Cayman Islands, Roatan)

Bus Companies

Fares are inexpensive, about $3 for most destinations and $10 for the longest routes. The buses are often old American schoolbuses, and they do not have lavatories or air-conditioning. Stops are frequent except for express buses. From Belize City to San Ignacio and Corozal takes about 2 hours; from Belize City to Dangriga, 4 hours; and to Punta Gorda, 10 hours.

Batty Bus Service
15 Mosul Street
Belize City
Tel. 2-72025
(points north and west)

Novelo's Bus Service
West Collet Canal
or Belize City
119 George Street
Benque Viejo
Tel. 2-77372
(points west)

Venus Bus Service
Magazine Road
Belize City
Tel. 2-73354 or 2-77390
(points north)

Z-Line Bus Service
Magazine Road/Pound Yard Bridge
Belize City
Tel. 2-73937, or 6-22211
(points south)

Boats and Ferries

If you arrive in Belize by private vessel, you must report your arrival to police or immigration immediately. No permits are required, but you need the usual official documents, clearance from the last port, and manifests for crew, passengers, stores, and cargo. No permits are required. Allowable points of entry are Belize City, Corozal/Consejo, Dangriga, San Pedro, Barranco, and Punta Gorda.

Private boats can be arranged between Consejo, Sarteneja, and other northern villages to Mexico's Yucatán. They can also be hired from Belize City, Placencia, Punta Gorda, and other places for trips into Guatemala and Honduras. A planned crossing between La Unión, Mexico, and Blue Creek in the Orange Walk District may be operable by the time you read this.

The passenger ferry *Indita Maya* provides regular twice-weekly (Tuesday and Friday at 2:00 p.m.) service from Punta Gorda to Puerto Barrios, Guatemala, with connections there to interior Guatemala and Honduras. The crossing takes about 3 hours, and you must have documents in order before embarking. Telephone: 7-22065. Tickets are about $4 one way, and it is best to purchase them in advance at Godoy's Shop in Punta Gorda. The ferry no longer stops in Lívingston, Guatemala.

Many boats ply the waters between Belize City, Caye Chapel, Caye Caulker, and Ambergris Caye. The *Andrea I* and *II* leave the Bellevue Hotel dock for San Pedro at 4:00 p.m. weekdays, 1:00 p.m. Saturdays. The return crossing is at 7:00 p.m. Trips take about 1 hour 15 minutes. A boat for Ambergris called the *Hustler* leaves the A & R Texaco Service Station on North Front Street at 4:00 p.m. weekdays and 9:00 a.m. on Sundays, returning at 7:00 a.m. Another, the *Thunderbolt*, leaves at 11:00 a.m. daily (10:00 a.m. Sunday) from the Front Street side of the Swing Bridge. The *Thunderbolt* departs from San Pedro at 7:00 a.m. daily for Belize City. The *Triple J* leaves for San Pedro at 9:00 a.m. daily from the Swing Bridge (with stops at Caulker and Chapel by request), returning at 3:00 p.m. Both the *Soledad* and the *Pegasus* shuttle between Belize City (the Texaco station on N. Front Street) and Caye Caulker on an irregular daily schedule. Travel time is about 45 minutes. Cruise ships visiting Belize include the American Canadian Caribbean Line (800-556-7450) and Odyssey America (800-221-3254).

Airplane Charters

ALL BASED IN BELIZE CITY

Cari-Bee Air Service, tel. 2-44253
Island Air Service (see above)
Javier's Flying Service, tel. 2-45332, fax 2-32731
Maya Airways (see above)
Su-Bec Air Service, tel. 2-44027 or 2-62170, fax 2-30389
Tropic Air (see above)

Godsman Ellis
Buena Vista Road
San Ignacio
Tel. 9-22109

Alistair King
Texaco Service Station
Box 67, Far West Street
Punta Gorda
Tel. 7-2126, fax 7-2104
(4-wheel drive available, vaild driver's license required; tours offered)

Car Rental

Avis Rent-A-Car
Radisson Ft. George Hotel
Belize City
Tel. 2-78367

Budget Rent-A-Car
771 Bella Vista
Belize City
Tel. 2-32435, fax 2-30237

Crystal Auto Rental
1.5 Mile, Northern Highway
Belize City
Tel. 2-31600, fax 2-31900
(rents used cars and arranges driveaway trips from Houston, valid driver's license and damage deposit required, all major credit cards accepted)

Maxima Car Rental
Maxima Hotel
Hudson Street
San Ignacio
Tel. 92-2265

Melmish Mayan Rentals
Box 934
Belize City
(based at international airport)
Tel. 2-45221, fax 2-77681

National Car Rental
International Airport
Belize City
Tel. 2-31586, fax 2-52272

Local Tour Guides and Travel Agencies

Belize City

Belize Global Travel Service
44 Albert Street
Tel. 2-77185, fax 2-75213
(full services: tickets, tours, hotels)

Ricardo Castillo Tours
Box 55, 59 N. Front Street
Tel. 2-44970 or VHF marine channel
68
(offshore and inland tours, cottages on Bluefield Range Caye)

Lisa Foreman Tours
11 Cadle Alley
Tel. 2-45578
(guided taxi service, nature tours, specializing in custom trips)

G & W Holiday
(Winston Seawell)
Box 820
Belize City
Tel. 2-31979 or 25-2461
(archaeology tours, historical sites; bookings for other tours, air charter, and resorts)

Jal's Travl and Tours
(Lombardo Riverol)
Box 918, 148 N. Front Street
Tel. 2-45407, fax 2-78852
(full-service travel agency; specializes in trips to see manatees; caving; bird-watching and Mayan ruins)

Native Guide Systems
(Homer S. Leslie)
Box 1045, 6 Water Lane
Tel. 2-75819, fax 2-74007
(natural history tours, custom trips a specialty)

Mayaland Tours
64 Bella Vista
Tel. 2-30515, fax 2-32241
(tours throughout Belize and adjacent parts of Mexico and Guatemala)

MayaWorld Safaris
Box 997
Belize City
Tel. 2-31063, fax 2-30263
(daily boat trips up New River from Orange Walk Town to Lamanai, tours of Mayan ruins and other sights)

Mesoamerica Tours Ltd.
(John Llewelyn)
Ramada Royal Reef Hotel
Barracks Road
Tel. 2-73383, fax 2-30750
Ambergris Caye tel. 2-62434
(custom and individual tours; destinations include Altun Ha, Crooked Tree Wildlife Sanctuary, Community Baboon Sanctuary, Xunantunich, Belize Zoo, Lamanai, Mountain Pine Ridge, Tikal)

Royal Palm Travel Services
Belize International Airport
Tel. 2-52534, fax 2-62329
(sightseeing, adventure, archaeology, and nature tours)

S & L Travel Services and Tours
(Lascelle and Sarita Tillett)
P.O. Box 700, 91 N. Front Street
Tel. 2-77593, fax 2-77594
(specializing in business trips and custom vacations, including adventure tours to the Cockscomb, Mountain Pine Ridge, Crooked Tree, Lamanai, and Baboon [Howler Monkey] Sanctuary, plus archaeology expeditions and sportfishing trips)

Sha-Bis Eco Tours
Box 265, Belize City
Tel. 2-45149
(tours of nature reserves, Mayan ruins, caves; bird-watching)

One Moore Tour & Travel Services
(Doug and Lou Moore)
19A Cleghorn Street
Box 1910, Belize City
Tel. 2-32331, fax 2-31711
(fishing, diving, reef, and interior trips; saltwater fly-fishing and "Belizean hospitality" specialist)

Belmopan

Tessa Fairweather
24 Santa María
Tel. 8-22412 or 8-23234
(nature tours, cave exploration specializing in Mayan archaeology)

Vincent Gillett
Department of Archaeology
Tel. 8-22106
(archaeology tours)

Cayes

Amigo Travel
San Pedro, Ambergris Caye
Tel. 2-62180, fax 2-62192
(full-service agency, moped rental, snorkeling, reef and interior tours)

Ramon Badillo
San Pedro, Ambergris Caye
Tel. 26-2158
(snorkeling, sightseeing, fishing, nature tours, glass-bottom boat)

Cari-Search Marine Consulting
(Ellen MacRae)
Caye Caulker
Tel. 2-22178
(tropical marine ecology seminars and tours)

San Pedro Tourist Center
(Josie Pollard)
San Pedro, Ambergris Caye
Tel. 26-2378, fax 26-2549
(complete travel and tour services)

Sea-Ing Is Belizing
(James Beveridge)
Frenchie's Dive Shop, Caye Caulker
Box 374, Belize City
Tel. 2-22234 or 2-22189
(underwater photography, camera safaris, snorkeling and diving expeditions)

Universal Travel/Belize Travel Haus
San Pedro, Ambergris Caye
Tel. 2-62031, fax 2-62185
in Belize City 2-30963
(boat charters, tours, archaeology, natural history, all travel arrangements)

Cayo District

Chaa Creek Inland Expeditions
(Mick and Lucy Fleming)
Box 53
San Ignacio
Tel. 9-22037, fax 9-22501
(guided expeditions to Mayan ruins, Mountain Pine Ridge, Vaca Plateau, Macal River, Tikal; horseback riding, nature trails, canoeing, trained mules for extended jungle trips)

The Divide Ltd.
(Neil Rogers, Jim Bevis)
Nord Farm, Mile 63 Western Highway
Central Farm, Cayo
Tel. 8-22149, fax 8-23235
(natural history tours, rafting, horseback trips, caving, waterfalls, Mayan ruins, wilderness camping)

Guacamallo Treks
(John and Beth Roberson)
c/o S& L Travel
Box 700
Belize City
Tel. 2-77593, fax 2-77594
(horseback trips throughout the Cayo)

Jungle Adventures
Caesar's Place
Box 48, Mile 62 Western Highway
San Ignacio
Tel. 9-2341
(hiking, fishing, boating, and camping trips)

Maya Mountain Lodge
(Bart and Suzi Mickler)
Box 46, San Ignacio
Tel. 9-2164, fax 92-2029
(similar to Chaa Creek services above, plus excursions to Caracol, Cockscomb Basin Wildlife Sanctuary, and barrier reef)

Pine Ridge Lodge
Chiquibul Road, Mountain Pine Ridge
U.S.A. (216) 781-6888
(caving, nature treks, birding, and archaeology tours)

Alwyn Smith
Bullet Tree Road
San Ignacio
Tel. 2155 or 3077
(taxi service and tour guide; Mayan ruins, Cayo, Tikal, Mexico)

Corozal District

Jal's Travl and Tours
49 4th Avenue
Corozal Town
Tel. 4-22163
(complete travel agency and tour services)

Menzies Travel and Tours, Ltd.
(Henry Menzies)
Ranchito Village
Corozal Town
Tel. 4-22725, fax 4-23414
(tours in northern Belize; archaeology tours; Mexico and Guatemala guided tours)

Orange Walk District

Godoy & Sons
(Luis and Carlos Godoy)
4 Trial Farm
Orange Walk Town
Tel. 3-22969
(specializes in the orchids and bromeliads of Belize, boat trips up New River to Lamanai and beyond)

Jungle River Tours
(Antonio and Herminio Novelo)
Box 95, 20 Lovers Lane
Orange Walk Town
Tel. 3-22293, fax 3-22201
*(river trips, jungle tours; Lamanai;
strong Belizean archaeology expert)*

Lamanai Outpost Lodge
(Colin and Ellen Howells)
Box 63
Orange Walk Town
Tel./fax 2-33578
*(windsurfing, boat trips, canoeing on New
River Lagoon in Orange Walk District)*

Atilano Narvallez
Guinea Grass
Tel. 3-22081
(boat rental, jungle river tours of Lamanai)

Stann Creek District

Allen Andrewin
Gales Point
Tel. 5-22087
(jungle and boat tours, guide services)

Dalton Eiley
Paradise Vacation Hotel
Placencia
Tel. 6-2046, ext. 119
*(natural history tours, guide to cayes, fish-
ing, diving, boating)*

Edison Eiley
Placencia
Tel. 6-2046, ext. 103
(fishing guide, boats for hire)

Rosado Tours
(Jorge Rosado)
35 Lemon Street
Dangriga
Tel. 5-2020 or 5-22119
*(nature trips, reef charters and accommoda-
tions, Mayan village and cave tours)*

David Vernon
Placencia Inland Tours
Tel. 6-2046, ext. 116
*(natural history, river trips, ruins, Cockscomb
Basin Wildlife Sanctuary)*

Toledo District

Dem Dats Doin
Box 73, Front Street at the Wharf
Punta Gorda
Tel. 7-22470
*(nature tours, Mayan village trips and
overnights, customized expeditions, permaculture farm, bed and breakfast)*

**Nature's Way Guest House/Belize
Adventure Travel**
(William "Chet" Schmidt)
Box 75, 65 Front Street
Punta Gorda
Tel. 7-22119
*(Mayan villages guest house and Garifuna
model village contact; boat trips
to cayes)*

Foreign Travel Agencies and "Adventure Travel" Outfitters Specializing in Belize

Above The Clouds Trekking
Box 398
Worchester, MA 01062
(800) 233-4499
(nature treks)

Adventure Associates
Box 16304
Seattle, WA 98116
(reef and interior tours)

Adventure Source International
5353 Manhattan Circle #103
Boulder, CO 80303
(800) 346-8666 or (303) 499-2296

Adventures and Delights
300 West 36th Ave., #1B
Anchorage, AK 99503
(907) 276-8282

Barefoot Vacations
7114 Moores Lane
Brentwood, TN 37027
(800) 251-1000, fax (615) 371-8891
*(Mayan ruins, scuba, deep-sea fishing, reef
trips)*

Belize Info
(Howard Benson)
24c Primrose Gardens
London, NW3 4TN, England
Tel. (0044) 71-586-0904
(tourist information service)

Belize Services/Houston
(Charles and Patrick Colby)
5959 Westheimer, Suite 124
Houston, TX 77057
(800) 880-MAYA or (713) 781-8274,
fax (713) 781-4629
(Belize travel specialists, including nature, reef, and Mayan ruin tours; hotel and airline bookings; car rental; special knowledge of Corozal and Orange Walk districts)

Belize Services/Austin
(Lin Sutherland)
8707-D Bluff Springs Road
Austin, TX 78744
(800) 880-MAYA or (512) 282-1607
(custom trips emphasizing nature, archaeology, and traditional Belizean hospitality; also see above listing)

Belize Tradewinds
8715 W. North Avenue
Wauwatosa, WI 53226
(800) 451-7776 or (414) 258-6687
(hotels; fishing and dive tours)

Best of Belize
(Jacqueline Tipton)
672 Las Gallinas Road
San Rafael, CA 94903
(800) 735-9520, fax (415) 479-2380
(hotel and airline booking; nature, diving, fishing, and snorkeling; also books Honduras, Guatemala, and Costa Rica)

Big Five Expeditions Ltd.
2151 E. Dublin-Granville Road
Columbus, OH 43229
(800) 541-2790
(nature and photography tours)

Club Class/Belize Holidays
12 Chamberlayne Road
London NW10 3JB
England
Tel. 081-960-8233, fax 081-969-4301

Bill Dvorak's Kayak & Rafting Expeditions
17921 US Hwy 285
Nathrop, CO 81236
(800) 824-3795
(white-water expeditions; supports river conservation)

Eco Adventures
632 Emerson Street
Palo Alto, CA 94301
(415) 321-1113
(customized itineraries for independent travelers)

Environmental Journeys/Earth Island Institute
300 Broadway, Suite 28
San Francisco, CA 94133-3312
Tel. (510) 655-4526, fax (510) 547-2881
(dolphin research, snorkeling, diving on Blackbird Caye through Oceanic Society Expeditions)

Ecosummer Expeditions & Tours
1516 Duranleau Street
Vancouver, B.C. V6H 3S4
Canada
Tel. (604) 669-7741, fax (604) 669-3244
U.S.A. (800) 688-8605
(sea kayaking, river running, caving, Mayan ruins, horseback riding, nature tours)

Great Trips
1616 W. 139th Street
Burnsville, MN 55337
(800) 522-3419 or (612) 890-4405
(interior, reef, and sportfishing trips)

Imagine Travel Alternatives
(Dyanne Kruger)
Box 27023
Seattle, WA 98125
(206) 624-7112
("soft adventure" tours of Belize, with extensions to Costa Rica and Guatemala; hiking, canoeing, Mayan village tours)

International Expeditions
(Steve Cox)
One Environs Park
Helena, AL 35080
(800) 633-4734 or (205) 428-1700, fax (205) 428-1714
(archaeological, barrier reef, and natural history tours; family trips; ecology workshops; extensions to Tikal; co-sponsors of Crooked Tree Cashew Festival)

International Program Tours
The Nature Conservancy
1815 N. Lynn Street
Arlington, VA 22209
(conservation-oriented tours to howler monkey and jaguar preserves as well as Tikal, the barrier reef, and Chan Chich; also Costa Rica, Panama, and Mexico)

Journeys
3516 NE 155th, Suite B-2
Seattle, WA 98155
(800) 345-4453
(conservation-oriented tours)

Massachusetts Audubon Society
5 S. Great Road
Lincoln, MA 01773
Tel. (617) 259-9500
(natural history tours guided by staff naturalists)

Mountain/Sobek Travel
6420 Fairmount Avenue
El Cerrito, CA 94530
Tel. (510) 527-8100
(conservation-oriented expeditions)

Ocean Connection
16734 El Camino Real
Houston, TX 77062
(800) 365-6232, fax (713) 486-8362
(diving, fishing, snorkeling, sailing, tours, hotels, airfare)

Oceanic Society Expeditions
Ft. Mason Center, Bldg. E
San Francisco, CA 94123
Tel. (415) 441-1106, fax (415) 474-3395
(dolphin research trips to Blackbird Caye, with extensions to Half Moon Caye, Tikal, Lamanai, and interior Belize)

Preferred Adventures
(Karen Johnson)
One West Water Street, Suite 300
St. Paul, MN 55107
Tel. (612) 222-8131, fax (612) 222-4221
(nature trips, bird-watching tours)

Remarkable Journeys
(Nancy Landau, Mark Scholl)
Box 31855
Houston, TX 77231-1855
(800) 800-1939, fax (713) 728-8334
(interior, reef, and sailing trips with Tikal extension)

River Travel Center
P.O. Box 6-B
Pt. Arena, CA 95468
(800) 882-7238
(emphasis on natural history)

Sierra Club Outings
730 Polk Street
San Francisco, CA 94109
(415) 776-2211
(nature trips)

Special Expeditions
(Sven-Olaf Lindblad)
720 Fifth Ave.
New York, NY 10019
(800) 762-0003 or (212) 765-7740
(conservation-oriented snorkeling, photography, and nature tours; reef and atoll trips, Tikal and Bay Islands extensions; based aboard shallow draft 238-foot, 80-passenger ship, the Polaris*)*

Tread Lightly
One Titus Road
Washington Depot, CT 06794
(800) 627-8227
(rain forest ecology, conservation; contributes to local environmental projects)

University Research Expeditions Program
University of California
Berkeley, CA 94720
(510) 642-6586
(research in environmental studies, archaeology, humanities, paleontology)

Victor Emanuel Nature Tours
Box 33008
Austin, TX 78764
(512) 328-5221
(bird-watching and other nature-oriented tours)

Voyagers International
Box 915
Ithaca, NY 14851
(607) 257-3091
(natural history, ornithology, and photography)

Wildland Adventures
3516 NE 155th Street
Seattle, WA 98155
(800) 345-4453
(tours specializing in Mayan archaeology, cultural diversity, tropical nature, and the barrier reef; hires local guides and contributes to conservation and community projects through the Earth Preservation Fund)

Winter Escapes
P.O. Box 429
Erickson, MB
Canada R0J 0P0
(204) 636-2968, fax (204) 636-2202
(nature and adventure tours)

Fishing and Diving Services

Belize Diving Services
(Janie and Frank Bounting)
Caye Caulker
Box 667, Belize City
Tel. 2-45937/2-22143, or marine VHF
channel 68
(complete dive shop)

Blackline Marine Service
Box 332, Mile 2 Northern Highway
Belize City
Tel. 2-44155, fax 2-31975,
marine VHF channel 70
(complete dive shop, hull and engine repairs, fishing/diving and sightseeing charters, marina with fuel, water, and ice)

Blue Planet Divers and Diving School
(Klaus Eiberle and Mark Van Thillo)
based on boat off Blackbird Caye,
Turneffe Islands
Box 1795
Belize City
Tel. 2-76770, fax 2-76203
U.S.A. (602) 825-5075
(NAUI scuba certification; dive trips; dive master and rescue diver courses; specialty in reef ecology and open water; group rates)

Blue Runner Guiding
(Kenny Villanueva)
Placencia Village
Tel. 6-23153 or 6-23130
(heavy and light tackle or trolling sportfishing trips; snorkeling; reef, river, and coast)

Bottom Time Dive Shop
San Pedro, Ambergris Caye
Tel. 26-2348, fax 26-2821
(dive shop, scuba instruction, night diving, sailing charters, equipment rental; located in Sun Breeze Hotel)

Caribbean Charter Services
Box 752, Mile 5 Northern Highway
Belize City
Tel. 2-45814
(boat charters, car rental, diving and fishing tours)

Coral Beach Hotel and Dive Club
San Pedro, Ambergris Caye
Tel. 2-62013 or 2-62001
(packages for snorkelers, divers, fishermen, beachcombers)

Kingfisher Sports Ltd.
(Robert Hardy and Charles Leslie)
Placencia
Tel. 6-23104, U.S.A. (512) 680-7647
(camping, bungalows, bar, boat rental, diving, flycast/spincast, inshore, offshore)

Kitty's Placencia Dive Shop
(Kitty Fox and Ran Villanueva)
Placencia
Tel. 6-22027
(complete dive shop, transportation to reef and atolls; also bicycle rentals, river trips, kayaking)

Lighthouse Reef Resort
Northern Two Caye, Lighthouse Reef
Box 26, Belize City
(complete fishing and diving services)

Manatee Lodge
Gales Point
Box 170, Belmopan
Tel. 8-23321, fax 8-23334
(sportfishing specialists)

Manta Resort
Glover's Reef
Box 215, 3 Eyre Street
Belize City
Tel. 2-31895 or (800) 342-0053, marine
VHF channel 70
(dive and fishing resort on 12-acre island)

One Moore Tour
(Doug and Lou Moore)
Box 1910, 19A Cleghorn Street
Belize City
Tel. 2-32331, fax 2-31711
(fishing specialist, guided inland and reef tours with emphasis on traditional hospitality)

Out Island Divers
Box 7
San Pedro, Ambergris Caye
Tel. 2-62151, U.S.A. (800) BLUE-
HOLE
(dive boat specialists)

Pow Cabral Flyfishing
Placencia
Tel. 6-23132, U.S.A. (800) 333-5691
(sport- and fly-fishing)

Pisces Dive Service
(Mike and Beverly McCarty)
Placencia
Tel. 6-23183
(certified NAUI and NASDS scuba instruction, photography services)

Placencia Cove Resort
Point Placencia
Tel. 6-2024
(sportfishing, diving, snorkeling, tours, beachcombing)

Reef Divers Ltd.
Ramon's Reef Resort
San Pedro, Ambergris Caye
Tel. 2-62371, fax 26-2028
(complete dive shop)

Ricardo's Adventure Tours
Caye Caulker
Tel. 2-22138
(river trips, island hopping, fishing, diving)

Rothschild Travel Consultants
900 West End Ave., Suite 1B
New York, NY 10025
(800) 359-0747
(diving and fishing packages, adventure trips)

Scuba Tours
5 Paterson Avenue
Little Falls, NJ 07424
(800) 526-1394, fax (201) 256-0591
(dive trips, live-aboard packages)

Sea & Explore
1809 Carol Sue Ave., Suite E
Gretna, LA 70056
(800) 345-9786, fax (504) 366-9986
(diving and fishing trips, represent several live-aboard dive boats)

Sea Safaris
3770 Highland Ave, Suite 102
Manhattan Beach, CA 90266
(800) 821-6670 or (213) 546-2464
(dive trips, live-aboard diving packages)

Sun Breeze Beach Hotel
San Pedro, Ambergris Caye
Tel. 2-62347, fax 2-62346
(dive shop, fishing trips, windsurfing, hotel, restaurant)

Travel Belize Ltd.
637-B S. Broadway
Boulder, CO 80303
(800) 626-3483
(dive trips)

Tropical Adventures Travel
11 Second Avenue
Seattle, WA 98109
(800) 247-3483 or (206) 441-3483
(scuba specialists)

Turneffe Flats
Blackbird Caye, Turneffe Islands
Tel. 2-45634
U.S.A. (605) 578-1304,
fax (605) 578-7540
(sportfishing and diving specialists)

Turneffe Islands Lodge
Caye Bokel, Turneffe Islands
Box 480
Belize City
(800) 338-8149, fax 3-0276
(diving specialists)

Joel Westby Fishing Guide
Placencia Village
Tel. 6-23138
(fishing guide specializing in fly-fishing)

Whiprey Caye Guiding
Point Placencia
Tel. 6-23130
(fly-fishing guide)

Richard Young, Jr.
Belize City
Tel. 2-74385
(light tackle fishing guide specializing in tarpon, snook, and bonefish on flats or rivers)

Live-Aboard Dive Boats

Belize Aggressor I and II (100-ft. dive boats)
based at Ft. George Pier, Belize City
Drawer K, Morgan City, LA 70381
(800) 348-2628 or 735-9520

Coral Bay (62-ft. dive boat) **and Off-shore Express**
Coral Beach Hotel
San Pedro, Ambergris Caye
Tel. 26-2001
U.S.A. (800) 433-7262 or (305) 563-1711

La Strega (85-ft. dive boat)
Box 673
Belize City
Tel. 2-3108, U.S.A. (800) 433-DIVE

M.V. Greet Reef (65-ft. dive boat)
Box 214A
Corpus Christi, TX 78415
(800) 255-8503 or (512) 854-0247

Out Island Divers
(operators of *Reef
Roamer I and II*)
Box 7
San Pedro, Ambergris Caye
Tel. 2-62138 or 2-62151,
U.S.A. (800) BLUE-HOLE

M.V. Manta IV
Box 13
San Pedro, Ambergris Caye
Tel. 2-62371, fax 2-62028
U.S.A. (800) 468-0123, fax (305) 473-6011
(overnight dive trips to Turneffe and Light-house atolls; interior tours)

Ramada Royal Reef Hotel
Barracks Road
Belize City
U.S.A. (800) 228-9898
(berth of various dive boats)

Wave Dancer (live-aboard dive boat)
based at Ft. George Pier, Belize City
Peter Hughes Diving
1390 S. Dixie Hwy., Suite 2213
Coral Gables, FL 33146
U.S.A. (800) 932-6237 or 735-9520

Mountain Biking, River Trips, Sea Kayaking, Sailing

Adios Charters
(Mike and Bonnie Cline)
Placencia
Tel. 6-23154
(36-ft. trimaran for day charters to area cayes for snorkeling)

Adventure Inn
Box 35
Corozal Town
Tel. 4-22187, fax 4-22243
(windsurfing, sailing, kayaking, bicycling in Corozal District)

Amigo Travel
San Pedro, Ambergris Caye
Tel. 26-2180
(scooter and bicycle rental, sailing, other services)

Bike Belize
104 New Road
Belize City
Tel. 2-33855
(mopeds, minibike, scooter, and bicycle rental; camping, guided tours throughout Belize)

Caye Caulker Sailboats
The Reef Hotel
Caye Caulker
Tel. 22-2196
(sailboat rentals)

Fanta-Sea Charters
(Michael and Donna Hill)
Box 768
Belize City
Tel. 2-33033, fax 2-3712
IU.S.A. (303) 226-1193
(day and overnight snorkel trips on 45-ft. catamaran, the Stingray, *based in Belize City at Ramada Reef Hotel marina)*

Float Belize
(Remo)
Box 48, 28 Benque Viejo Road
San Ignacio
Tel. 9-23213 or 9-22188
(canoe and raft rental, camping, river trips, horesback riding)

Heritage Navigation
Paradise Hotel Dock
San Pedro, Ambergris Caye
Te.l. 26-2394
(island and reef cruises on 66-ft. sailboat, the Winnie Estelle*)*

Hinterland Tours
3 Eve Street
San Ignacio
Tel. 92-2475
(river, ruin, and jungle trips)

Island Expeditions
4585 Commercial Street
Vancouver, BC V5N 4G8 Canada
(800) 667-1630 or (604) 879-9800, fax (604) 684-3255
(sea kayaking)

Kayak & Rafting Expeditions
17921 S. Highway 285
Nathrop, CO 81236
(sea kayaking, river trips)

Paradise Bicycle Tours
(Tom Hoskins)
P.O. Box 1726
Evergreen, CO 80439
Tel. (800) 626-8271
(bicycle tours)

Pegasus Boat Charter
Box 743
Tel. 2-31138
(boat charter for reef, river, and caye trips)

Red Rooster Peddle & Paddle Tours
(Tom, Jeanette, and Shaw Ellis)
Red Rooster Bar & Grill
2 Far West Street
San Ignacio
Tel. 9-23016, fax 92-2057
(mountain biking trips, raft trips, bicycle rental)

Sailing Fantasy
Ramon's Reef Resort
San Pedro, Ambergris Caye
Tel. 2-62439
(catamaran trips and rental, operators of El Tigre)

Slickrock Adventures
Box 1400
Moab, UT 84532
(801) 259-6996
(sea kayaking)

Sunrise Boat Tours and Charters
(Jim Novelo)
Caye Caulker
Tel. 2-22195
(trips to cayes near and far, including weekly excursion to Half Moon Caye)

Timeless Tours
2304 Massachusetts Avenue
Cambridge, MA 02140
Tel. 7-2119, U.S.A. (800) 370-0142
(7- to 12-day sailing/camping excursions with 38-ft. schooner based in Punta Gorda, overnight on cayes and jungle rivers)

Toni Canoes
22 Burns Avenue
San Ignacio
Tel. 92-2267
(river and canoe trips)

Wilderness Alaska/Mexico
(Ron Yarnell)
1231 Sundance Loop
Fairbanks, AK 99709
Tel. (907) 479-8203
(sea kayaking)

Archaeological Expeditions

Earthwatch
Box 403, 680 Mt. Auburn Street
Watertown, MA 02272
(work-study archaeological tours)

Far Horizons Archaeological and Discovery Trips
(Mary Dell Lucas)
P.O. Box 91900
Albuquerque, NM 87199-1900
(800) 552-4575 or (505) 822-9100, fax (505) 828-1500
("cultural discovery" trips to Mayan villages and ruins, led by archaeologists trained in Belize; can arrange canoeing, horseback riding, fishing and boat trips)

Foundation for Field Research
Box 2010
Alpine, CA 91903
(619) 445-9264
(archaeological field research sites)

Institute of Mayan Antiquities
(Ron Whipple)
6828 Wofford Drive
Dallas, TX 75227
(214) 381-2311
(remote-sensing research trips to Mayan ruins in Belize and Guatemala)

Smithsonian Odyssey Tours & Research Expeditions
1100 Jefferson Dr. S.W.
Washington, D.C. 20560
(800) 524-4125 or (202) 357-4700
(study tours and research expeditions)

University Research Expeditions Program
Univerisity of California
Berkeley, CA 94720
(510) 642-6586
(research expeditions in archaeology; develops cooperative projects with scientists of developing nations)

Appendix

Government-Protected Areas

Aguas Turbias Nature Reserve
Bladen Nature Reserve
Blue Hole National Park
Burdon Canal Nature Reserve
Chiquibul National Park
Cockscomb Basin Wildlife Sanctuary
Crooked Tree Wildlife Sanctuary
Crown Reserve Bird Sanctuaries (6)
Five Blues Lake and Indian Creek Caves
Guanacaste National Park
Half Moon Caye National Monument
Hol Chan Marine Reserve
Laughingbird Caye National Park
Manatee Special Development Area
Monkey Bay Nature Reserve
Paynes Creek/Monkey River Wildlife Sanctuary
Río Blanco Falls Nature Reserve
Río Grande Reserve
Temash and Sarstoon Delta Wildlife Sanctuary
(*The above does not include forest reserves and government-protected Mayan "archaeological monument" sites, such as Caracol, Xunantunich, Lamanai, and Altun Ha.*)

Privately Protected Areas

Belize Agroforestry Research Center
Belize Zoo and Tropical Education Center
Carrie Bow Caye and Twin Cayes Research Station
Community Baboon Sanctuary
Gales Point Manatee Community Sanctuary
Hidden Valley Institute for Environmental Studies
Ix Chel Farm and Tropical Research Center
Man o' War Caye
Monkey Bay Wildlife Sanctuary
Parrot Hill Farm
Possum Point Biological Station
Río Bravo Conservation and Management Area
Shawfields Nature Reserve
Shipstern Nature Reserve
Siwa-Ban Nature Preserve
Slate Creek Preserve
Society Hall Nature Reserve
Wee Wee Caye Research Station

Conservation Groups

Local Conservation Contacts

Belize Audubon Society
Box 1001, 29 Regent Street
Belize City
Tel. 2-77369

Belize Center for Environmental Studies/Belize Youth Conservation Corps
(Lou Nicolait)
Box 666, 55 Eve Street.
Belize City
Tel. 2-45739

Belize Department of Archaeology
(John Morris, Commissioner)
Belmopan
Tel. 8-22106, fax 8-23345

Belize Natural History Society
(Bruce Miller)
Gallon Jug, Orange Walk District

Belize Zoo & Tropical Education Center
(Sharon Matola, Amy Bodwell)
Mile 30, Western Highway
Box 1787, Belize City

Community Baboon Sanctuary
Bermudian Landing, Belize District
Tel. 2-44405 or 2-77369

Ix Chel Tropical Research Foundation
(Rosita Arvigo)
San Ignacio, Cayo District
Tel. 92-3310

Programme for Belize
(Joy Grant)
1 King Street (at Church St.)
Belize City
Tel. 2-75616, fax 2-75635

Slate Creek Reserve
(Jim and Marguerite Bevis)
Central Farm P.O., Cayo
Tel. 92-3452

Some International Conservation Groups Working in Belize

LightHawk
(Steele Wotkyns, Charlie Luthin)
P.O. Box 8163
Santa Fe, NM 87504
(505) 982-9656

Manomet Bird Observatory
P.O. Box 936
Manomet, MA 02345
(508) 224-6521

New York Botanical Garden
(Michael J. Balick)
Dept. of Ethnobotany
Bronx, NY 10458
(212) 220-8763

Tropical Conservation Foundation
P.O. Box 31
CH-2074
Marin-Ne, Switzerland
(038) 334344

Wildlife Conservation International
New York Zoological Society
185th St. and So. Blvd., Bldg. A
Bronx, NY 10460
(212) 220-5155

World Wildlife Fund—U.S.
1250 24th St., NW
Washington, D.C. 20037
(202) 293-4800

Prohibitions

The following activities are prohibited by law in Belize: the removal, sale, and exportation of black or any other kind of coral without a license; hunting without a license; picking wild orchids in a forest reserve; removing, defacing, or destroying archaeological artifacts; spearfishing or collecting crustaceans while wearing scuba diving apparel without a special Fisheries Department permit; possessing or exporting turtles or materials made from turtles without a license; overnight camping in any public place, including a forest reserve, without permission from the proper authorities; collecting out of season any lobster (March 15-July 14), conch (July 1-September 30), or sea turtle (June 1-August 31).

The U.S. Customs Service and the Fish and Wildlife Service bar items made with crocodile, alligator, lizard, and snake skins as well as anything made of sea turtle shells or ostrich skins. Souvenirs made of feathers are also banned, as are dried butterflies or turtles and any jaguar or ocelot skin. A complete list of such items is available through most travel agents or federal offices.

Art Galleries and Museums

The government of Belize has established a Department of Museums and committed itself to construction of a facility that would properly display the many priceless Mayan artifacts now held in storage by the Department of Archaeology in Belmopan. The new museum, to be located in the capital, should open during the mid-1990s.

Arts & Crafts of Central America
1 Waight Street
San Ignacio
Tel. 9-32351
(arts and crafts from Belize, Guatemala, and their neighbors; located next to bus station)

Baron Bliss Institute
1 Bliss Parade
Belize City
Tel. 2-77267
(Mayan artifacts, public library, art and culture exhibits)

Community Baboon Sanctuary Natural History Museum
Bermudian Landing, Belize District
(local artifacts, howler monkey displays, natural history)

El Caracol Gallery & Gift Shop
32 Macaw Avenue
Belmopan
Tel. 8-22394
(stone carvings, sculptures, ceramics, jewelry, basketry, prints, musical instruments)

Galeria Hicaco
Caye Caulker
Tel. 2-22178
(photos, prints, arts and crafts)

García Sisters Museum & Gift Shop
Box 75
San Ignacio
(museum and gift shop on Cristo Rey Road in San Antonio Village; slate carvings on Mayan themes, handmade cards, medicinal herbs and teas)

Go Graphics and Gifts
23 Regent Street
Belize City
Tel. 2-74082
(T-shirts, handicrafts, books, carvings, souvenirs)

Itzamna' Gift Shop and Museum
San Antonio Village, Cayo District
(Mayan stone and wood carvings by the Magaña family, also tapestries)

Mayan Artifact Vault
Department of Archaeology
Belmopan
Tel. 8-22106, fax 8-23345
(vault containing Mayan artifacts, open by appointment two days in advance on Monday, Wednesday and Friday only from 1:30 to 4:30 p.m.)

Melinda's Historical Museum
21 St. Vincent's Street
Dangriga
Tel. 5-22266
(Garifuna handicrafts and artifacts; open daily except Thursday and Sunday; $1 admission)

Mexican Cultural Center
Barracks Road
Belize City
(Mexican-funded museum and visitors center emphasizing Mayan history and archaeology; located near Ramada Royal Reef Hotel)

National Handicraft Sales Center
Box 291, Fort Street
Belize City
Tel. 2-33833, fax 2-33636
(wide variety of native handicrafts at reasonable prices; wholesale and retail sales)

New Hope Trading Company
Buena Vista Road
San Ignacio
Tel. 9-22188
(exotic wood crafts)

Rachael's Art Gallery
39 West Albert Street
Belize City
Tel. 2-77488
(contemporary Belizean art, novelties, art supplies)

Stone Maiden Arts & Crafts Shop
Western Highway at Xunantunich Ferry
San José Succotz, Cayo District
(contemporary Mayan arts and crafts)

Embassies and Consulates

Note: The following is a partial list.

British High Commissioner
Embassy Square, 34 Halfmoon Avenue
Belmopan
Tel. 8-22146

Costa Rican Consulate
8 Eighteenth Street
Belize City
Tel. 2-44796

German Honorary Consul
2 Cork Street
Belize City
Tel. 2-77316

Guatemalan Embassy
Mile 5.5, Northern Highway
Belize City

Guatemalan Consulate
Western Highway
San José Succotz

Honduran Consulate
91 North Front Street
Belize City
Tel. 2-45889

Mexican Embassy
20 North Park Street
Belize City
Tel. 2-30193 or 2-30194

United States Embassy
29 Gabourel Lane (at Hutson St.)
Belize City
Tel. 2-77161

Scientific Names of Flora and Fauna Mentioned

Note: This is *not* a comprehensive list of Belize's flora and fauna. Those species listed below, with the exceptions of insects and crustaceans, are only those mentioned in the text.

Birds

Agami heron *(Agamia agami)*
American coot *(Fulica americana)*
American redstart *(Setophaca ruticilla)*
Aztec parakeet *(Aratinga astec)*
barred forest falcon *(Micrastur ruficollis)*
barred antshrike *(Thamnophilus doliatus)*
black-headed trogon *(Trogon melanocephalus)*
blue grosbeak *(Guiraca caerulea)*
brown-hooded parrot *(Pionopsitta haemotosis)*
brown jay *(Psilorhinus morio)*
citreoline trogon *(Trogon citreolus)*
collared aracari *(Pteroglossus torquatus)*
collared forest falcon *(Micrastur semitorquatus)*
common woodnymph *(Thalurania furcata)*
crested guan *(Penelope purpurascens)*
emerald toucanet *(Avlacorhynchus prosinus)*
eye-ringed flatbill *(Rhynchocyclus brevirostris)*
great curassow *(Crax rubra)*
great blue heron *(Ardea herodias)*
green-backed heron *(Butorides striatus)*
green-winged teal *(Anas crecca)*
jabiru stork *(Jabiru mycteria)*
keel-billed motmot *(Electron carinatum)*
keel-billed toucan *(Ramphastos sulfuratus)*
king vulture *(Sarcoramphus papa)*
least grebe *(Tachybaptus dominicus)*
limpkin *(Aramus guarauna)*
magnificent frigatebird *(Fregata magnificens)*
mangrove warbler *(Dendroica erithacorides)*
mealy parrot *(Amazona farinosa)*
Montezuma oropendola *(Psarocolius montezuma)*
northern jacana *(Jacana spinosa)*

ocellated turkey *(Agriocharis ocellata)*
olivaceous cormorant *(Phalacrocorax olivaceus)*
orange-breasted falcon *(Falco deiroleucus)*
prothonotary warbler *(Protonotaria citrea)*
pygmy kingfisher *(Chloroceryle aenea)*
red-footed booby *(Sula sula)*
red-lored parrot *(Amazona antumnalis)*
ringed kingfisher *(Ceryle torquata)*
roadside hawk *(Buteo nitidus)*
rose-throated becard *(Pachyramphus major)*
roseate spoonbill *(Ajaia ajaja)*
roseate tern *(Sterna dougalli)*
rough-winged swallow *(Stelgidopteryx ruficollis)*
rufous-capped warbler *(Basileuterus belli)*
scaly-throated foliage gleaner *(Anabacerthia variegaticeps)* scarlet macaw *(Ara macao)*
slaty-breasted tinamou *(Crypturellus boucardi)*
smoky brown woodpecker *(Veniliorus fumigatus)*
snail kite *(Rostrhamus sociabilis)*
sooty tern *(Sterna fuscata)*
squirrel cuckoo *(Piaya cayana)*
tropical mockingbird *(Mimus gilvus)*
vermiculated screech-owl *(Otus guatemalae)*
vermillion flycatcher *(Pyrocephalus rubinus)*
white ibis *(Eudocimus albus)*
white hawk *(Leucopternis albicollis)*
white-crowned parrot *(Pronis senilis)*
white-crowned pigeon *(Columba leucocephala)*
white-fronted parrot *(Amazona albifrons)*
white-necked jacobin *(Florisuga mellivora)*
wood stork *(Mycteria americana)*
yellow-billed cacique *(Amblycercus holosericeus)*
yellow-headed parrot *(Amazona ochrocephala)*
yellow-lored parrot *(Amazona xantholora)*
yellow-throated euphonia *(Euphonia hirundinacea)*
Yucatan jay *(Cyanocorax yucatanicus)*

Mammals

agouti *(Dasyprocta punctata)*
armadillo *(Dasypus novemcinctus)*
Atlantic bottlenose dolphin *(Tursiops truncatus)*
Baird's tapir *(Tapirus bairdii)*
black howler monkey *(Alouatta pigra)*
brocket deer *(Mazama americana)*
Central American river otter *(Lutra longicaudus)*
coati *(Nasua nasua)*
Geoffroy's spider monkey *(Ateles geoffroyi)*
gray fox *(Urocyon cinereoargenteus)*
jaguar *(Panthera onca)*
jaguarundi *(Felis yagouaroundi)*
kinkajou *(Potos flavus)*
margay *(Felis wiedii)*
ocelot *(Felis paradalis)*
paca (Agouti paca)
puma *(Felis concolor)*
spinner dolphin *(Stenella longirosrus)*
tayra *(Eira barbara)*
Virginia opossum *(Didelphis virginiana)*
West Indian manatee *(Trichechus manatus)*
white-lipped peccary *(Tapirus pecari)*
white-tailed deer *(Odocoileus virginiana)*

Reptiles

hawksbill turtle *(Eretmochelys imbricata)*
hickatee *(Cermatemys mawii)*
iguana *(Iguana iguana)*
loggerhead turtle *(Staurotypus triporcatus)*
Morelet's crocodile *(Crocodylus moreleti)*

Fishes

Atlantic sailfish *(Istiophorus albicans)*
blue marlin *(Makaira nigricans)*
blue-striped grunt *(Haemulon criurus)*
great barracuda *(Sphyaena barracuda)*
grouper, 5 species (see "Belize: Country Environmental Profile")
horse-eye jack *(Caranx latus)*
king mackerel *(Scomberomorus cavalla)*
snapper, 15 species (see "Belize: Country Environmental Profile")
Spanish mackerel *(Scombermorus maculatus)*
tarpon *(Tarpon atlanticus)*
wahoo *(Acanthocybium solandi)*
white marlin *(Tetrapturus albidus)*
yellow-tail snapper *(Ocyurus chrysurus)*

Trees

banak *(Virola koschnyi)*
barba jolote *(Pithecellobium arboreum)*
black mangrove *(Avicennia)*
breadnut *(Brosimum alicastrum)*
bullhoof *(Drypetes brownii)*
ceiba *(Ceiba pentandra)*
coconut *(Cocos nucifera)*
cohune palm *(Orbignya cohune)*
copal *(Protium copal)*
guanacaste *(Enterolobium cyclocarpum)*
gombolimbo *(Bursera simaruba)*
ironwood *(Dialium guianense)*
logwood *(Haematoxylon campechianum)*
mahogany *(Swietenia macrophylla)*
mamee apple *(Pouteria mammosa)*
mapola *(Bernoullia flammea)*
mylady *(Aspidosperma cruenta)*
negrito *(Simarubra glauca)*
palmetto palm *(Acoellorhaphe wrightii)*
quamwood *(Schizolobium parahybum)*
red breadnut *(Trophis racemosa)*
red mangrove *(Rhizophora mangle)*
Santa María *(Calophyllum brasileinse var. rekoi)*
sapodilla *(Manilkara zapota)*
Spanish cedar *(Cedrela odorata)*
waika chewstick *(Symphonia globulifera)*
wild mammee *(Alseis yucatanensis)*
yemeri *(Vochysia hondurensis)*
ziricote *(Cordia sebestena)*

Glossary of Belizean English

The Creole dialect spoken by the majority of Belizeans is sometimes difficult for outsiders to understand. It has not only a lilting Caribbean cadence but a grammatical structure that borrows heavily from the African languages used by slaves who were originally brought to Belize from West Africa to work in the logging and sugarcane industries. When talking among themselves, the Creole can be almost completely unintelligible to foreigners; however, they are used to quizzical looks and gracious about answering questions in more standardized English. Here is a brief translation of some Creole words and phrases.

Baboon ya de fu we	We're for the baboons
Bacra (also spelled backra)	White man
Bad ting nebah gat owner	An unfortunate event never has an owner
Bettah belly bus den good bikkle waste	Better to eat too much than to waste good food
Boil up	Fish stew
Bush (or Belize breeze)	Local marijuana
Cow no bidness eena hoss glop	A cow has no business in a horse race
Coward man kep soun bone	The cautious fellow lives longer
Dat boy done mek she fat	That boy made her pregnant
Dis de fu we chicken	This is our chicken (slogan of Quality Poultry Products, a Mennonite-owned poultry firm)
Fishaman nevah say he fish tink	A fisherman never says his fish stinks (Self-criticism never happens)
He a two-eye mon in a one-eye town	He is smart
He kin skin a dog wid he tongue	(Reference to a popular but erroneous Creole myth that the docile tapir will kill dogs and other domestic animals)
High bush	Dense jungle
If you drink de Belize watta, you mus com bak	One visit to Belize is not enough
I study B-Town and I don' mess around	I know Belize City; therefore, I am careful.
Jimba	Cane fishing pole
Jump up	A festive dance
Nak yo own tang	Do your own thing
Nebba caal de crocodile bit mout til you done cross de ribba	Don't make trouble until you are safely out of danger
No put puss fo mind butter	Don't leave known thieves in positions of trust
Only daag bahk an chase	Only dogs bark and chase (Do one thing at a time)
Sleeping policeman	An asphalt speed-bump placed across a roadway
Tea	The evening meal (as in England and Australia)
Teef neva prospa	Thieves never prosper
Tell me ears now	Talk to me
Wah fu happen haffu happen.	What is to happen has to happen.
Wah way a goin?	What way are you going?
Wah way a won?	What do you want?
Yah mon!	Yes!
Yu pahk up a go?	Are you leaving?

Suggested Reading

Travel Guides

Adventure Guide to Belize, Harry S. Pariser. Edison, N.J.: Hunter Publishing, 1992.

Adventuring in Belize, Eric Hoffman. San Francisco: Sierra Club Books, 1993.

Belize Guide, Paul Glassman. 2d ed. Champlain, N.Y.: Passport Press, 1991.

Belize Handbook, Chicki Mallan. Chico, Calif.: Moon Publications, 1991.

Bicycling in Latin America, Walter Sienko. Seattle: Mountaineers Publishing, 1993.

Central America on a Shoestring and *La Ruta Maya: A Travel Survival Kit,* Tom Brosnahan, ed. Oakland: Lonely Planet Publications, 1992.

Fodor's Costa Rica, Belize, Guatemala: The Complete Guide with the Best Beaches, Parks, and Ruins, Carolyn Price, ed. New York: Fodor's/Random House, 1993.

The Real Guide to Guatemala and Belize, Mark Whatmore and Peter Eltringham. New York: Prentice Hall 1990.

World of the Maya

The Ancient Maya, S. Morley and G. W. Brainerd. 3d ed. Stanford: Stanford University Press, 1956.

The Blood of Kings: Dynasty and Ritual in Maya Art, Linda Schele and Mary Ellen Miller. Ft. Worth: Kimbell Art Museum, 1986.

The Complete Visitor's Guide to Mesoamerican Ruins, Joyce Kelly. Norman: University of Oklahoma Press, 1982.

Guide to Ancient Maya Ruins, C. Bruce Hunter. Norman: University of Oklahoma Press, 1986.

Time Among the Maya, Ronald Wright. New York: Weidenfeld & Nicholson, 1989.

Warlords and Maize Men: A Guide to the Maya Sites of Belize, Byron Foster, ed. Belize City: Cubola Publications, 1989.

Flora and Fauna

A Belizean Rain Forest: The Community Baboon Sanctuary, Robert Horwich and Jon Lyon. Gay Mills, Wisc.: Orang-utan Press, 1990.

Belize: A Country Environmental Profile and Field Study, Robert Nicolait and Associates. San José, Costa Rica: Hnos Sucs, S.A., 1984.

Birds of Mexico and Central America, Steve Howell and Sophie Webb. New York: Oxford Press, 1993.

The Bladen Branch Wilderness: A Special Report, Nicholas Brokaw and Trevor Lloyd-Evans. Manomet Bird Observatory, 1987.

"Checklist of the Birds of Belize," Wood, Leberman, and Weyer. Pittsburgh: Carnegie Museum of Natural History Special Publication No. 12.

The Diversity of Life, Edward O. Wilson. Cambridge: Belknap Press of Harvard University Press, 1992.

Field Guide to Mexican Birds, Roger Tory Peterson and Edward L. Chalif. Boston: Houghton Mifflin, 1973.

Guide to Corals and Fishes, Jerry Greenberg. Miami: Seahawk Press, 1972.

Jaguar, Alan Rabinowitz. New York: Arbor House, 1986.

Jungle Walk: Birds and Beasts of Belize, Katie Stevens. Belize City: Angelus Press, 1989.

A Neotropical Companion: An Introduction to the Animals, Plants, and Ecosystems of New World Tropics, John C. Kricher. Princeton: Princeton University Press.

Neotropical Rainforest Mammals: A Field Guide, Louise H. Emmons. Chicago and London: University of Chicago Press.

One Hundred Birds of Belize, Carolyn M. Miller. Washington: International Council for Bird Preservation.

Orchids of Guatemala and Belize, Oakes Ames and Donovan Stewart Correll. New York: Dover, 1985.

Reef Fish and Reef Creatures, Paul Humann. Jacksonville: New World Publications.

History and Culture

Belize: A Country Guide, Tom Barry. Albuquerque: Inter-Hemispheric Education Research Center, 1989.

Caye Caulker: Economic Success in a Belizean Fishing Village, Anne Sutherland. Benque Viejo, Belize: Cubola Publications.

A Profile of the New Nation of Belize, William David Setzekorn. Athens: Ohio University Press, 1981.

Creole Proverbs of Belize, Colville N. Young. Belize City: National Printers Ltd., 1988.

Hey Dad, This Is Belize, Emory King. Belize City: Tropical Books, 1984.

I Spent It All In Belize, Emory King. Belize City: Tropical Books, 1986.

On Heroes, Lizards and Passion, Zoila Ellis. Benque Viejo, Belize: Cubola Publications, 1989.

Profile of Belize, Society for the Promotion of Education and Research. Belize City: Cubola Publications/SPEAR Press, 1990.

Spirit Possession in the Garifuna Community of Belize, Byron Foster. Benque Viejo, Belize: Cubola Publications.

Publications Available in Belize

"Belize Business & Travel Directory," Henson & Associates. Belize City: Angelus Press, 1988.

Emory King's Driver's Guide to Beautiful Belize, Emory King. Belize City: Tropical Books, 1990.

Magazines and Newspapers Available in Belize

Amandala
(weekly independent newspaper)
3304 Partridge Street
Belize City

Belize Currents
(semi-annual general interest magazine)
2159 Summer Avenue
Memphis, TN 38112

Belize Magazine
(quarterly general interest and conservation magazine)
P.O. Box 74
San Pedro, Belize
or
Box 803283
Dallas, TX 75380

Belize Natural History Society Papers
c/o Bruce Miller
Gallon Jug, Orange Walk District

Belize Review
(monthly general interest and conservation magazine)
7 Church Street
Belize City

Belize Times
(weekly PUP newspaper)
Box 506, 3 Queen St.
Belize City

Belize Tourism News
(monthly newsletter)
Belize Tourist Board
15 Penn Plaza, 415 Seventh Ave., 18th Floor
New York, NY 10001

Belize Today
(bimonthly free business-oriented magazine)
Belize Information Service
Box 60
Belmopan

Belizean Bullet
(occasional archaeology magazine)
Department of Archaeology
Belmopan

Center Forum
(bimonthly conservation magazine)
Belize Center for Environmental Studies
Box 666, 55 Eve Street
Belize City

Chamber Update
(monthly business magazine)
Belize Chamber of Commerce & Industry
Box 291, 63 Regent Street
Belize City

San Pedro Sun
(weekly independent newspaper)
Box 35
San Pedro, Ambergris Caye

People's Pulse & Beacon
(weekly UDP newspaper)
7 Church Street
Belize City

Reporter
(independent weekly)
Box 1217
Belize City

Index

Index

Cerros 86, 171, 212-213
Chaa Creek 153-154, 159, 167
Chan Chich 28, 176, 178-179
Chase, Arlen and Diane 200-202
Chetumal, Mexico 34, 51, 86-87, 94, 173
Chichén Itzá, Mexico 4
chicle: *See* sapodilla
Chiquibul: caves 163-164, 167, 202; forest 163, 166-167, 195; wilderness 164, 166-167, 199
citrus industry 22, 89, 94, 129-130, 136, 138, 169, 181
climate 31-32, 52, 83, 85, 161
clothing 41, 191
coatimundi 119, 121, 243
Cockscomb Basin Wildlife Sanctuary 19, 23, 25, 102, 115, 130, 132, 194-201
Colha 222
Columbus Caye 68
Community Baboon (Howler Monkey) Sanctuary 23, 25, 103, 110-117, 171, 186
conservation 17-30, 47-49, 55-58, 67-68, 70-71, 76-81, 83, 91-96, 102, 108, 112-116, 119-121, 139, 144, 162, 171-172, 175-179, 180-195; organizations 25-29, 102, 108-110, 121, 147, 159, 168, 172, 175, 185-187, 192, 194, 298
consulates: *See* embassies
Corozal District 87-90; hotels 279; restaurants 283; tour guides and travel agents 288
Corozal Town 6, 32, 54, 85-87, 95, 99
Costa Rica 100, 126
credit cards 44
Creole: history 9, 10, 12, 33, 46, 83, 115, 134; language 34, 115-116; proverbs 303
Crooked Tree Wildlife Sanctuary 25, 28, 103-104, 107-110, 171
Crown Reserve Bird Sanctuaries 91
Crystal Skull 232
Cuello 210-212
Dangriga 33, 54, 69, 71, 131-137, 140, 148, 169, 182, 185, 191
diving 241-247; hazards 20-21, 47, 56-58, 246-247; instruction 53, 77; outfitters 53, 58-59, 62-64, 68, 70, 82, 84, 292-295
economy 14-16, 51-52, 77, 79, 88-89, 96, 112-113, 136-138, 145, 151, 156, 164; foreign debt 14-15
Ecotourism Society 29
education 14, 70-71, 76-78, 92, 114, 117-121, 162, 165, 175
El Mundo Maya 140, 176
El Salvador 3, 19, 22, 140
elections 13
embassies 35, 45, 284, 300
England: *See* Great Britain
English Caye 65-67
exchange rate: *See* money
exit visa 33-34, 137
fax 42, 45, 102
fer-de-lance 35, 245-246
ferries 39, 148, 286. *See also* boats
flatfishing: *See* sportfishing

flyfishing: *See* sportfishing
food 15-16, 53-54, 59-60, 87, 90-91, 101-102, 129, 132, 134-135, 145, 151-152, 158, 191. *See also* restaurants
Gales Point 124-125, 128-131
Garifuna 125-129: history 10, 125-126; language 33, 125-129, 133, 142; Village Project 141-143
gasoline 40-41, 116, 130, 133, 151
glossary 303
Glover's Reef 25, 74-75, 82-84, 137
Godfrey, Glenn 16, 20
Goff's Caye 65, 67
Gonzales, Victor 20, 192
Great Britain 7-10, 12-14, 37, 92, 133; embassy 278
Guanacaste: National Park 25, 171-172; tree 121, 171-172 Guatemala 1, 3, 8-10, 12-13, 16, 19, 22, 34, 38-41, 68, 74, 96, 103, 105-106, 112-113, 116, 126, 136-137, 139-140, 148-149, 165, 172-174, 176, 197
Half Moon Caye 79-82; national monument, 25, 79-81, 168. *See also* Lighthouse Reef
Haulover Creek 99
hickatee 115, 244
Hidden Valley Falls 161-162, 180
highways: Hummingbird 123-124, 130, 168-169, 171; Northern 39, 103-104, 106-107, 110, 116; Southern 124, 130-132, 136-138, 148, 170, 182, 190; Western 13, 39, 42, 118-122, 149, 152-154, 159, 180
history 1-16, 50-52, 58, 63, 65, 73, 78-79, 81, 83, 85-86, 90, 97-101, 103-106, 125-128, 133-134, 139, 142, 144, 152, 176. *See also* Maya
Hol Chan Marine Reserve 55-58, 102, 171, 228
holidays 8, 54, 63, 86, 94, 99, 126-129
homesite farming 23-24,141-142, 145, 148
Honduras 3, 10, 12-13, 19, 22, 33, 38-39, 63, 74, 83, 100, 110, 126-127, 137, 140
Hopkins 131-132
horseback riding 153, 161-162
hotels 272-281. *See also* specific cities or districts
Hunting Caye 73
hurricanes 61, 64, 66, 71, 79, 121, 124, 138, 141, 191, 244-245I
iguana 72, 80, 121, 124, 133, 141, 191, 244-245
immigration 33-34
immunization 35-37
Independence 136-137
Indian: archaeological sites 57, 73-75, 83-84, 87-88, 94, 97, 103-107, 139-140, 149, 151, 164-165, 169, 183, 193; artifacts 65, 100, 105, 119, 121, 163, 170; Black Carib 33, 122, 125, 142; Carib 46, 128; languages 32; population 140; tribal groups 50, 112, 122. *See also* Maya
Ix Chel Farm 153-159
jabiru stork 103, 107-108, 131, 237